The Prime Minister's Ironing Board

The Prime Minister's Ironing Board And Other State Secrets

True Stories from the Government Archives

Adam Macqueen

W F HOWES LTD

This large print edition published in 2014 by
W F Howes Ltd
Unit 4, Rearsby Business Park, Gaddesby Lane,
Rearsby, Leicester LE7 4YH

1 3 5 7 9 10 8 6 4 2

First published in the United Kingdom in 2013
by Little, Brown

A CIP catalogue record for this book is available
from the British Library

ISBN 978 1 47125 423 9

Typeset by Palimpsest Book Production Limited,
Falkirk, Stirlingshire
Printed and bound by
www.printondemand-worldwide.com of Peterborough, England

For Janie Macqueen
Because she's brilliant, and she always has been

CONTENTS

INTRODUCTION –
FOR RECIPIENT'S EYES ONLY

These are the things they didn't want you to know.

The inner thoughts of prime ministers from Lloyd George to Margaret Thatcher. The missives from the Palace that the royals wanted kept away from prying eyes. The things the Cabinet were only prepared to discuss behind closed doors, on the strict understanding that no one would find out about it until long after they were safely picking up their pensions. The secrets so worrying to the powers-that-be that they decreed they should be kept locked away for decades.

And in many cases, it's very hard to see why.

Would it really have hurt the nation to know that Mrs Thatcher was incandescent at public funds being spent on a new ironing board for Number 10? That Winston Churchill graciously offered to hold his Cabinet meetings elsewhere so Clement Attlee and his wife could take their time moving out of Downing Street? Or that the Queen disliked the film *Beau Brummel* so much that she threatened to stop going to the cinema altogether?

1

Other documents make hair-raising reading. The admission in a top-secret briefing on Britain's preparedness for nuclear war in 1960 that 'the provision of facilities on the scale considered necessary for the continued survival of those who outlived the attack was not undertaken because of the cost'. The plans made 50 years before 9/11 to counter the 'most serious threat' of undetectable atomic bombs being smuggled into the UK on board ships and planes, which consisted in full of 'putting on a bold front' and hoping the Russians fell for it. Or even the heartfelt worries of one of Harold Wilson's ministers – expressed in a hand-written note 'because I did not want the office to know about it' – that Prince Charles might have been brainwashed into supporting terrorists.

These are the inside stories of those crises and everyday dramas – and the reactions of the very ordinary men and women who had to deal with them: their frustration and fury, incredulity and occasional outright horror. They range over eight decades and administrations of every political persuasion, but a peculiarly British sensibility runs through them all: a determination to avoid awkward questions, to defuse pomp and, wherever possible, indulge in a little light piss-taking. They reveal first-hand, and in many cases for the first time, what one senior Number 10 official termed the 'mixture of sweet reasonableness and low cunning' that kept the country functioning throughout the twentieth century.

A brief history of confidentiality

All the source material for this book comes from the declassified official papers which take up over 100 miles of shelving at the National Archives. It wasn't until 1916 that anyone thought it might be a good idea to keep formal records of what was said in Cabinet, which is why the earliest item you will find here is 'an appreciation' of how the First World War was progressing (in short: not terribly well). For a long time there was no question of letting anyone outside of Whitehall ever see them: as a Cabinet Precedent Book makes clear a few decades later, 'official information is the property of the Crown. Any person, whether a servant of the Crown or not, who publishes or otherwise discloses official information, without official authority, is liable to prosecution under the Official Secrets Act of 1911 and 1920.' Even decades after declassification, there is still quite a thrill to opening up a file that has 'SECRET' or even 'TOP SECRET' stamped in large red letters across its cover. Although I have to say the one that also had the reference number '007' on it turned out to be considerably less exciting than it ought to have been.

It was not until 1958 that the law decreed that government paperwork should be automatically opened up to the public after 50 years had passed. This came as an unpleasant surprise to former PM Anthony Eden, who had left Downing Street a year before that, when he came to write his memoirs. 'I found it very disturbing,' he complained after the Cabinet Office informed him he would not be allowed to look at all his own correspondence until he had reached the grand old age of 110. 'So far as I can recall, I knew nothing about the Public Records Act of 1958, and if I did I would certainly have put forward some arguments at the time.'

The deadline, which was designed to ensure that anyone who featured in the paperwork as it was released would be beyond the reach of recriminations due to retirement or death, came down to the more familiar '30-year rule' the following decade. 'If criticisms are to be made of me, and of my conduct of affairs, I would rather be alive to answer them,' announced Prime Minister Harold Wilson in 1966. He died exactly 29 years later.

There was a vain attempt to put the genie back in the bottle in 1985, when maverick politician Enoch Powell, by that point a backbencher for the Ulster Unionists, tabled a parliamentary motion attempting to extend the secret period beyond three decades in order to avoid embarrassing any ministers who might be 'still active in public life'. By an astonishing coincidence, the thirtieth anniversary of his own first government job was fast approaching.

In 2000, Tony Blair's government introduced the Freedom of Information Act, which opened up all but the highest-security government departments to anyone who knew exactly what to ask for and had the stamina to hold out against obfuscating civil servants until they got what they were looking for. So proud was Blair of this particular bit of legislation that he described it as 'imbecility' and himself as a 'naive, foolish, irresponsible nincompoop' for ever considering it. The 30-year rule itself, however, remained unchanged for another seven years, until his successor Gordon Brown – a man who was regularly accused of keeping secret from Blair what he was up to when serving as his Chancellor – commissioned a review of the way the nation deals with its secrets from his unlikely pal Paul Dacre, editor of the *Daily Mail*. This concluded that the limit should be dropped to 15 years as 'a small but significant contribution to a more mature democracy in which there is a greater trust between the electors and the elected'. The report was released in 2009, just before the MPs' expenses scandal broke. A year later the government said it would drop the deadline – but only to 20 years, and it won't be fully phased in until 2023.

This book, by its very nature, is something of a lucky dip. I've rummaged in the archives and blown the dust off the things that surprised, enlightened and amused me. I hope they do the same for you. If you enjoy it, tell your friends. If you don't, it is absolutely imperative in the interests of national security that you tell no one.

NUCLEAR FAMILY

'As if God himself had appeared
among us' – 1945

The message from the British Ambassador to the USA which arrived by cipher telegram in Whitehall was simple and clear. 'Experiment took place this morning and is reported to have been successful.'

The account he attached from an eyewitness was more effusive. 'It was a wonderful, even fantastic, experience which I shall not attempt to describe now, as I am rather tired and should get things in wrong proportion,' wrote Sir James Chadwick. 'The implosion "gadget", containing 6 kg of 49, was fired this morning . . . The test appears to have been completely successful. There is no doubt that the nuclear reaction took place . . . The ball of fire was intensely bright, equivalent to several suns by general estimate, so that it seems reasonably certain that the explosion was equivalent to more than 1000 tons of TNT and possibly several thousand. This I call completely successful.'

It was 16 July 1945. Chadwick, who headed the British mission to what was code-named the Manhattan Project, had watched something that no one had ever seen before; that very few people in the world even suspected might be possible: the explosion of a nuclear bomb.

It took place at a remote army airfield in New Mexico, almost literally the middle of nowhere, five hours' drive from the Los Alamos laboratory where the scientists had been beavering away for the previous two and a half years. But the blast was so enormous that it could be seen, heard and felt up to 100 miles away: a cover story had to be contrived about the 'severe explosion of an ammunition dump with considerable pyro-technic effect'. Even that excuse was on a strictly need-to-know basis: as ambassador Lord Halifax informed his superiors in London, 'This statement will only be published in the New Mexico papers and will not be carried by any news agencies or published in other states, though some leakage is, of course, possible.'

By 23 July Chadwick had recovered his composure sufficiently to deliver a fuller report to Sir John Anderson in the War Cabinet Offices, the man whose eponymous bomb shelters he had just rendered obsolete. Chadwick may have been a physicist by training – he won the Nobel Prize in 1935 for proving the existence of neutrons, one of the discoveries that paved the way for the creation of the atomic bomb – but he wrote like a poet as he described his viewpoint 20 miles from the explosion site.

> The first grey light of dawn was appearing as we lay or sat on the ground. Except for the faint twitterings of a few early birds there was complete silence. Then a great blinding light lit up the sky and earth as if God himself had appeared among us.
> After a second or so I peeped round the dark glass with which I was shielding my eyes, but the light was still so intense that I was almost blinded. Then I saw . . . the ball of flame, the blue and purple luminosities, etc. After about 100 seconds there came the result of the explosion, sudden and sharp as if the skies had cracked. Then the hills themselves took alarm and uttered rumbling protest for what seemed several minutes. Meanwhile a column of gas had risen and it continued to rise in a fairly definite cylinder with a mushroom top. It rose with surprising speed. There was an inversion at about 17,000 feet, and here the cloud spread out to some extent, but the central portion pushed through this layer and continued to rise. After some minutes, the column had reached a height which I estimated, by rough measurement, to be about 40,000 feet.
> My anxieties over the uncertainties of the

9

test had made me somewhat nervous, and the awe-inspiring nature of the outcome quite overwhelmed me. Although everything happened almost exactly as I had imagined it, the reality was shattering. Even now, a week later, I am filled with awe when I look back on this moment. It was a vision from the Book of Revelation.

His colleague James L. Tuck, who watched from alongside him, provided a series of sketches, in childish coloured pencil, of the phases of the explosion: the 'beautiful poplar tree shaped cloud, in turbulent motion, whose colour rapidly changed from dark orange through red to brown black'; the 'buff brown cloud on a stalk above the site, reaching halfway to the cloud base' and the 'strong, dark blue violet glow' that billowed in its margins. Most terrifying, however, is Chadwick's account of the aftermath.

The steel tower (100 ft high) on which the gadget was placed has completely disappeared, probably vaporised in the great heat. There is a crater of about 140 feet in diameter, surrounded by a green area of some 1100 feet diameter. This is probably a vitreous surface formed by the action of the heat on the sand, a kind of bottle glass . . .
Some estimates have been made of the amount of energy released, but they are still

very rough . . . More accurate figures can do no more than confirm the main facts, which are already perfectly clear. The nuclear reaction works, and, as far as can be judged from the first analysis of the observations, exactly as predicted. The implosion method of assembly, even in this first form, is successful. The efficiency of the nuclear reaction is high enough to give a weapon of military significance.

It would be less than a month before it was put into use.

When everything changed – 1945

It looks like nothing. Handwritten, barely legible, scrawled on a few sheets of yellow lined paper, evidently torn from an academic notepad. But for the words 'Top Secret', scrawled not once but twice across the top of the pages in bright red capitals, you might take it for a student's lecture notes. It is only as you read on that you realise exactly what you are holding in your hands.

Outline plan for employment of Special
  Weapon
1. Targets considered suitable.
HIROSHIMA. KYOTO. NIIGATA.

The latter two cities were dropped from the list in the weeks that followed, and Nagasaki was added. But this is an account of how things stood on 30 May 1945, when Field Marshal Henry Maitland Wilson, head of the British Joint Staff Mission in Washington, which was overseeing the Allied war effort, reported back to the government in London. His account came from James Chadwick, the chief British scientist on the atomic bomb project, ahead of official confirmation, as he explained to Sir John Anderson in Whitehall. 'I expect the American Chiefs of Staff will discuss it with me at a later date, but I feel it is most important that the Prime Minister and yourself should know what is contemplated before it is admitted officially.'

For plans were already at a very advanced stage. Chadwick's notes detail the height from which what was still being referred to as 'the TA Weapon' would be dropped, the time settings for its detonation, and the expected results:

RADIUS of demolition based on explosion
   of 5000 tons
Complete demolition ½ mile
Non-repairable structural damage 1 mile

The notes featured two comic names, which would soon come to sound far from funny:

Bomb LITTLE BOY to be ready to drop
   Aug 10–15

FATMAN month beginning 2nd week in
    August

and a measured, mathematical statement of
requirements:

ESTIMATED EFFECT
HIROSHIMA AND NIIGATA require
    2 Bombs
KYOTO requires 4 Bombs
Complete destruction of 3 Targets should
    be expected by Xmas 1945

It all came in well ahead of time. On 3 August, Sir John received a top-secret telegram from the Joint Staff Mission – 'The date of the operation will almost certainly be tomorrow' – only for it to be cancelled less than 24 hours later – 'Following for Sir John Anderson from Field Marshal Wilson: Operation postponed owing to bad weather.'

Just one Little Boy was dropped on Hiroshima, on 6 August. The scientists had been far too modest in their estimates. An area of more than a square mile was completely flattened, and two thirds of the buildings in the city were destroyed by the blast and ensuing fires. More than 100,000 people died. Tens of thousands more would perish from the long-term effects of radiation. Survivors suffered horrendous flash burns which seared the patterns of the clothing they had been wearing permanently on to their flesh. Three days later, another atomic bomb was dropped on Nagasaki, annihilating another 74,000 men, women and children.

'Somewhat disturbing' was Field Marshal Wilson's verdict of a report he passed on to London on 21 August, a week after the Japanese finally surrendered. But he was not talking about the unprecedented death and destruction. What was really exercising the British was that their chaps had very nearly not been allowed to take part.

'General Lemay [the US commander in charge of air attacks on Japan] did not wish to speak to me but Farrell [the military representative of the project to create the atomic bomb] asked him on my behalf whether I might take part in the operation as an observer,' reported RAF Group Captain Leonard Cheshire, who had been sent out to the American base in Guam to represent British interests alongside scientist William Penney. 'Lemay said there was no question whatsoever of this as he refused to allow anyone in the aeroplanes who was not vital to the operation . . . It was by this time obvious that I was being prevented from participating because of some policy decision and that the Americans were trying to make it appear as though it were due merely to a number of unfortunate technicalities.'

Clearly, this was outrageous. 'To a man everyone expressed great regret that we were not permitted to fly and stated openly that they considered it an insult to the British Empire,' Cheshire pointed out. 'They furthermore said that it was very different to the treatment they had received from the British when they were over in the European Theatre.'

The pair had to smuggle out a complaint to Lemay's superiors in Washington – 'since we were not allowed to send any communication to British authorities without first submitting it to Farrell' – and got word, just three hours before the bombers took off for Nagasaki, that they were to be permitted on board the observation plane. Cheshire was still not impressed. 'I was surprised at the lack of organisation and co-ordination,' his eminently detached account continues. 'Although the operation itself was a comparatively simple and routine affair, there was a great deal of excitement and confusion . . . There was, furthermore, a certain amount of friction between the air crews and some of the scientists, neither of whom showed any great inclination for each other's company.'

Nor were the military men any good at taking instruction. 'Neither of the operators were accustomed to photography and consequently no photographs of any value were obtained. The bomb aimer who operated the 16mm was so astonished at what he saw, in spite of a very adequate briefing from Penney, that he missed the explosion completely and thereafter, with the exception of a few feet of film, appears to have aimed his camera at the sky and not at the smoke . . . Both Penney and I recommended on several occasions that urgent steps should be taken to obtain adequate photographic cover of the operation. We suggested that this would not only provide valuable technical information but was the only means of providing history with a tangible and accurate account of something that the world might never see again.'

Penney, a mathematician by training, appears to have been just as emotionless an observer. Leading the scientific survey of Hiroshima and Nagasaki that September, his chief complaint was that 'many peculiar effects due to fire winds were noted but not reported very accurately by the Japanese', who were rather busy being incinerated by them at the time.

The biggest concern all round, however, appears to have been that American bolshiness. 'It is hard to appreciate whether it was due to resentment on the part of some of the officers concerned at British participation in what hitherto has been regarded as a purely American theatre of operations, or whether there is something behind the idea mentioned by the scientists that the American Army Air Force will try to get complete control of the TA project in the future,' wrote Wilson to his political masters across the Atlantic. He urged them to swiftly come up with 'some agreed policy concerning TA to cover the interim period until definite decisions as to its future can be made'.

Back in London, the new prime minister Clement Attlee was wrestling with just that. 'What is to be done about the atomic bomb?' he wrote to his

Cabinet colleagues on 28 August, in a memorandum that carries that smack of authentic desperation so absent from Cheshire and Penney's accounts:

> Scientists agree that we cannot stop the march of discovery. We can assume that any attempt to keep this as a secret in the hands of the USA and UK is useless. Scientists in other countries are certain in time to hit upon the secret.
>
> The most we have is a few years start. The question is what use are we to make of that few years start.
>
> We might presumably on the strength of our knowledge and of the advanced stage reached in technical development in the USA seek to set up an Anglo-American Hegemony in the world using our power to enforce a worldwide rigid inspection of all laboratories and plants.
>
> I do not think that this is desirable or practicable. We should not be able to penetrate the curtain that conceals the vast area of Russia. To attempt this would be to invite a world war leading to the destruction of civilization in a dozen years or so.
>
> The only course which seems to me to be feasible and to offer a reasonable hope of staving off imminent disaster for the

world is joint action by the USA, UK and Russia based upon stark reality.

We should declare that this invention has made it essential to end wars. The new World Order must start now.

While steps must be taken to prevent the development of this weapon in any country, this will be futile unless the whole conception of war is banished from people's minds and from the calculation of governments. This means that every vexed question will have to be settled without the use of force . . . The USSR must abandon, if it still holds them, its dreams of revolution by force or intrigue. The UK and the USA must abandon, if they have them, any dreams of overturning Left Governments. All nations must give up their dreams of realising some historic expansion at the expense of their neighbours. They must look to a peaceful future instead of a warlike past.

This sort of thing has in the past been considered a Utopian dream. It has become today the essential condition of the survival of civilisation and possibly of life on this planet.

When the boat comes in – 1950

How dull does the Imports Research Committee sound? Very dull indeed. Which is deliberate. It made it less likely that anyone would ask questions about it. So no one would ever get round to wondering why, along with representatives of the Board of Customs and Excise, the Ministry of Transport and the Ministry of Supply, it also had senior figures from the Ministry of Defence, Directorate of Scientific Intelligence and Security Service sitting on it.

Because the committee, formed shortly after British troops had been sent into Korea to help stop the communists overrunning the whole country, was set up to look into one very specific import: one that no one wanted to see arriving on our shores. 'The Chiefs of Staff recently considered a report by the Joint Intelligence Committee on the clandestine introduction of weapons into the UK, from which they conclude that the most serious threat seems to be the atomic bomb concealed in a merchant ship and exploded in harbour,' explained its newly appointed chair, Mr G. Wheeler of the MoD, on 6 September 1950. 'I need hardly say that the subject is of the greatest secrecy.'

Each of the eight members of the committee was circulated a copy of Dr Robert Oppenheimer's testimony to the US Senate hearings on atomic energy which had been held five years previously. It was a chilling read. 'The active material which makes it an atomic bomb is usually not near the surface, and I think that just by walking along past a crate you would not be able to tell that in that crate there was an atomic bomb. It would not tick,' pointed out the man who had spearheaded the development of nuclear weapons. 'If you hired me to walk through the cellars of Washington to see whether there were atomic bombs, I think my most important tool would be a screwdriver to open the crates and look. I think that just walking by, swinging a little gadget, would not give me the information.'

So they were faced with a weapon that was not only the deadliest in the world, but almost impossible to detect. It was difficult to imagine anything more terrifying. But at their first meeting, held on 28 September, the committee tried their hardest.

In discussion it was pointed out that to produce the maximum effect an enemy might well use every means at once including

1) the merchant ship in harbour
2) a civil aircraft carrying a bomb to be detonated at a low altitude
3) detonation in a submarine . . .

It would be possible to conceal a complete bomb, ready for detonation, in the structure of a ship so that no normal Customs search would find it. Alternatively, if it came concealed as ordinary merchandise there seemed no reason why it should necessarily come on a Russian or satellite ship. It could be arranged for it to come from any port, in any ship, with such transhipment as was necessary.

. . . The detonation of the bomb in the aircraft at a low altitude would have to be undertaken by a suicide squad.

It took the committee's members two months – some of which they may well have spent sitting under the table gibbering – to come to an inescapable conclusion: 'there are no practicable and efficacious steps that can be taken in peace time to prepare against any of these threats'.

There were a few suggestions that might have helped a bit. Customs officers should look out for cargoes containing 'at least one package of the size of a grand piano', which probably covered most of them. And Mr G. L. Turney from the Directorate of Scientific Intelligence proposed that 'Russian and satellite shipping should be directed to some specified port, presumably one of the less important' to discourage attacks. 'The enemy would probably not think it worth while for the sake of destroying one minor port. Admittedly, the results might be unfortunate for the port chosen.'

Otherwise, Britain was just going to have to bluff it out. The committee recommended that 'there should be some deterrent value in a display of confident assurance on our part that we have an adequate answer to the threat'. They didn't, but hey. Whistling a happy tune to fool the people she feared worked for Anna in *The King and I*, which opened on Broadway the following spring, so it might do the trick here too.

As one unnamed official scribbled on the minutes, 'it will deceive our own people more than the Russians, but I suppose we must put on a bold front'.

Thermonuclear power? Yes please – 1954

In the summer of 1954, the Chiefs of Staff, the country's most senior military leaders, prepared a memorandum for the Cabinet on the 'Likely Form of a Future Global War'. It was the stuff of nightmares.

Although they estimated that the Soviets were unlikely to develop nuclear weapons long-range enough to reach the United States before 1970, this was not good news for the UK. In fact, the news was about as bad as it could get.

> The Russians will, we believe, appreciate that, apart from its importance as a strategic base, the United Kingdom is the major political target in Western Europe; and that the extinction of the United Kingdom would quickly lead to the disintegration of Western Europe and the break up of the Commonwealth and would greatly strengthen the Soviet position in

any negotiations which they might hope to open with the United States. We therefore consider that, whatever the Russians' ability to attack the United States – and for the next few years they are not likely to be able to deliver more than sporadic attacks – the United Kingdom will be the primary military target for initial attack in any future war, and will be subjected to devastating attack by a large part of the Russian bomber effort together with any ground-to-ground missile capacity which she may possess.

Our defence system within the foreseeable future will not be able to provide the complete protection necessary against air attack employing weapons of mass destruction . . . Thus, if war did break out, we should have to expect that the United Kingdom would be devastated in the opening days to such an extent that it could no longer function as a main support area. Indeed, the real problem might be one of mere physical survival.

Unsurprisingly, the chiefs concluded that 'More than ever the aim of United Kingdom policy must be to prevent war.' How best to do so? They recommended immediate upgrading of the UK's own nuclear deterrent to the latest thermonuclear or hydrogen bombs, hundreds of times more powerful than those dropped on Hiroshima and Nagasaki nine years previously.

This proposal, however, led to a difficult ethical question with which the Cabinet wrestled at their meeting of 8 July. 'Was it morally right that we should manufacture weapons with this vast destructive power? There was no doubt that a decision to make hydrogen bombs would offend the conscience of substantial numbers of people in this country.'

The solution? Blame the opposition. Winston Churchill's crew concluded that 'there was no sharp distinction in kind between atomic and thermo-nuclear weapons, and that, in so far as any moral principle was involved, it had already been breached by the decision of the Labour Government to make the atomic bomb'. The announcement that 'after fully considering all the implications of this step the Government had decided to proceed with their development and production' came the following February.

Be prepared . . . to die – 1960

The good news is, we'd have a full hour and a half's warning of a nuclear attack. The bad news is, quite soon after that almost everyone except the government would perish horribly.

This was the conclusion of the Home Defence Review Committee in a report submitted to the Cabinet in December 1960, slightly under two years before the Cuban Missile Crisis would bring the world as close as it has ever been to nuclear annihilation. Soviet nuclear strikes would, it cheerily predicted, be 'at present launched primarily by manned bombers . . . There would be about ninety minutes warning of the moment of a Soviet attack on the United Kingdom.' However, 'if ballistic missiles were used now there could be no warning. By 1963 the threat could be entirely from ballistic missiles.'

Fortunately, the UK, along with America, was already putting the finishing touches to a Ballistic Missile Early Warning System – those great golf balls that dominate the landscape at Fylingdales in North Yorkshire – which meant that 'warning of the moment of attack might be as little as three minutes or as much as 12 minutes'. The latter left plenty of time for a leisurely stroll down to the cellar. You would even have time to pop out and buy a pint of milk and a snack on the way.

Actually, that might be a good idea: the report also admits that the last set of official recommendations for nuclear preparedness, issued in 1955, had largely been ignored – 'the stockpiling of food, the safeguarding of water supplies and the provision of other facilities on the scale then considered necessary for the continued survival of those who outlived the attack was not undertaken because of the cost'.

One of the committee's immediate recommendations was that an emergency food scheme, with 'just about enough to provide a Spartan diet for the survivors of attack' should be established by 1965. This was despite concerns that 'the printing of ration books, which could not be kept secret, might arouse public concern about the risk of war'. And probably also a terrible sinking feeling, given that the country had only been free of food rationing for six years: the end of restrictions on meat and bacon had been carnivorously celebrated in 1954, with members of the magnificently named London Housewives' Association hosting a special ceremony in Trafalgar Square.

Another topic considered at length was whether to instigate an official evacuation procedure, not just from cities to the countryside but also a mass move westwards to remove citizens from the vicinity of all those RAF bases that lined the eastern side of the country and were assumed to be primary targets for the Russians. Not everyone should bother packing a suitcase. Four 'priority classes' for evacuation had been proposed in a 1950s plan: 'children, adolescents, expectant mothers and the aged and infirm'. Now, however, this was to be – literally – drastically culled. 'Leaving out some 800,000 adolescents, aged and infirm, it would be possible to have more, or somewhat larger, evacuation areas.'

Poor teenagers. They had only just been invented and they were already being thrown on the thermonuclear scrapheap. If they, or anyone else left behind, raised any objections, it was hoped the

British sense of fair play would kick in: 'the Government of the day could appeal to the public sense of duty, state that there was no room in the reception areas for unofficial evacuees and give a warning about the risks from fall-out for people caught in the open; and it might be that their appeal for non-priority classes to stay put would in these circumstances meet with a considerable response'. Well, it might. But the committee was wise enough to point out that 'unorganised panic evacuation might bring the life of the country to a standstill'.

The committee was at least 'unanimous that there is one type of home defence measure which must be maintained, whatever view is taken of other measures'. Can you guess what it was? Yes, looking after their own: 'Preparations for carrying on the government of the country, including the provision of emergency headquarters for the central Government . . . staffed mainly from the Civil Service and the armed forces.' This appears to have been about the only thing the country *was* prepared for: 'the emergency underground headquarters for the central Government is due for completion in 1961–62'.

Though the report didn't say so – the information was far too sensitive even for a document stamped 'TOP SECRET' at the top and bottom of every one of its 36 pages – this bunker, code-named Burlington, was, and still is, located 100 feet beneath the town of Corsham near Bath. It had room for 4,000 key personnel, its own water supply and treatment plant and fuel to keep its four generators running and the air at a pleasant 20 degrees for up to three months. An operation code-named Visitation would see RAF helicopters landing in Horse Guards Parade to evacuate the Prime Minister and 23 ministers and officials via the back garden of 10 Downing Street and whisk them to Wiltshire, and safety.

The outlook was rather chillier for everyone else, despite the fortifications that still stood in many back gardens, pressed into peacetime service as sheds or chicken coops. 'Much shelter still exists from the last war, but the amount is steadily decreasing, and a good deal of it would be unsuitable for prolonged occupation. There is at present useful shelter for only a very small proportion of the population.' Besides, what existed was all but useless: cast iron and brick-work might have seen the bulk of the population through the Blitz two decades before, but 'the committee are unable to recommend any special provision at the present time for protection against blast and heat' from the new generation of weapons.

To look on the bright side, this was not the main threat: 'An initial attack on this scale would not, comparatively speaking, cause a great number of casualties but with present home defence preparations fall-out would account for millions of deaths, the number depending largely on the wind

28

direction at the time of attack.' Decent shelters could cut the number of victims from 'more than thirteen millions to less than one million', but 'to provide such protection for a substantial proportion of city dwellers would be beyond our resources'. Oh, and no one would know when the deadly material was drifting in their direction anyway: 'there is no provision for warning the public against fall-out'.

So what was to be done in the face of what appeared to be certain doom for the bulk of the population? Er, 'further examination of these and other difficult problems is needed before any suggestions can be put to Ministers . . . for the present Ministers are asked only to note that these studies are contemplated'.

Was it surprising that, as the report warned, 'many people have tended to conclude that the Government has lost faith in the practicability of this country's surviving a nuclear attack'? The report even apologetically reveals that some members of the committee held that view themselves. 'There is a minority view that home defence preparations have no place in our defence policy, since we could not afford to undertake preparations on a scale that would provide adequate protection against attack.'

In short: we were pretty much doomed. It was lucky that, that year at least, the Soviet premier seemed to be content with no more aggressive action than banging his shoe on the podium at the

UN, and UK retaliation went no further than the notorious *Daily Mirror* headline: 'MR K! DON'T BE SO BLOODY RUDE!'

Mothers' milk – 1961

Like all the best supervillains from Herod onwards, the biggest danger the Soviets posed was to babies. The undeveloped thyroid glands of those under one year old can't cope with the radioactive isotope Iodine-131 in the way those of children and adults can; babies also drink a lot more milk, which soaks up high levels of the substance even after it's been processed through both grass and a cow (leafy vegetables like spinach take in a lot of it too, which is another good reason to refuse to eat your greens). And the obsessive nuclear testing programme the Russians were undertaking in central Siberia and the Arctic Circle during the autumn of 1961 – sometimes they were blowing up two or three atomic devices per day – meant that if the wind was blowing in the wrong direction, Britain's infants were at risk.

'The fall-out from the Russian explosion on 23rd October could, if the bomb was of large size and if all conditions are adverse, be such that the contamination of UK milk would approach the maximum acceptable dose for the year,' warned the Ministry of Defence after consulting with the Met Office. 'It is estimated that the dangerous concentration would arrive here between 12th and 16th November [someone has ringed the dates in biro]. If this happens, babies under 12 months should stop having fresh milk.' Instructions from the Ministry of Health were clear: 'We must start planning now for the suspension of fresh milk supplies and we cannot wait to see how serious a situation may develop.'

On 25 October, instructions went out to all local health authorities in England. If Iodine-131 levels reached danger levels – calculated at an average of more than 130 micro-microcuries over a year – 'a public announcement on radio and television and in the press' would be made. They would all receive thousands of 16oz tins of evaporated milk which they were to hand out to parents from 'special points nominated by the authority'. Along with them they were to distribute the following instructions:

How to feed your baby. Infants under 12 months should not be given fresh liquid milk whether as a drink or mixed with solid foods such as cereals, whether cooked or not. For the time being it is bad for them because of radioactivity from recent nuclear tests. They should only be given dried or tinned milk, and only dried or tinned milk should be used in preparing solid foods for them.

Thankfully, the measures were never necessary. Although the figures got up to frightening levels – 190 in Scotland, 160 in Northern Ireland – they didn't remain there long enough to take the yearly average up into the danger zone, and the tins remained in storage. Still, it is good to see that the government really had thought through all the possibilities. The file also contains a lengthy and detailed correspondence between the Ministries of Science and Health fretting about the danger of people in remote areas who weren't on mains water recontaminating their emergency dried milk supplies by mixing it up with rainwater which had absorbed its own hefty dose of radiation. They concluded that 'we consider it unlikely that more than 50,000 persons drink water obtained in this way, though some persons who normally use streams or wells may of course turn to collected rainwater in exceptionally dry periods'.

Don't panic! – 1979

It happened at ten to four on a Friday afternoon, 9 November 1979. In the House of Commons, Leon Brittan had just embarked on a long-winded speech about the Representation of the People Bill. 'Diddy' David Hamilton was hammering out the hits on Radio 2's afternoon show. Across the country, little ones were being plonked down in front of the telly ready for *Play School* as their older brothers and sisters arrived home from school looking forward to *Crackerjack*. And an alert went off at the Pentagon that a massive nuclear attack was under way.

American pilots sprang into action at bases in Oregon and Michigan. The Canadian Air Force dispatched ten F-111s from British Columbia. The 'doomsday plane' from which President Carter would have been able to oversee the destruction of his country and most of the rest of the planet was launched. Across the Atlantic, the message flashed through to the UK's early warning station at Fylingdales at eight minutes past four: advanced alert state. The crew of our own interception aircraft were automatically put on 'cockpit readiness', prepared to take to the skies at ten minutes' notice.

But before the pilots had even got as far as their planes, some happy news came through from America: it was a false alarm. The attack was just a pretend one: a simulation intended to test operators at the North American Air Defense command centre in Colorado. Only its contents had somehow been transmitted to two other military command centres, in Maryland and at the Pentagon – 'through possible mechanical malfunction', according to the US Defense Department, although a later investigation discovered that someone had actually just put the tape in the wrong machine – which immediately assumed the worst. But for now, everything was fine. The American and Canadian planes were recalled to their bases. And everyone swiftly agreed that there was no need to tell the President about it.

It was a different matter in Downing Street. 'Prime Minister – you may wonder why you were not involved in the false alarm concerning US strategic forces yesterday evening' begins a nervous handwritten note dispatched by Michael Alexander, Mrs Thatcher's foreign affairs adviser. He was at least able to insert a note of jingoism into his explanation. 'The early warning station at Fylingdales was alerted and identified the alert as a false alarm within 30 seconds – evidently rather more rapidly than the Americans themselves – so you were not troubled.'

But this was not enough for the Prime Minister. Beside a further reassurance from the Ministry of Defence that 'there was no indication from the Fylingdales radars of any threat to the UK, and indeed within seconds the information was shown to be suspect', she scribbled the single word 'How?'

She got an explanation that, stripped of its hi-tech language and acronyms, basically amounted to 'they had a look and couldn't see any bombs'. 'Fylingdales found no corroborative information on their own displays of the supposed missile attack,' wrote D. T. Piper of the MoD. 'NORAD was receiving no information from any of the three BMEWS – the other two are in Alaska

34

and Greenland – that would confirm the warning, nor had any other US warning system indicated a danger.' The world was safe. And that is why no one now talks about the catastrophic attacks of 11/9.

ROYAL REVELATIONS

The King is (nearly) dead, long live
the King – 1935

'**M**OST SECRET' reads the large red stamp on the first page of the dossier. 'TO BE KEPT UNDER LOCK AND KEY'. It is not surprising that Stanley Baldwin's government didn't want its contents to leak. Because the meeting it documented, held at Whitehall Gardens, that Sleeping Beauty's castle just downriver from the Houses of Parliament, on 20 December 1935, was held to discuss exactly what should be done about the death of the King. And he wasn't dead yet.

But George V was far from well. He was suffering from chronic lung disease and had to be regularly administered with oxygen; he had had a brush with death from bronchial pneumonia seven years earlier and been obliged to spend much of his time in Bognor for the good of his health, which is enough to make anyone long for the end. And of course, although no one likes to admit it, there is nothing unusual about forward planning for a royal death: I can remember reading the copious obituaries for the Queen Mother thanks to a few idle moments computer-hacking during a shift on the *Daily Telegraph* in 1999; they were already laid out on the page even though she still had three years to live at the time.

The media were an important part of plans then, too: one of the attendees at the secret meeting was Sir John Reith, the forbidding first director general of the BBC. His fellow attendees were representatives of various government departments who had their parts to play in such vital issues as precisely how many guns should be ceremonially fired to mark the King's passing, and who should give the orders for the 'half-masting of flags at flag stations under the control of the Service Departments'.

All departments were issued that month with an instruction manual titled 'SECRET – DEMISE OF THE CROWN': it gave full details of what the Privy Council would have to wear to proclaim the next monarch ('Levee Dress with crepe band on the left arm'), and what order they should be summonsed in ('Any Princes of the Royal Blood who are in this country' first, followed by the Archbishops of Canterbury and York, the Bishop of London and then members of the Cabinet). 'A letter should also be sent to the Home Office asking that special police facilities may be afforded on the occasion of the Meeting. Drafts of the necessary letters, forms of summons, and envelopes are, so far as practicable, kept ready.'

Appendices listed the many officials who would be obliged to proclaim the new king just in case anyone had missed the news: the chancellors of the universities of Oxford and Cambridge, the lieutenant governors of the Isle of Man, Jersey and Guernsey, the Constable of the Tower of London, and the mayors of various cities around Britain. Item one on the list of things to do, however, was this: 'Immediate steps should be taken to ascertain what style the King wishes to assume, in order that the draft Proclamations and Orders may be completed without delay.' Despite being known to his family and friends as David, the Prince of Wales stuck with tradition and plumped for Edward VIII as his regal title; pleasingly, he decided to abdicate less than a year later and put his younger brother on the throne, ensuring that the list of kings between Victoria and Elizabeth would be an easily memorable Edward-George-Edward-George.

The elder George's last bronchial breath did not emerge until the last minutes of 20 January 1936 – hastened, it emerged many decades later, by a fatal dose of morphine and cocaine administered by his doctor, Lord Dawson, something he rather glossed over in the bulletin he issued to *The Times*: 'The King's life is drawing peacefully to its close.' Someone was on duty at Downing Street that night: in the files are their handwritten instructions for whom to call if the worst news came through from Sandringham. Sir Maurice Hankey, the

Cabinet Secretary, would be at the United Services Club; the contact at the Prince of Wales's official residence was Mr Henty on Whitehall 3007. Another handwritten note headed '12.3 a.m.' records exactly what happened: the call came through from George V's assistant private secretary Sir Alan Lascelles to say that 'The King Passed peacefully away at a few minutes before 12 (11.58). I told Sir John Reith that I could confirm the demise of the Crown and gave him the above. He had not had his message and was due he said to issue a bulletin in 6 minutes. He wanted to use our message, but I said that as he was himself on the Sandringham list he ought not to do that. He rang up later to say he had broadcast our message at 12.15 on the strength of what appeared before them on the tape.'

The rest of the file is taken up with a plethora of paperwork concerning the proclamation of the new king and arrangements for a two-minute silence in memory of the old one (plans for a bank holiday on the day of his funeral were abandoned because it 'might be unpopular, involving as it would loss of work and wages to great numbers of people'). Every single piece of official notepaper – in compliance with the order from the Earl Marshal that 'all persons upon the present occasion of the death of His Late Majesty of blessed and glorious memory do put themselves into mourning to begin on Wednesday the 22nd of this instant, such mourning to continue until after His

Late Majesty's Funeral' – was specially printed with a black border.

And what would you like your great-grandchildren to be called, ma'am? – 1952

Two months before the coronation of Queen Elizabeth II, the Lord Chancellor, Lord Simonds, distributed a message from Her Majesty to his colleagues. 'I hereby declare My Will and Pleasure that I and My children shall be styled and known as the House and Family of Windsor, and that My descendants, other than female descendants who marry and their descendants, shall bear the name of Windsor.'

This was not entirely surprising. Any chance of them being known as the Schleswig-Holstein-Sonderburg-Glucksburgs had sadly died when her husband Prince Philip had adopted the surname Mountbatten on becoming a British subject (it wasn't his first choice: apparently he fancied being Mr Oldburgh). But the memorandum clears up any possibility of the Queen's kids following the custom of her subjects and taking their father's surname: 'when King George VI conferred a dukedom upon HRH the Duke of Edinburgh he did not intend that the name of Edinburgh should supersede that of Windsor as the name of the Royal House'. Besides, the two children they had at this point were unique in another way: 'King George VI issued Letters Patent by which He declared that the children of that marriage should enjoy the style of Royal Highness and the titular dignity of Prince or Princess prefixed to their Christian names in addition to any other titles of honour which might belong to them thereafter. Thus from their birth Prince Charles and Princess Anne came within these Letters Patent and neither had nor needed any surname.' It must be hell when they're filling out forms.

There was, however, one exception, albeit one that has yet to become relevant given that at time of writing Prince Harry still shows no signs of broodiness: 'the sons of grandsons of the Queen (other than the eldest son of the eldest son of the Prince of Wales) will not be within the Proclamation or the Letters Patent of 1917 and, if they have a surname at all, will have the surname of Mountbatten'.

Well, we couldn't have that, could we? Why, the name of Windsor was an ancient one, dating back all of 35 years to the point when George V had renounced the title of Saxe-Coburg-Gotha to avoid the same kind of jingoistic wartime senti- ment that had seen dachshunds being attacked in the street for being too German. The Cabinet swiftly approved the Queen's declaration, and her descendants were set to be named after her favourite of all her castles for ever more.

Or at least for eight years. Because in January 1960, with the Queen eight months pregnant with her third child, she decided she fancied another rebranding, to Mountbatten-Windsor. And it wasn't just because it sounded posher. She wished, according to her press secretary, 'to associate the name of her husband with her own and his descendants. The Queen has had this in mind for a long time and it is close to her heart.'

Not everyone was convinced. 'I do understand and if I may say so thoroughly sympathise with the Queen's desire,' wrote a fretful Reginald Manningham-Buller, the Attorney General, to Home Secretary Rab Butler. 'But it is a reversal of the decision made only eight years ago and I fear very much that the announcement will not be popular and will seriously affect the magnificent position the Royal Family now enjoy . . . I fear that one consequence may well be suspicion as to the influence Prince Philip has over the Queen; and to his actions in future being viewed with unjustified suspicion. I fear that this change will not enhance his position and prestige . . . I do feel that we ought to be certain before any public Declaration is made that Prince Philip is aware of the effect that the change may have on his position in the eyes of the public. If, having considered the matter, he would also like it to be done, then we should do all that we can to promote the acceptance of the change.'

Certainly the rumour has always been that Prince Philip had been cross about having his name removed from the credits despite his hard work as executive producer, and that his pushy uncle

Lord Louis Mountbatten had been lobbying behind the scenes. The fact that extensive chunks of the ensuing correspondence have been redacted from the relevant files and closed until 2060 does little to discourage the belief. But as the Queen's due date approached, Simonds' successor as Lord Chancellor, Lord Kilmuir, managed to convince the government that it was better to act sooner than later:

> REASONS FOR THE CHANGE: If the baby is a boy, his grandchildren will require a surname while those of the Prince of Wales will not . . . It is right that the name of his (the boy's) descendants should include the name of his father. This applies especially in view of the services of Prince Philip to Britain and the Commonwealth.

And so, on 8 February, 11 days before Prince Andrew popped out, his mother declared that her descendants – 'apart from those enjoying certain styles or titular dignities' – would be Mountbatten-Windsors, and that was her final word on the matter. It was, however, made very clear that they would be collectively 'styled and known as the House and Family of Windsor'.

Confused yet? It won't help that the first grandchild who actually qualifies to bear the name Mountbatten-Windsor, Prince Edward's eldest, born in 2003, goes by the title Lady Louise

Windsor. Her little brother, meanwhile, is called Viscount Severn. Which makes him sound like a special-offer packet of biscuits.

The flying duke – 1955

You'd think being married to the Queen meant you could pretty much do what you liked, but in the 1950s, the Duke of Edinburgh seemed to have to go crawling to the Cabinet every time he wanted to have any fun. At least if he wanted to have it several hundred feet above the ground.

If Winston Churchill had had his way, he would never have been allowed. When the Secretary of State for Air, Lord De L'Isle, broke the news in October 1952 that 'HRH the Duke of Edinburgh was anxious to learn to fly', the Prime Minister expressed 'grave doubts about the proposal . . . In view of his public position and responsibilities, His Royal Highness should not expose himself to unnecessary risks.' Cabinet minutes record that the Commonwealth Secretary and the Lord Privy Seal agreed with him, but their less fuddy-duddy colleagues were having none of it. 'Flying was now widely regarded as a normal means of transport, and young men who were in a position to learn to fly thought it little more hazardous than learning to drive a motor-car.'

They got their way when it came to the second stage of the Duke's training, which commenced the following January. Churchill was absent in

America at the time, jaw-jawing with the newly elected Eisenhower, and a Cabinet led by Foreign Secretary Anthony Eden agreed to give His Royal Flyness the go-ahead to continue to the advanced stage, on the grounds, recorded in the Cabinet Secretary's notebook at the time, that it would be 'much more dangerous if he isn't allowed to complete his training'. The notebook also shows that they insisted the Duke stick to the single-engine Harvard plane recommended by his instructors: 'Not Balliol, which is less well tried – tho he wd prefer it.' The Chief of the Air Staff was summoned to reassure ministers that 'the Duke had said that he would not at any time pilot an aircraft in which the Queen was a passenger', and 'the Cabinet re-affirmed their earlier view that the Duke of Edinburgh should not fly jet aircraft'.

He seems to have fancied a go on everything else, though. A 'Top Secret – Most Confidential Record' from July 1955, two years after the Duke was awarded his RAF 'wings' in a private ceremony at Buckingham Palace, marks the first of many ticklish problems for the Secretary of State for Air: 'it was thought that HRH the Duke of Edinburgh might wish to fly in a glider when he visited the National Gliding Championships meeting' in a few days' time. The Cabinet agreed that he could be allowed to if 'the Chairman of the Royal Air Force Gliding Association decided that a suitable two-seater glider could be used and that an experienced pilot was available to accompany the Duke', but 'if not, the Duke of Edinburgh would be dissuaded from flying in a glider'. Whose job it would be to do so was left unspecified.

Eight months later he was back: 'The Prime Minister said that HRH the Duke of Edinburgh had expressed a wish to fly a helicopter from the deck of an aircraft carrier,' the Cabinet were told in March 1956. Eden, now in the top seat in his own right, was quick to assure ministers that 'the Duke was assessed as a first class helicopter pilot . . . there was no doubt of his competence to do this, nor was it regarded as a specially dangerous flight', but they do not appear to have been entirely convinced. 'Discussion showed that it was the general view of the Cabinet that any extension of the Duke of Edinburgh's flying activities increased the risk which he was accepting.' Rather sweetly, they insisted on checking with his wife first: 'The Prime Minister might take a suitable opportunity to ascertain whether The Queen herself was concerned at the additional risk involved in a flight of this nature; but unless Her Majesty felt anxiety about it, it would be preferable that no objection should be raised to it.'

Give him an inch . . . back came another hapless Secretary of State for Air, George Ward, in October 1959. 'HRH The Duke of Edinburgh had recently been interested in the extension of the activities of flying clubs and in that connection had shown particular interest in a single-seater light aircraft known as the Rollason Turbulent.' Despite its less than reassuring name, he had 'expressed a wish to fly this aircraft himself, not as a means of transport from one point to another, but in order to gain first-hand experience of its operation'.

This time, the Cabinet could barely be bothered to put up any opposition. Permission was granted, 'provided that suitable safety precautions were observed. For example, the flight would be limited to an area within sight of the airfield; it should take place when the weather was clear and not liable to sudden deterioration; and no other flying would be allowed at the airfield while the Duke of Edinburgh was in the air.'

The best medicine – 1963

'I fear that I have had to go to hospital for an operation for prostatic obstruction,' wrote Prime Minister Harold Macmillan to the Queen on 9 October 1963, sounding like he wasn't quite sure. 'The fact is that at about 9 p.m. on Monday, October 7 I was suddenly overtaken by intolerable pain and discomfort.'

Never fear, her Majesty knew just what would sort him out. 'Today I received Your Majesty's reviver which encourages me to think that I am on the way to recovery,' wrote the grateful PM on the 14th.

Someone has written in the margin: 'Champagne.'

Plenty of people wanted to congratulate Harold Wilson on his election victory in October 1964. There is a thick file of telegrams from presidents and prime ministers from every corner of the world, all filed neatly with the Foreign Office's suggested replies for Downing Street's approval. But perhaps the most unlikely, given that Wilson led the Labour Party into Downing Street on a wave of guff about youth, modernity and the 'white heat of the technological revolution', came from a man not generally noted as being at the forefront of the Swinging Sixties scene: the Duke of Edinburgh. 'Delighted to see that resident of Duchy of Cornwall is new tenant at Downing Street. Signed Philip.'

Resident was pushing it a bit. Although Harold and Mary Wilson did indeed own a holiday bungalow on St Mary's, one of the Isles of Scilly that have been part of the royal estate providing an income for successive Princes of Wales since the fourteenth century, they had spent most of their time in Hampstead Garden Suburb. It was a bit easier for getting to Parliament. But Wilson was obviously touched: he scribbled his instructions directly on to the telegram:

Please discuss earliest line of reply, possibly on following lines

(a) Presenting humble duty or whatever form is
(b) Thanks
(c) He feels he might point out that while, thanks to the generous and liberal attitude of the Duchy, his residence within the Duchy of Cornwall is a freehold, his Downing Street residence has the status of a tied cottage.

His private secretary Malcolm Reid, whom he had inherited from his Eton-educated predecessor Sir Alec Douglas-Home, quietly tidied up his etiquette errors; a discreet note advised: 'Prime Minister: It is not necessary to telegraph in the third person or to present your humble duty to the Duke of Edinburgh (but only to the Sovereign).'

What do you buy for the prince who has everything? –1966

In October 1966, private secretary Michael Halls passed a note on to Prime Minister Harold Wilson reminding him that Prince Charles's eighteenth birthday was fast approaching.

The public in general does think that the 18th birthday of the Royal Family marks their coming of age and you may feel that

49

some special gesture is warranted. In 1944 when the Queen was 18 Mr Churchill privately sent her a present of his own works . . . Would you like:-

To send the usual telegram?

To send a present?

To combine 1 or 2 with any form of entertainment when he is in London at Christmas?

Wilson replied in his usual green pen. 'Telegram. 2. Is no good because my written works would not be of any interest.' This seems unduly harsh. What 18-year-old could fail to be thrilled by Wilson's 1945 debut *New Deal for Coal,* his Fabian tract *Post War Economic Policies in Britain*, or the 1957 potboiler he co-authored with Hugh Gaitskell, *Remedies for Inflation:A series of Manchester Guardian Articles*?

He did, however, think the third suggestion merited some thought. '?3 – I remember Clem [Attlee] entertaining the Prince and HM following their engagement with young friends there.'

On 23 November, nine days after Charles had celebrated his birthday by cutting a rug with 150 friends in the Crimson Drawing Room at Windsor Castle to the sounds of The Quiet Five (biggest hit: 'When the Morning Sun Dries the Dew', number 45 in the hit parade in May 1965), Halls penned another reminder. 'It was suggested that you might like to entertain the Prince when he is

50

in London over Christmas. Do you wish to pursue this, please?'

Alas, the Wincarnis would stay corked and Mary Wilson would not have to prepare a finger buffet: the PM had had second thoughts. 'Perhaps better not,' he replied to Halls. 'Palace might think I was [here his handwriting becomes infuriatingly indecipherable] – esp. if it got into press. There could be adverse political reaction too, if known.'

Prince Charles, sleeper agent? – 1969

George Thomas was a worried man. 'I have written this letter because I did not want the office to know about it,' the Secretary of State for Wales confided at the top of a handwritten note to Prime Minister Harold Wilson in July 1969. 'A dangerous situation is developing.' The object of his concerns? Charles, the bright shiny new Prince of Wales invested at Caernarfon Castle amid much pomp and pageantry just three weeks previously. Thomas thought he might be a terrorist.

Well, a useful idiot, anyway. 'I am concerned by the speeches made by the Prince of Wales . . . On two occasions he has made public speeches which have political implications. In my presence in Cardiff he referred to the cultural and political awakening in Wales. This is most useful for the Nationalists.'

This was a matter of more concern than it would

51

be now. The Welsh Nationalists of '69 vintage were not the cuddly Plaid Cymru crew currently playing at pretend parliaments in Cardiff: that very month had seen the jailing of six members of the Free Wales Army for public order offences, although their claims of hidden aeroplanes and dogs trained to carry explosives at a secret base in the Black Mountains turned out to have about as much truth to them as the Mabinogion. More seriously, Mudiad Amddiffyn Cymru, the Movement for the Defence of Wales, had managed to blow up several water pipes and electricity pylons as well as a couple of their own members on the morning of the investiture. 'If the prince is writing his own speeches he may well be tempted to go further,' fretted Thomas. 'The enthusiasm of youth is a marvellous spur, but it may lead to speeches that cause real difficulty.'

So where might Charles have become indoctrinated in such radicalism? In the run-up to his investiture, the Prince had spent a term at Aberystwyth University, studying Welsh and Welsh history and living in the Pantycelyn hall of residence just like any other student (although he was probably the only one with his own security team). 'He was subjected to concentrated attention by Welsh nationalists,' Thomas informed the Prime Minister. 'His tutor, his neighbour in the next room, and the Principal were all dedicated Nationalists. It has become quite evident to me that the Aberystwyth experience has influenced the Prince to a considerable extent.' Maybe his next-door neighbour sang 'Land of My Fathers' through the wall while Charles was asleep?

'The only constructive suggestions I have are that a discreet word to the Queen might help,' Thomas continued, 'but you are a better judge of that than I am.' Wilson's private secretary Michael Halls offered the opinion that Charles 'may perhaps be modelling himself on his father. But he is in a different constitutional position.' The PM asked him to have a 'low key' word with the Queen's private secretary, Sir Michael Adeane, and 'suggest that any subject on which the Prince became interested or any subject on which he wished to refer in a speech he should be encouraged to secure briefing from the appropriate Minister'.

While Thomas's fears turned out to be groundless in the long run – it seems fairly unlikely that Charles is going to lob a firebomb through the window of his son William's home in Anglesey any time soon in revenge for him being an 'incomer'– this invitation opened a whole new can of worms. More than 30 years later, ministers from another Labour government would be complaining publicly about their endless flow of correspondence from the heir to the throne. 'It wasted people's time. They thought he was a bit of a loon,' Gordon Brown's spin doctor Charlie Whelan said in 2006. They had only Harold Wilson to blame.

Mind you, Wilson may have quite quickly been kicking himself, judging by the contents of another Number 10 file from the summer of '69. After Charles gave a speech to the London Welsh Association about salmon fishing, the PM requested a briefing on the subject from MAFF (the Ministry of Agriculture, Fisheries and Food), which he then passed on to the Prince himself with an obsequious covering note: 'I am, Sir, Your Royal Highness's obedient servant.' He got six sides of neat handwriting on Balmoral note-paper in return. 'It was good of you to have bothered to do so when you must have been so busy with many other time-consuming problems . . . People are notoriously short-sighted when it comes to questions of wildlife and several species have been wiped out because no-one has woken up in time to the danger . . . You may not have fished yourself, but to do so for salmon is immensely exciting . . . when you come up here next weekend I shall attack you on the subject again!'

Wearily, Wilson requested a 'further note' from MAFF on the topic ahead of what he might have been hoping would be a relaxing weekend break at Balmoral. In return he got a vast, closely typed report, complete with multiple appendices and tables of statistics on salmon stock, which a further note records he went through in detail with the Prince during his Highland stay. The hours must have just flown by.

No proxy for poxy monarch – 1971

The Queen has got lovely handwriting. Even when she's poorly. Great big letters, open loops, a confident roundness to her vowels. Signs, allegedly, of an outgoing and confident personality, someone who enjoys the limelight, and is happy to compromise in order to please people. All of which must come in quite handy, what with being Queen.

While most of Her Majesty's correspondence comes in typed form via various private secretaries and ladies-in-waiting, she picked up her own fountain pen to dash off a thank-you note to Edward Heath when he wrote her a (typed) get-well-soon message after she went down with chickenpox in November 1971.

My dear Prime Minister

How very kind of you to write and sympathise – it seems a ridiculous disease to catch, especially when it isn't even from one's own children!

The doctors say that I have had chicken pox quite mildly for a grown-up – but it is not much consolation when one is covered in spots!

I trust by Tuesday I shall be completely free of all possible infection, but I have been told not to go amongst crowds in case of re-infection from them – one can't win from a virus!

Yours sincerely

Elizabeth R

It's not entirely clear why the British people choose to celebrate royal weddings through the medium of mugs and shiny coins in presentation cases, but they do, and the Royal Mint were not about to miss out when Princess Anne announced her engagement to Captain Mark Phillips in 1973. 'The Deputy Master [Harold Glover] is keen to strike a silver medal to commemorate Princess Anne's forthcoming wedding. He is sure this would be popular,' runs a memo to the Treasury from 8 June that year.

There was a problem, however. 'To produce a medal of this sort he needs the consent of the Queen and for the design to be approved by his Advisory Committee, the Chairman of which is the Duke of Edinburgh. When the design of a Silver Wedding Crown was being discussed, the Duke of Edinburgh apparently grumbled about none of the profits on what was basically a domestic matter accruing to the Palace, and referred to the scale of the Civil List. Mr Glover fears that this point will be raised again.'

What family wedding hasn't been accompanied by the father of the bride moaning about the cost of it all? But the man from the Mint had a cunning plan to keep Prince Philip quiet (and it wasn't just to park him near the bar and keep his glass topped up). Instead, he would offer to share the profits on each commemorative medal with the Palace, or 'some worthy cause' of their choice.

'After consultation I told the Deputy Master we saw considerable objections to these proposals bearing in mind that a new Civil List had been fixed . . . at a level which would permit the Royal Family to operate on its present basis, including the celebration of Royal occasions such as wedding anniversaries and the like,' Treasury official Joan Kelley reported to her bosses. 'As far as allocating a fraction of the profits to some worthy cause was concerned we saw public expenditure objections to this.'

Glover – who was himself immortalised on a Royal Mint medal when he left the following year; they did his glasses beautifully – then came up with an alternative plan to get in the royal good books. 'In suggesting to the Queen's Private Secretary that the medal should be issued and put on sale, he would like to be able to offer to supply the Queen, without charge, a certain number of the medals for her to give to guests at the wedding . . . He thought this would be an appropriate gesture of appreciation to the Palace . . . At a metal cost of £2 a time this would work out at £400, only a fraction of the profits on the operation which might be around £¼ million.'

Taking care of the wedding favours, leaving the royals with even more of the budget to spend on booze and the mobile disco? It had to be a winner. After all, the buffet was already sorted: Mark

Phillips's father worked for Wall's Sausages and would definitely see them right. 'I agree that this is reasonable,' wrote Kelley on 11 June, giving Glover the go-ahead to present his plan to the Palace.

Perhaps it was his final point that clinched it: 'Whatever is done on this occasion would of course provide a precedent for similar action when and if Prince Charles marries.' And it did. Both times.

Kidnap? Bloody likely – 1974

When a lone gunman brought Princess Anne's Rolls-Royce to a halt at the top of the Mall in 1974, shot and injured her driver and bodyguard and attempted to force her out of the car, there was just one question on the mind of the Queen's private secretary, Martin Charteris. 'It seems to me that it is important to establish whether this horrible business was just the act of a nutcase or something more serious.'

His counterpart at Number 10, Robert Armstrong, was able to reassure him – and by extension the Queen, who was at the time on a tour of Indonesia – in an exchange of top-priority 'flash' telegrams. 'All the indications are that this man was operating entirely on his own, and without political motive. He had obviously worked out the details of his idea with care and attention to detail, but the whole framework was lunatic . . . At the time of writing we do not know the motive, but it sounds to me like an attempt to imitate the Hearst kidnapping.' Patty Hearst, the American heiress to a vast media empire, had been snatched from her home the previous month by the world's most pretentious terrorist group, the Symbionese Liberation Army. At the time of Armstrong's telegram she was still their captive, and well on the way to being brainwashed into robbing banks alongside them. There is no evidence that Ian Ball intended to do anything similar with Princess Anne, but who knows, if things had worked out differently maybe she would have popped up a few months later trying to hold up a branch of the Midland.

Back to reality. On 21 March, the day after the kidnap attempt, Home Secretary Roy Jenkins made a statement to the House explaining that 'the examination of the issues and the conclusions reached must remain confidential if they are to be effective in enabling us to achieve the greatest degree of security that can be obtained'. But his boss, Harold Wilson, had already received a secret briefing on the whole affair, courtesy of Crown Equerry Colonel John Miller, who had been in a car behind the Princess and her husband, returning from the same event. He wrote to Wilson that morning asking if he could spare five minutes for an eyewitness account: 'I have of course not told anybody that I have written to you, and I certainly do not wish it to be known.'

In the event, Wilson was unable to see Miller,

but Armstrong gave him a thorough debriefing which was fully minuted for the PM. According to Miller, having blocked the path of the royal Rolls, 'Ball came round to the side of the car, pointed a gun at Princess Anne and said "I want you to come with me for a day or two, because I want £2 million. Will you get out of the car?" Princess Anne replied "Bloody likely; and I haven't got £2 million."

'Apparently this conversation continued for a time, with Ball trying to persuade Princess Anne to get out of the car, and Princess Anne refusing to do so. She said afterwards to Colonel Miller "It was all so infuriating; I kept saying I didn't want to get out of the car. I nearly lost my temper with him, but I knew that if I did, I should hit him and he would shoot me."

'It seems that Princess Anne then decided that if she made as if to get out of the door on the opposite side of the car, Ball would go round there and could be apprehended. So she made a dive for the door, and sure enough Ball fell for it.' He was bundled to the ground by several policemen, disarmed and arrested. He later pleaded guilty to attempted murder, and was detained indefinitely under the Mental Health Act. He is still in Broadmoor, but he has his own website on which he explains that the whole affair was a hoax caused by a policeman called Frank who managed to persuade him to live his life exactly one year out of sync from everyone else in the world. It's a cracking read.

Wilson hand-wrote a comment in the margin of Miller's account: 'A very good story. Pity the Palace can't let it come out.'

How Harold Wilson saved the Queen Mother from blowing up – 1975

In May 1974, the Shah of Iran wrote a nice letter to the Queen Mother inviting her for a visit. The 74-year-old dowager said she would love to come, but she had better just check with the Foreign Office first. They were very enthusiastic indeed. 'Iran is very important to us for a variety of reasons, particularly trade and oil supply, and relations between our two countries are extremely close and friendly,' came the reply to Clarence House, demonstrating just how much global politics can change in the space of four decades. 'For these reasons Mr Callaghan would welcome it if Queen Elizabeth [senior] decided to accept the Shah's invitation. The Foreign and Commonwealth Office would be prepared to sponsor the visit. As to timing, we agree that late April or May 1975 would be suitable; the weather in Iran at that season should not be too trying.'

Then someone came up with an even more wizard wheeze: why not send the Queen Mum over there on Concorde? The supersonic passenger plane co-developed with the French had so far cost something approaching a billion pounds, and with several prototype aircraft up and running, both countries desperately needed to get some orders in to start covering their costs (Wilson's administration had come close to scrapping the whole project due to the escalating price the previous year). Prince Philip had already done his bit for sales by joining a test flight: what better way to showcase the shiny new sales opportunity than by putting his mother-in-law on board another? The government were hoping that the Shah himself would want to stop her and buy one (or preferably several: they were banking on selling around 200 of the planes). Granted, Concorde hadn't actually been granted its Certificate of Airworthiness yet, but that was just a formality. Wasn't it?

The first inkling that something was wrong came in a Foreign Office telex on 18 February. 'It has now been concluded that meteorological conditions will not permit the trials to be phased to coincide with the Royal visit.' That order was rapidly reversed – and then re-reversed on 25 March in a further cryptic message: 'because of higher priority requirements relating to the certific- ation programme, Concorde can not repeat not now be made available to fly the Queen Mother to Tehran'.

'This is getting embarrassing,' wrote Our Man in Tehran, Sir Anthony Parsons. 'At the time of [the Queen Mother's Private Secretary] Sir Martin Gillat's reconnaissance visit we gave the court to understand that it was probable that Her Majesty would come in Concorde. Later we told them that Concorde was definitely off. A week or so ago we told them that it was definitely on again. The response from the court to my latest communication was a little sharp. If we now change our minds again the Shah will wonder what we are up to. What reason would we give? We could hardly tell the court that Concorde had a more important mission to carry out. Equally I do not have to emphasise the positive publicity value of Her Majesty arriving in Concorde, particularly if the Iranians' own contract for Concorde is signed at about the same time. Could the latest decision not be re-considered?'

What Parsons did not know – what very few people would know for a further 30 years – was what was contained in a confidential memo from Peter Shore, the Trade Secretary, to Downing Street. 'About three weeks ago the operation of one of Concorde's engines was discovered to be unsatisfactory. If the engine is run in the wrong mode there is some risk of fracture of the compressor blades, which could have serious consequences if it occurred.'

The Airworthiness Requirements Board had concluded that Concorde was perfectly safe to fly as long as 'an experienced pilot and flight crew' kept an eye on things and made sure the plane wasn't put into the mode where it would, er, blow up in mid-air. 'This being so both the Secretary of State for Industry and I are inclined to agree that the flight should proceed,' Shore advised. But the Prime Minister was having none of it. 'I do not feel that in the case of an aircraft carrying the Queen Mother we should have to rely on a test pilot for this purpose,' wrote Harold Wilson in a personal minute on 9 April. 'We should be in an indefensible position if it became known that the Queen Mother had been allowed to fly in the aircraft at a time when there was a problem over its engine. I do not therefore think that Concorde should be used for this flight.'

So the nation's favourite grandmother was saved to fly another day. She went to Tehran on what her biographer William Shawcross describes as 'what was by now a rather elderly RAF Comet', and had a lovely time by all accounts. Concorde passed its Certificate of Airworthiness in December that year and managed not to blow up in flight for a further 25 years, at which point all of the 14 planes that had eventually been sold were withdrawn from flight. By then, in July 2000, the Shah, Wilson, Gillat and Parsons had all passed on too, leaving the Queen Mother, at the age of 100, as the slightly unlikely sole survivor of the episode.

Bombers and bouquets – 1979

The telegram operator charged with transmitting the news to the Foreign Office on the afternoon of 27 August 1979 did not spot its significance: he prefaced it and the second message that followed swiftly on its heels with some jaunty backchat, now forever recorded for posterity: 'Got two short Tels for U pal ok? . . . Ere Goes.'

EXPLOSION ON LORD MOUNT-BATTEN'S BOAT

AT 1235 WE WERE INFORMED BY THE GARDA THAT THERE HAD BEEN AN EXPLOSION ON LORD MOUNT-BATTEN'S BOAT IN SLIGO.

LORD MOUNTBATTEN IS MISSING. THE BOATMAN AND TIMOTHY KNATCHBULL ONE OF LORD BRABOURNE'S SONS ARE BOTH DEAD AND THEIR BODIES HAVE BEEN RECOVERED. LORD AND LADY BRABOURNE HAVE BEEN RESCUED. THEY ARE INJURED. WE ASSUME YOU WILL CONTACT THE PALACE.

Also preserved are the handwritten notes of an official, obviously made during a frantic phone call to find out more information. 'Embassy people leave about 4 p.m.,' he scrawled in a panic. 'Paul' was written down and scribbled out. 'Boatman' was written next to it. Beside that: 'Timothy Knatchbull head injury'. Some of the nameless official's confusion is explained in the next telegram:

65

THE GARDA INFORMED US AT 1520 THAT THEY HAVE NOW RECOVERED THREE BODIES. THOSE OF LORD MOUNTBATTEN, PAUL MAXWELL, THE BOATMAN, AND NICHOLAS KNATCHBULL (NOT TIMOTHY KNATCHBULL AS WE WERE PREVIOUSLY TOLD).

Timothy, Lord Mountbatten's 14-year-old grandson, had survived the attack. His twin brother was not so lucky. Nor was the 82-year-old Lady Brabourne, another passenger on the boat, despite the telegram's assurance that she was 'in hospital in Sligo. Reported to be not seriously injured.' She died the following day.

Lord Mountbatten, the Queen's cousin, former Viceroy of India and Chief of the Defence Staff, was one of the IRA's most prominent and significant victims, and his murder a low point in their decades-long campaign of terror. But the file on his death shows how quickly the initial shock gave way to routine paperwork. Typewritten drafts of statements to be issued by the Prime Minister, expressing how the attack 'has reinforced the repugnance felt for those who seek to advance their political ends by these evil means'. Letters of condolence from world leaders – President Jimmy Carter, the President-elect of Nigeria, the 'Government and people of South Africa', Chancellor Schmidt and 'the whole German people' and dozens more. Each comes with its own covering note from the respective ambassador or high commissioner; then with a note from a Downing Street official drafting a reply from the Prime Minister, then with a covering note for that reply. Most of the replies are identical. Some people didn't get one – officials decreed that 'no substantive reply is necessary to the message of condolence from the Uttar Pradesh Legislative Assembly'. Roy Jenkins, then President of the European Commission, got two, prompting an icy note from the Prime Minister's private secretary to his counterpart at the Foreign Office: 'An excess of zeal on your part, perhaps?'

Denis Thatcher was also the victim of a doubling-up. On the same day that an instruction was put out that 'the Prime Minister would like as many senior Ministers as possible to be present' at Mountbatten's funeral – she was even moving the time of Cabinet, so they wouldn't have an excuse – her husband replied to an enquiry as to his own intentions in elaborately curlicued handwriting: 'I much regret that I will be in the Midlands on that day at a Board Meeting.' Pressed on the point, in a handwritten note from his wife's private secretary, he was rather more terse: 'NO.'

Practicalities are discussed. A letter from Number 10 to the Lord Chamberlain's office points out that 'a number of former Prime Ministers will be accompanied by their private detectives. I expect that this will be true of others attending the Service, and I wonder what your plan for this will be – find a place, probably standing, quietly somewhere?'

Then there is what is not there. Paperwork relating to the pathologist's examination of Mountbatten's body has been excised, with a neat handwritten note: 'Passages deleted and closed, 40 years, under an FOI exemption.' So too has a 'letter from Prime Minister to the Queen dated 27th August 1979'.

In the midst of it all, other human touches. A note of 'information passed on' assuring the PM that the Foreign Office had requested 'discreet surveillance of Carol Thatcher in Canberra in view of IRA Australian activity reported'. And her mother's handwritten instructions for a government wreath to be sent to Mountbatten's funeral: 'Please – a very beautiful one if possible all in white.'

And someone – a Mr Peterson – has taken the trouble to write back. 'The wreath was beautiful. A large circle of all white flowers, carnations, roses, freesias, orchids, shaggy chrysanthemums, large ordinary chrysanthemums – and a raised top part of white tiger lilies with pale green spots on a background of dark foliage.' An appreciation is scrawled on the top of his note. 'Many thanks.'

FOREIGN FIELDS

Lions led by donkeys: a donkey
writes – 1915

Much to everyone's surprise, it wasn't over by Christmas.

And so, in January 1915, the Committee of Imperial Defence requested 'an appreciation by Lord Esher' of 'THE WAR – after six months'.

For Esher, a behind-the-scenes fixer who had chaired a committee that recommended the wholesale reorganisation of the army following the Boer War, it was all a question of WWND – What Would Napoleon Do? 'Although according to Napoleon, the whole art of war consists in a well-reasoned and strictly judicious defensive, he added that this should, in all cases, be followed by audacious and rapid attack,' he noted. 'So far, except in sporadic instances, this has been found impossible.' There was a very good reason for that. The French and British troops on one side and the Germans on the other were bogged down in a series of freshly dug trenches which stretched through northern France and up through Belgium: they wouldn't move much for the next three and a half years. 'This deadlock may be partly occasioned by severe winter conditions,' noted Lord Esher, 'but on the other hand, it may be caused by the physical and material conditions of modern war, that appear to tend rather in the direction of siege than of free manoeuvre.'

So what would happen next? As far as Esher was concerned, the best way to work this out was to 'endeavour to ascertain the moral factors at work among the peoples engaged in strife, as well as among the neutral nations more directly affected'. And this was exactly what he provided.

The bad news first: the Germans were looking like winners. 'It may safely be assumed that the German Armies have not succeeded in effecting all that was hoped for by German statesmen, they have nevertheless accomplished a great deal . . . it cannot be claimed that, on balance, the advantage of the war, so far as it has been fought, is on the side of the Allies.'

There was better news concerning Germany's partners in the conflict. 'In the past Austria has constantly failed as a fighting power. Her failure, therefore, to-day is no new thing. In the Napoleonic wars she was beaten over and over again.' Why so? Esher was inclined to blame it on 'her ever-present racial problem', which arose from being cobbled together out of bits of other nations in an 1867 union so tenuous it was officially called the Austro-Hungarian compromise. 'Her armies are not homogenous,' he pointed out. There were 'internal disagreements and the ever-present conflict between the German and Hungarian temperament'.

Germany's other ally, Turkey, posed a different problem – one familiar to modern military strategists: 'The great value of Turkey to Germany is to demobilise in the central area of conflict considerable forces of Russian and British troops and to rouse a certain amount of friction in the Mahommedan world.' But he had reassuring news for those lining up against the troops of the Ottoman Empire in the area that was not yet known as Iraq: 'Turkish troops are not an entirely negligible factor, although they are not of the quality which distinguished them forty years ago in the Shipka Pass.' Not many of the troops on the ground would recognise the name of this key battle from the Russo-Turkish War of 1877. But within months, everyone would come to know the name Gallipoli, as the disastrous offensive launched that April saw 286,000 British, French and Anzac soldiers killed or wounded. Few of those humiliatingly evacuated from the peninsula the following winter would concur with Esher's opinion of their enemy's negligibility.

What about those on our side? Esher stopped short of calling the French cheese-eating surrender monkeys, as the more rabid supporters of another war would 90 years later, but he was not impressed. 'The Committee of Imperial Defence had been told over and over again by the General Staff that France was so ready for war and that her armies were so admirably commanded, trained, and provided, that there could be no question of an immediate invasion on a large scale of French territory, and, furthermore, that if the assistance of Great Britain was immediately forthcoming, that France could not be invaded at all . . . The rapid advance of the German Armies and the retreat of the Franco-British force came therefore as a surprise.'

This could, however, 'only have a historic interest'. The fact was that both French and British troops were now bogged down in their trenches, and the strategists in Paris were sounding a lot less optimistic. 'It remains to be seen whether, as many French officers believe, troops subjected for a long period to warfare of this kind degenerate and become incapable of active operations,' wrote Esher. He noted that 'many French officers have told me that they view with misgiving the manner in which their men have accommodated themselves to trench life, so foreign to their previous notions and to the French temperament'. It's unlikely the British troops were exactly jumping for joy about it either.

The Russians were frankly a bit of a let-down too. 'Up to the present time Russia has failed to make good the expectations of her Allies . . . It was anticipated when war broke out that before this date the Russian armies would be well within the boundaries of the German Empire.' No such luck. So disastrous had the Russian advance been that the general in charge, Alexander Samsonov, had committed suicide rather than report back to the Tsar.

So, as usual, it was all down to Great Britain, or, as Esher insisted on calling it, England. 'If England was left standing alone, she would, thanks to her intangibility, have nothing to fear from the result of the conflict with Germany,' he frothed, slipping into the third-person feminine in his patriotic fervour. This was despite the fact that 'she has gone further in the direction of continental warfare than the traditions of the country and its ancient policy would have suggested. The hatred, if so strong a word may be used, of the English people for continental wars has been one of their strongest characteristics, and it was this hatred that Pitt made the foundation of what he called "his system of strategy". Pitt's legacy to his country was a well-adjusted combination of land and sea force, and the successes of 1759 – that immortal year – were due to the use that he made of the amphibious power of this country.'

Just how irrelevant this nostalgic navel-gazing was would become apparent over the next few years, as tanks, aeroplanes and ever more advanced machine guns took over from cavalry charges as the deciding factors of war.

About one thing, however, Esher was right. 'The response of the country under a voluntary system of recruitment to Lord Kitchener's call, has produced results that prove beyond all question the determination and capacity of the English people to fight through this war to a successful finish.' They did so, but not without the sacrifice of nearly a million men. Needless to say, Esher was not among them.

Getting to know these new-fangled Bolsheviks – 1917

It was nine months since the Russian Revolution, but the Cabinet couldn't help feeling that they hadn't really got the measure of these new chaps who had taken over.

The reports they were receiving from the Foreign Office didn't always help. 'The Russian situation is more obscure than ever,' reported assistant secretary William Ormsby-Gore (or, as he rather splendidly signed his pre-PC reports, WOG), days after the new administration declared an armistice with Germany in December 1917, a major blow to the Allied war effort. 'Trotsky is evidently a genuine Karl Marxian Jewish Internationalist, who is seeking to spread this new anti-national dispensation.'

His department had at least managed to obtain a text of the armistice agreement – by the cunning method of reading *The Times*, which printed it in full on 19 December. They had also received telegrams from the British Ambassador to Moscow concerning the fate of the pro-war Constitutional Democratic Party, or Cadets, but they were slightly unsure about some of the unfamiliar phrases being bandied about: 'the Cadet party had been declared by the government to be (?enemies of the people) and ordered the arrest of its leaders'. The ambassador, Sir George Buchanan, faced a further problem in finding out exactly what was going on: although he had been a close personal friend of Tsar Nicholas, the new foreign commissar, a fellow by the name of Leon Trotsky, had informed Sir George that 'he was accredited to a non-existent government by one which did not recognise the Bolsheviks, so that technically he was nothing more than a private individual'.

Matters had become slightly clearer by the new year, when WOG checked in again with news from the High Commissioner to Russia. 'Mr Lindley's telegram of the 7th January is most interesting, and confirms previous estimates that have been formed here regarding the principles and aims of the Bolshevik leaders,' he informed the Cabinet. 'Mr Lindley telegraphed that the Bolshevik movement was completely in the hands of MM Trotsky and Lenin, and they had fully explained their aims and policy, which might be summed up as social revolution throughout the world, with the entire suppression of nationality, property and religion . . . [they] would do all they could to discredit all existing Governments and prevent either of the belligerent sides scoring a success. They were particularly hostile to everything British and would do what they could to upset our rule in Egypt and India.'

Still, the new regime were at least keeping up some of the old traditions and providing a diplomatic representative to London. It wasn't quite an announcement in *The Times*, but a decree had been published 'in the official organ of the Soviet Government' – the catchily titled *News of the Central Executive Committee of the Soviets of Working and Military Deputies*, or *Izvestiya* – that 'In the name of Soviets of Workmen, Soldiers and Peasants' Deputies, Citizen Litvinoff is hereby appointed provisional plenipotentiary in London by the People's Commissariat of Foreign Affairs. All members of the embassy, the military mission in general, all officials of the Russian Republic actually residing in Great Britain engaged on official duties are invited at the first demand of Citizen Litvinoff to hand over to him all current affairs, documents, and public moneys of the Russian Republic which may be at their disposal. Any opposition to the orders of Litvinoff given in the above-indicated sense will be dealt with as a crime against the State.'

Not that these people sounded like the sort we wanted to have anything to do with. A further memorandum distributed by Ormsby-Gore at the end of the month noted that, as well as something called a 'Congress of Sovyets' held in St Petersburg and an 'All-Russian Anarchist Congress' in

76

Petrograd, Moscow had seen 'a Bolshevik demonstration on the previous day in which soldiers, the Red Guard, and roughs had taken part'.

There may be trouble ahead – 1919

The secret British Empire Report prepared for the Cabinet in December 1919 noted that the Governor General of the Union of South Africa had visited a new student hostel for Transvaal University College, where he made perhaps the most optimistic prediction in history.

'His Excellency the Governor-General praised the work which Mr Justice Bristowe had done for the institution, which had probably been so successful because it was neither a racial nor a denominational establishment. Unfortunately, His Excellency added, the racial question was still a serious one in South Africa, and it might occasion some slight trouble in the future, but he was confident that the Union would increase in prosperity and eventually become a happy and contented land.'

Rubbish for Russia – 1921

Around five million people are estimated to have died in the Russian famine of 1921, the result of a prolonged drought and the chaos and civil war that followed the revolutions of 1917. It took Lenin some time to concede that a population that was alive due to aid from filthy foreign capitalists was preferable to an ideologically sound but extinct one, but once he did so, an international relief effort sprang into action thanks to organisations like the recently formed Save the Children and the Quakers. Pathé cameras recorded sacks of grain and boxes of tinned goods being loaded on to ships in the London docks, and in November 1921, despite public grumblings about the Bolsheviks' failure to make good on the war debts run up by their predecessors in government, Lloyd George's administration decided to get in on the act by donating, for distribution by the Red Cross, what was described to journalists as 'certain war surpluses held by the Disposals Board, consisting of medical stores, clothing, etc. which cost about £250,000 when purchased'.

This was a less than honest picture, as the Prime Minister conceded in a Cabinet meeting the following March. It is probably no accident that his admission was preceded by a discussion of leaks to the press, which concluded that the minutes of meetings should henceforth be restricted to stop details of discussions being publicly aired. Because Lloyd George was about to speak very frankly indeed.

'The Prime Minister deeply deplored a decision which, in his view, would involve this country in a good deal of discredit. He would ask the Cabinet to review the question of the grant of stores. He had given an answer in the House of Commons to the effect that we had made a gift of stores to Russia. He was now informed that these stores were rubbish. We were entitled to refuse help to a starving population, but it was utterly unworthy, while pretending to help, to send gifts of useless stores. He asked that at least the Cabinet should make good the gift which he had announced in Parliament.'

No one demurred. It would have been very hard to object, given that reports were coming in of families reduced to eating grass and the bark from trees to survive. 'The Secretary of State for the Colonies agreed that it was disgraceful to take credit for a worthless gift, and that we should send a fresh parcel to Russia.' A further £100,000 worth of stores – all food, this time – was dispatched that month.

But it didn't mean the government were about to 'fess up to the worthlessness of the first batch. 'Every effort will be made to add to the supply of medical stores already placed at the disposal of the Red Cross Society,' Cabinet minister Austen Chamberlain disingenuously told the House of Commons when he was urged to do more for the starving just two days after the meeting. 'I believe the horror of the situation in Russia can hardly be exaggerated, but we must have regard to what we have already done.'

Wales goes to India – 1922

In July 1922, Prime Minister David Lloyd George called a special meeting at Number 10 to discuss the situation in India. Mohandas Gandhi was leading a campaign of peaceful civil disobedience against British rule: the 1919 Government of India Act, an attempt to extend the involvement of actual Indians in the government of their country while retaining all the important powers for their colonial masters had not gone down as well with the locals as everyone had hoped. Clearly, Lloyd George needed some advice from an expert. So he invited the Prince of Wales along.

The Prince of Wales in 1922 was known subsequently for a brief period as King Edward VIII, and forever after as 'the one that abdicated and married Mrs Simpson', but the secret minutes of the Downing Street meeting record him as 'HRH The Prince of Wales, KG, KT, GCSI, GCMG, GCIE, GCVG, GBSSC'. His knowledge of India – other than the third and fifth set of initials there, which indicated that he was a Knight Grand Commander of the Order of the Star of India and a Knight Grand Commander of the Order of the Indian Empire – derived from the fact that he had visited the country the previous year: at every stop during his royal tour he had been faced by protests against the import of cotton from Britain as Gandhi tried to establish the country's own industry. Joining him at Number 10 were the Secretary of State for India, Viscount Peel; the Parliamentary Secretary to the Indian Office, Earl Winterton; Sir Malcolm Hailey, a member of

India's Executive Council, effectively the country's Cabinet under the Viceroy; and a couple of other fellows with Sir in front of their name and letters afterwards. And if a prince, a viscount, an earl and three knights couldn't sort out a problem, who could?

Lloyd George – who was, incidentally, common as you like – laid on the flattery with a trowel. 'The Prince of Wales had already given him much useful information arising out of His Royal Highness's recent visit.' Now he wanted to sound him out about the idea of providing the Viceroy with extra support in government by boosting up his Executive Council. 'The Prime Minister said he did not see how the Viceroy could govern such a huge country with only two or three advisers in these difficult times.' Naturally, he wasn't talking about appointing natives, but 'persons drawn from outside India'.

As it stood, the council was made up of an equal number of Indians and Brits, and Lord Peel pointed out that 'if two more British members were added the question would be raised as to whether the position of the Indian members of the Council was not being weakened'. But, he assured his colleagues, there should be no question of putting more Indians in charge of their own country: 'they could not be relied on to keep matters secret'. Hailey agreed: 'It was very difficult for the Indians, surrounded as they were by their relations and friends, not to mention in

81

conversation what had taken place at the Council.' Far better to appoint that eternal solution for all governments: 'some competent City man', although Peel pointed out that the salary on offer was a mere £6,000 a year, and 'it was very difficult to obtain such, as they were already doing too well'.

The Prince appears to have only made minimal contributions to the discussion. He said 'his impression in India had been that men like Sir Malcolm Hailey had a great deal too much to do', something which, given that his own time was mostly devoted to drinking, dancing and seducing other people's wives, he may not have been in the best position to judge.

He was more worried about other things: the shortage of qualified doctors in India, which he reckoned 'hit the white women most of all'. Quite so, said Hailey: 'even if English women could overcome the racial aversion, they had no confidence in the Indian doctors'. Lord Winterton was determined not to be left out of the racist fun: he chimed in that 'in Palestine the men serving under him in the Camel Corps had complained at being attended by Indian doctors, in whom they had no confidence'. The Prince's other great contribution was to shoot down the tentative suggestion by the Prime Minister, who had attended his local village school in Wales, that civil servants in India might choose to educate their children locally rather than sending them back home to boarding school at great expense: 'The Prince of Wales said it was very bad for British boys to get their education in India.' At which point the discussion appears to have been closed.

French kissing – 1939

Walter Monckton faced many problems when he was appointed director general of the government's Press & Censorship Bureau at the outbreak of war in 1939, but the one that blew up in mid-December was probably the most pleasurably resolved.

The 1st Canadian Division set off from Halifax, Nova Scotia, for Europe on 10 December; they were made up of both English- and French-speaking troops, so, as Monckton pointed out, 'the French were naturally specially interested'. Someone, however, had forgotten to inform the French press of the embarkation: they not only had no photographs of the convoy as it set out across the Atlantic, but they only heard about it second-hand.

'They were naturally angry, and will splutter a bit,' Monckton informed his superiors on 20 December. But not to worry; he was bringing them not a problem but a solution. 'I gave about 20 of them luncheon at Claridges today and I think we can say we kissed (thank God not literally) and all is prettier again in the garden. A good time was had by all.'

What I did on my holidays,
by Harold Macmillan – 1958

On his return from a two-month tour of the Commonwealth in February 1958, Harold Macmillan ordered the Cabinet Secretary to distribute a 'Commentary' on what he had been up to. And boy, did he have a lot to say for himself.

The Prime Minister and his wife were accompanied on their 33,000-mile round trip by his valet and her personal maid, as well as a crowd of officials who seem to have been entirely devoted to sucking up to them. By everyone's assessment – each of them amplified and emphasised in Macmillan's account – the trip was considered to have been 'a personal triumph for the Prime Minister and Lady Dorothy Macmillan, who inspired friendship and respect (and a sense of warmth and exhilaration) wherever they went. Many of the Prime Minister's speeches touched his hearers very deeply.' His stop-off in Australia was 'beyond all question a wonderful success'. India was 'outstandingly successful'. And the 'natural gaiety and geniality of the people in Ceylon' meant that his visit was 'a real success both at the popular level and among thinking people'. The tribal leaders at the Khyber Pass liked him so much they gave him some sheep.

This was despite a startling lack of tact when it came to Commonwealth relations: when Macmillan discussed the Indian leader Nehru with his New

Zealand counterpart, he referred to 'Kashmir as very much the nigger in the woodpile'. He gave Nehru a lecture on the position of his own Congress Party and how it was 'in a sense in the position of the Irish Party after Home Rule – it cannot just live on the claim that it made the revolution. In the same way, the Whig party could not continue indefinitely on in fear of Jacobiteism.' If this went slightly over the Indian Prime Minister's head, he threw in his own impressive attempt to bamboozle the British PM a few minutes later: 'He tried to argue in favour of suspension of nuclear tests, the abandonment of nuclear weapons, and all the rest of it . . . He said that somebody had told him you could make an H-bomb in your back garden. I said that this was not our experience.'

Macmillan was, however, particularly proud of the way he had dealt with the Mayor of Singapore, who had 'not long before indulged in acts of discourtesy to the Crown. The Prime Minister however behaved towards him with a courtesy that appeared to embarrass him.' And guess what? 'The Prime Minister was received everywhere with a welcoming interest.'

But then – disaster! Macmillan 'contracted a chill at Singapore and remained in the aircraft sleeping under drugs on medical advice' when he arrived in Sydney, meaning that the Commonwealth Minister for Air could not be received. Thankfully within 24 hours he had recovered sufficiently to enjoy a full programme in New Zealand: amongst other thrilling activities, the PM 'inspected cars taking part in a vintage car race, which he then officially started' and, best of all, 'visited an albatross sanctuary and had a picnic tea with the Mayor'.

This exhaustive account goes on for an unbelievable 98 pages. The Cabinet were probably just grateful he didn't make them sit down and watch a slideshow of his holiday snaps.

Dancing with danger – 1959

Margot Fonteyn was the most famous ballerina in the world, star of the Royal Ballet, muse of the choreographer Frederick Ashton and a Dame of the British Empire. So Ian Henderson, the British Ambassador to Panama, was quite surprised to be woken in the early hours of the morning on 21 April 1959 and told that she was in prison in the country's capital.

He knew that she had been on a yachting holiday off the coast of the country with her Panamanian husband Roberto Arias, not least because she had 'enthusiastically accepted an invitation' to a reception at his embassy for the visiting Duke of Edinburgh two days previously (the couple never showed up). But how she had come to be arrested was a mystery.

'Panamanian police confirm information reaching me that Dame Margot Fonteyn was detained for questioning late last night at Panama City Prison,' he cabled London at 4.25 a.m. 'I have asked Minister for Foreign Affairs for permission to visit her myself urgently. I understand that she has British nationality.'

'The Panamanian authorities will surely realise that Margot Fonteyn is such a public figure that the way in which they treat her case is bound to attract a great deal of attention here and may have a corresponding effect on Anglo/Panamanian relations,' the Foreign Office wrote back. They still did not know what the ballerina was supposed to have done. But the next thing they heard was that she had not only been released but had left the country. 'The Embassy have now confirmed that Dame Margot has left Panama,' came the news in the early hours of the following morning. 'Confirm Miss Fonteyn left by air at own request at 0505.'

What the hell was going on? A clue arrived with Henderson's next bulletin. 'Newspapers report that Dame Margot Fonteyn's husband Doctor Roberto Arias, having transferred from yacht to a fishing vessel, has landed some of band of armed men on the Pacific coast about one hundred miles north of Panama City. Government spokesmen report that he is in flight from the National Guard.'

'All very mysterious,' noted a Foreign Office official back in London. 'The Arias were up to no good.' He was not wrong. Roberto Arias was the son of a former Panamanian president and a long-standing opponent of the current regime. 'It has long been known to this Embassy that he has been conspiring against the Panamanian Government and that his intentions have not excluded armed rebellion,' Henderson reported.

Meanwhile in London the luvvies were leaping into action. 'Lord Drogheda rang up just after you had left tonight,' runs a note to the Foreign Office's permanent undersecretary, 'to say that he, as Chairman of Covent Garden and his Committee had been having a meeting to consider what they could do for their "beloved ballerina".' In the Commons, MPs were just as sure of the dancer's innocence. William Yates, member for that well-known ballet-loving constituency the Wrekin, tabled a question demanding a government statement 'on the circumstances in which Dame Margot Fonteyn was tricked by the Panamanian police authorities'.

In the Foreign Office, officials were more sceptical. 'This episode has many puzzling features,' noted one. 'Why did Dame Margot leave the safety of the Canal Zone [controlled by the USA] for Panama knowing, as she must have done, that she would probably be questioned by the police and possibly arrested? Was she, in fact, as suggested in some agency reports, an accomplice in the plot?'

'Latest reports are that Roberto Arias has taken asylum in the Brazilian Embassy in Panama,' is the news of 25 April, by which point Fonteyn was on her way back to London. 'An invasion force of 32 men and a woman have been put ashore at

Santa Isabel on the Atlantic coast about 50 miles from Panama City. 3 members have been captured by the National Guard . . . They had apparently been sent ahead to explore the ground.' And, having let Fonteyn go, the Panamanian president had told local journalists that he was considering demanding her extradition back again.

At last a full account arrived from Henderson of his visit to Fonteyn in prison. 'I am most happy to say that I found her physically well, though naturally a little confused at first, and with no complaints about her accommodation. I rather fancy that she had been allotted the Prison "Presidential Suite", generally reserved for political prisoners of high standing, and the English-speaking Second Lieutenant detailed to look after her was careful to provide fresh flowers for her dressing table.'

All right for some! Her interrogators might have held back on the bouquets had she told them what she told Henderson 'in conspiratorial whispers which I discouraged in front of the police . . . She knew her husband was gun-running, she knew that he was accompanied by rebels and at one point she used her yacht to decoy Government boats and aircraft away from the direction which her husband was taking.' The ambassador was certainly in no hurry to shower her with flowers himself. 'I do not regard her conduct as fitting in any British Subject, let alone one who has been highly honoured by Her Majesty the Queen . . . The "holiday" of Dame Margot in Panama has been disastrous. She has most complicated our relations with this little country . . . Her conduct has been highly reprehensible and irresponsible to a degree.'

A week later in London, Fonteyn personally confirmed all this and more to the Secretary of State for the Foreign Office, a little-known chap by the name of John Profumo. 'It is quite plain that she has been, and still is, deeply involved in Panamanian political matters,' he noted. 'She admitted visiting Cuba in January and, together with her husband, seeing Dr Castro . . . She was a bit hazy about the extent of the aid offered because, she said, the talks were in Spanish, but she was certain the aid included both arms and men. She gave me to understand that quite a large-scale operation had been planned but that it had gone wrong at the last minute. The plan was to land somewhere and collect in the hills, but the gaff was blown (by fishermen, she said) so it was hurriedly decided that the game was up and her husband must go into hiding, she going back to Panama City to try to put people off the scent.'

There was yet another cock-up before they had finished: 'She threw some white armbands (intended to distinguish the rebels when they landed) into the sea in mistake for some incriminating letters and documents and her husband's address book, which were hastily packed with some machine-guns and ammunition and landed with her husband and her followers . . . This book contained several of the addresses of Dr Arias' faithful rebels and those of several Hollywood personalities with whom he had in the past had business dealings. That is how the names of John Wayne, Errol Flynn, etc. came into all this.'

The moral of the story? If you're fomenting an armed insurrection, don't get a ballerina to organise it. 'I had to pinch myself several times during her visit to be sure I wasn't dreaming the comic opera story which she unfolded,' wrote a bemused Profumo.

Libya and let live – 1969

In September 1969, a group of army officers seized control of the Libyan government and abolished the monarchy while King Idris was out of the country for medical treatment. They called themselves the Revolutionary Command Council, and a 27-year-old newly promoted colonel swiftly emerged as their leader and head of state. His name was Muammar Gaddafi.

It wasn't a problem as far as Britain were concerned. 'There had been no hostile demonstrations against the United Kingdom or British subjects,' Foreign Secretary Michael Stewart informed the Cabinet three days after the coup. 'The RCC had stated that they would honour Libya's international obligations and had addressed a warm message of friendship to the British

Government. It was important to be on good terms with whatever Government controlled Libya. BP and Shell had an investment in the country of about £100 million . . . As regards recognition, the RCC appeared to be reaching one of the criteria which we considered necessary, namely, effective control of the country.'

Stewart had had a message from the deposed King Idris, 'who had urged that we should intervene in Libya to save lives and property'. But he assured his colleagues that 'This was not a proposition that we need consider seriously.'

Monkey business – 1971

There are few more important jobs than Foreign Secretary. Its holder is responsible for the UK's relations with every other country in the world; he or she manages our relationship with international institutions such as NATO, the UN, the EU and the Commonwealth, and is first point of contact for the 14 Overseas Territories that are spread across the globe. He manages a vast international network of embassies and consulates in every corner of the world, and oversees the work of the secret intelligence service MI6. Plus he's in charge of the monkeys.

Specifically the ones that live on the Rock of Gibraltar, that peculiar British toehold in the Mediterranean that's been annoying the Spanish for three centuries now. 'As you will see from the attached submission the Governor makes a return every six months of the names and ages of all the apes,' wrote an official on 7 September 1971 to Alec Douglas-Home, who had taken over the third great office of state in Ted Heath's government after having a bash at the first the previous decade. 'I have attached the latest up-to-date summary of the ape situation in which you will see that we are up to a healthy 37.'

And indeed, beneath a fierce 'CONFIDENTIAL' heading, every one of the monkeys (they are macaques, although everyone calls them apes) on Gibraltar is listed in neat typescript, along with their birthdays, just in case the Foreign Secretary felt like sending them a card. Those names in full:

QUEEN'S GATE PACK
Tessa
Deidre
Fiona
Sam
Venus
Eliott
Barbara
Lesley-Anne
Jimmy
Richard
Roger
Bob (named after the Chief Minister)
Frances

MIDDLE HILL PACK
Wilma
Caroline
Bridget
Charlotte
Joan
Bernard
Paris
Helen
Patrice
Peter
Marie Celeste
Val
Mike
Ian
Charlie
Rosemary
Dorothy
Sybil
Olga
Marie Claire
Rodney (named after Admiral Sturdee)
Alfredo (named after the Mayor, Mr Vasquez)
Hex (named after the former senior RAF
  officer)
Pop

'The origin of this return stems, of course, from
the old tradition that our tenure of the Rock would
lapse if the apes should disappear,' explained the
official. This is one of those widely held beliefs,

like the one about the ravens in the Tower of London, which people tend to preface with phrases like 'legend has it' or 'an ancient prophecy states', or other euphemisms for 'someone made this up'. It had, however, convinced Winston Churchill, who instructed in September 1944 (when he really did have more important things to be getting on with) that 'The establishment of the apes should be 24. Action should be taken to bring them up to this number at once and maintain it thereafter.'

It is possible that not everyone took the situation quite as seriously as Churchill did. In February 1967, Saville Garner, the permanent undersecretary at the Commonwealth Relations Office, telegraphed Gibraltar Governor Sir Gerald Lathbury on the topic of a gender imbalance that could threaten the future of the two troops. He chose to do so in verse:

We're a little bit perturbed
About the Apes,
After studying their sizes
And their shapes.
As we see it, at first glance
There seems at least a chance
Of some lesbianism, or sodomy,
Or rapes.
For nine girls of Middle Hill
May well decide
That they can't by five mere males

Be satisfied.
While the Queen's Gate lads, one fears
May become a bunch of queers
If by sex-imbalance nature
Is denied . . .

Provided with a copy of the poem in 1971 'for a little light relief if you have a moment', Douglas-Home wrote politely in the margin: 'VG but unusable I fear?'

Shrinks and Scots – 1975

Ugandan President Idi Amin went in for a very direct style of literary criticism. When he learned that Denis Hills, a British-born lecturer at Makerere University, had referred to him as a 'village tyrant' and 'black Nero' in the manuscript of his as-yet-unpublished memoir *The White Pumpkin* in April 1975, he ordered the security police to arrest him. When a magistrate declined to press charges against Hills, Amin intervened personally to order that he be tried by a military tribunal. More amenable, they found him guilty of treason and espionage and sentenced him to death by firing squad. For good measure, Amin announced that all the other 700 British citizens in his country were also spies, and threatened to shoot them too.

Foreign Secretary James Callaghan offered to visit Uganda for discussions if Hills was reprieved. It was 'indicated to President Amin through

President Kenyatta [of neighbouring Kenya] that following a reprieve the spare parts he required would also be made available quickly'. The Queen – who Amin told Hills was a good friend of his – intervened with a personal plea. So did the Archbishop of Canterbury. And Prime Minister Harold Wilson wrote to the Ugandan leader personally several times, assuring the Cabinet that 'in all these dealings with President Amin he had received advice from a leading psychiatrist'.

It will have come in handy. Amin was as barmy as he was brutal. He had slaughtered up to half a million of his own people, often for completely arbitrary reasons, and kicked 80,000 Asians settled in Uganda out of the country, blaming them for its economic problems when they actually ran many of its most successful businesses. He was rumoured to keep severed heads in his fridge and feed his enemies to crocodiles. He set up an army unit called the Revolutionary Suicide Mechanised Regiment and took a teenage dancer from their regimental band as his fifth (concurrent) wife. He draped himself in medals he had invented himself, like the 'Victorious Cross', and declared himself President for Life, 'Big Dada', 'Lord of All the Beasts of the Earth and Fishes of the Seas and Conqueror of the British Empire in Africa in General and Uganda in Particular' and 'King of Scotland'.

It was this last title that gave Wilson his final brilliant idea, which he unveiled to the Cabinet on 19 June: 'It should not be forgotten that President Amin seemed to have a particular affection for Scottish institutions. It was possible that a message from the Moderator of the Church of Scotland or the Colonel of a Scottish regiment would have some effect: the Secretary of State for Scotland should consider this possibility urgently and let the Foreign and Commonwealth Secretary have his advice later that day.'

In the event, it wasn't necessary to roll out the tartan: Amin declared that Callaghan would do. The Foreign Secretary flew out to Kampala on 10 July, spent an hour with the Caledoniphile president, and then flew back with Hills aboard his plane. 'I have kept my word to release Mr Hills,' Amin announced to the world's press. 'This proves I am not mad as British newspapers said.'

Diplomatic debag – 1979

'SECRET UK EYES' is stamped on a memo submitted to Jim Callaghan in February 1979. The handwritten covering note reads 'Prime Minister: A nasty incident.'

And it must indeed have been horrible for the two diplomats and their wives who were attacked by a mob as they walked through Leningrad, taken prisoner for several hours and interrogated by Soviet military intelligence officers. Not least because it came during a very icy period of the

Cold War. So you're not to laugh when we get to the bit where one of them loses his trousers.

'A serious incident involving Lt Cmdrs Pyke and Clapham and wives took place at 1510 local Feb on Smiths Embankment Leningrad,' the account reads. 'The four observers were attacked, thrown to the ground and robbed by a group of 20–25 persons including three women. Observers were frisked, Pyke had his trousers removed, handbags were broken open.' Average temperatures in Leningrad in February were around -10°C, and the river they were strolling beside is usually frozen solid until April. Let's hope he had his thermals on.

The group were dragged off to a nearby factory where they were held for two and a half hours. They apparently 'proclaimed their diplomatic status from the outset', but the official account of their activities doesn't exactly make their day out sound like an innocent one: 'Four exposed films and notebooks were forcibly removed from Pyke and Clapham before they had opportunity to destroy them. Films were processed during the period that observers were held captive. Observers were not shown proofs but were accused of photographing industrial installations. Films were in fact of naval targets in Leningrad.' Both Pyke, who rejoiced in the Christian name Aubone, and Ian Clapham were military attachés to the British Embassy in Moscow: their job was specifically to pass back intelligence about what the armed forces

99

there were up to. If they weren't actually spying at the time they were detained, they were certainly guilty of taking their wives on the most boring sightseeing tour ever. Eventually a 'militia officer' arrived to interrogate them: it is devoutly to be hoped that when he demanded their names Lieutenant Commander Clapham took the opportunity to say 'Don't tell him, Pyke.'

According to the USSR ministry of foreign affairs, the mob consisted of civic-minded 'workers of the Baltiska factory' who had noticed the quartet's suspicious behaviour, and any violence that ensued was the fault of the Brits. 'When explaining the reasons for their suspicious behaviour Pyke and Clapham conducted themselves provocatively and attempted to start a fight. All the evidence points to the fact that representatives of the British Embassy have grossly violated the rules of behaviour of foreign diplomats on the territory of the USSR.'

Our side were equally cross. The British Ambassador to Moscow had already had a stroppy meeting with a representative of the Soviet foreign ministry in which he pointed out that the incident appeared to 'implicate the Soviet authorities in a clear breach of the Vienna Convention', the international treaty which allows diplomats to get on with doing pretty much whatever they want on each other's soil. At that point, however, the official went curiously cagey and declared that 'an investigation would not be in the interests of either side and there was no need for publicity'. Why so? The Prime Minister requested the opinion of George Walden, the most senior diplomat at the Foreign Office, who took a shrewd guess: 'This may well have been because of the arrival in Moscow on 5th March of HRH the Duke of Edinburgh for a 4-day unofficial visit on Equestrian Federation business related to the Olympic Games', which were to be held in Moscow that summer.

Last word must go to Pyke himself, tracked down by the *Daily Mail* in 2010. 'They pulled my trousers straight down. It was to stop me running away or struggling and it was very effective. I can tell you it was bloody cold and my wife was very worried about the obvious effects.'

Thatcher-san, karate lady – 1979

The BBC's coverage of the general election on 3 May 1979 had many highlights: graphics of the faces of Jim Callaghan and Margaret Thatcher made out of little Xs, Robin Day smoking an enormous cigar in his own special corner of the beige studio, an assurance from a youthful David Dimbleby that 'the computer has not ousted our old friend the Swingometer' and Richard Stilgoe making up a tooth-grinding song about the whole thing that Sue Lawley had to pretend to laugh at. But it was a throwaway line during Richard Baker's news bulletins that caused the greatest concern to the incoming residents of Number 10: in a report on Japanese preparations for the economic summit that was to take place the following month, it was mentioned that in the event of Mrs Thatcher being elected and heading the British delegation, she would be attended by '20 karate ladies'.

The Cabinet Secretary was instructed to bring this up as a matter of urgency during a preparatory meeting of bureaucrats for the summit in Washington a fortnight later, rather brilliantly known as the Sherpas' Meeting (their personal assistants are referred to as Yaks for the duration). 'Sir John Hunt raised this with his Japanese colleague; the latter told him that this report is in fact true,' reported a representative of the Conference and Visits section of the Protocol and Conference Department, who, ever mindful of protocol, signed herself E. A. Deeves (Miss). 'Sir John said that Mrs Thatcher will attend the Summit as Prime Minister and not as a woman per se and he was sure that she would not want these ladies; press reaction in particular would be unacceptable.'

For goodness' sake! Did she have no imagination? The only thing that could possibly be cooler than a squad of karate ladies was fembots, but Maggie would probably have turned them down as well. On the other hand, you can see her point: Thatcher was fighting a constant battle not to be defined by her gender; to force people's views away from her body of a weak and feeble woman and on to her heart of a king, or at least a prime minister as good as any of her predecessors in trousers. She was the first female leader of any of the G7 countries that attended the summits (extra pub quiz points if you can name the five female heads of government who preceded her elsewhere in the world).* This was to be her very first appearance on the world stage: if she materialised amid a gaggle of glamazons it would provide a defining image for both the summit and herself. No one would notice anything else at all.

'The Prime Minister would like to be treated in exactly the same manner as the other visiting Heads of Delegation,' pointed out Miss Deeves in a confidential memo to the private secretary to the Lord Privy Seal, whose job title disguised his responsibility for such overseas visits. 'It is not the <u>degree</u> of protection that is in question but the particular means of carrying it out. If other Delegation leaders, for example are each being assigned 20 karate gentlemen, the Prime Minister would have no objection to this; but she does not wish to be singled out. She has not had in the past and does not have now, any female Special Branch officers.'

The Lord Privy Seal leapt into action, and pressed

---

* Sirimavo Bandaranaike of Sri Lanka, Indira Gandhi of India, Golda Meir of Israel, Isabel Martinez de Peron of Argentina and Elisabeth Domitien of the Central African Republic. Don't lie, you didn't have a clue. The Peron isn't even the one out of *Evita*, so stop pretending.

the issue at a lunch with the Japanese foreign minister the very next day: he reported back to Downing Street that he was 'satisfied that the point has been well taken and appreciated'. And so Mrs Thatcher never got to do her Tiger Tanaka act.

The summit did not, however, go by entirely without reference to her femininity. A Japanese interviewer told her that 'the Japanese people are very much interested in you as a person – many women in particular would like to know how you combine a job with a home life, what you like to do when you have time to spare, that sort of thing', which she dealt with briskly and rather admirably by pointing out that 'we cope because the whole family recognises that I have a job to do and they all think, thank goodness, that I am the right person to do it so they help in every possible way'.

More flatteringly, she was a big hit with the German Chancellor. A Foreign Office telegram sent from Bonn the week after the conference ended reported the claim of high-level government sources 'that Chancellor Schmidt had spoken in glowing terms of Mrs Thatcher's contribution. Schmidt, as you know, does not glow easily.'

WHITEHALL FARCES

Artistic differences – 1919

In 1914 the artist Sigismund Goetze, fired up by a speech made by the Archbishop of Canterbury, offered to paint a series of murals for the Foreign Office. Since he proposed to complete and hang them in the Grand Staircase, the overblown and ornate entrance hall to the Empire's headquarters, at his own expense, the government gratefully accepted – but then got rather distracted by the First World War for the next few years. So it came as something of a surprise when Mr Goetze turned up to install the first section of the murals five years later.

'The first I heard of the matter was in January 1919, when I assumed acting charge of the Foreign Office,' Lord Curzon of Kedleston reported to his Cabinet colleagues. 'Without professing in the smallest degree to be an art-expert, I have yet been so much associated with art in various forms, and particularly with pictorial art, that I could not fail to form some opinion on the experiment thus made. That opinion was entirely unfavourable. I was convinced that the Foreign Office was about to be made the victim of a form of mural decoration not only quite unsuited to the character and style of the building, but recalling some of the least attractive features of modern German and Austrian pictorial art.' There was more than a hint of post-war xenophobia here, but Goetze's name was actually the most Teutonic thing about him: he was British-born and had proved his devotion to his home country with a series of rather nice landscapes of Northumberland and the Scottish Highlands.

While Lord Curzon may not have known much about art, he knew what he didn't like. 'Without presuming to criticise the skill or ability, or even the technical accomplishment of the artist, I felt that both the conception and the execution of his scheme were foreign to an English public building like the Foreign Office, and that to decorate in this way the main hall of that office, where the official receptions used to be and may again be held, would excite the severest criticism, if not of the world of art – for whom I could not speak – at any rate of the public at large . . . The staff at the Foreign Office were unanimously and fiercely opposed to the project.'

Oh dear. What was to be done? Lord Curzon admitted that he 'felt most reluctant to do anything that would injure the feelings of the artist who had planned the work with so much generosity and had devoted so much time and labour to carrying it out'. So he attempted to palm the mural off on someone else instead. County Hall, the imposing headquarters of what would later become the GLC (and even later the home of the London Aquarium and London Dungeon), was nearing completion on the south bank of the Thames opposite Parliament. Wouldn't a set of frescoes depicting 'the origin, education, development, expansion and triumph of the British Empire, leading up to the Covenant of the League of Nations' make the perfect backdrop for councillors as they debated the capital's rates and road improvement schemes? The London County Council's chairman, Lord Downham, popped across the river to have a look at Goetze's work, and 'very courteously offered to provide wall space for the entire series'.

Problem solved? Er, no. Curzon informed Goetze of the new plan in August 1919. 'He rejected it with indignation, declined to entertain any proposal other than the fixing of the panels in the places for which they had been designed, and invited me to see the remainder of the series at his studio . . . I unfortunately found the impressions which had been left upon me by the single panel at the Foreign Office more than confirmed by the rest of the series. These were of a character that would, I thought, produce a shock of great surprise if placed permanently on the walls of the Foreign Office.' On the grounds that they 'may possess artistic merits which I am incapable of appreciating', he offered to get expert second opinions from the directors of the National Gallery, the Tate, the V&A and Royal Academy, but a furious Goetze rejected this idea too.

By now Curzon was in an equally spectacular bate. 'I do not imagine that it can be suggested that any man is bound in law to accept a gift because he said he would, or bound in law to put up in his house a picture which he does not like because he said he would,' he stropped to his colleagues. 'Neither do I believe that any successor of [former ministers] Lord Beauchamp or Lord Grey can be bound by any obligation (if such there was, which I dispute) incurred by him. To argue that such a successor could not decide at any time that the gifts should be removed would be in effect to contend that the artistic idiosyncrasies of an individual First Commissioner of Works could for all time disfigure the walls of our public institutions. Such a view is of course absurd.' He really, really didn't like these paintings.

It was left to the First Commissioner of Works – not the one who had agreed to take the paintings in the first place: he had wisely left the scene years before – to try and broker a peace. 'I have been endeavouring to bring the views of the Secretary of State for Foreign Affairs and the artist into some line of agreement,' wrote Sir Alfred Mond wearily to the Cabinet in October 1920. Although the pair were still bickering over the best way to hang the paintings (it wasn't as if Curzon had anything better to do), 'the position at the moment is that the Foreign Secretary agrees to these Frescoes . . . to remain there for a sufficiently long period to enable a considered judgement upon their merits to be given'.

How long would that period be? Ninety-three years and counting. Goetze's murals of Britannia Sponsa, Britannia Nutrix, Britannia Bellatrix and Britannia Mater Colonorum remain around the Grand Staircase of the Foreign Office to this day after Prime Minister Lloyd George finally over-ruled Curzon and said they had to stay. They even survived Robin Cook's cull of 'ideologically unsound' paintings when he arrived as Foreign Secretary in 1997 (he replaced several with mirrors so he could look at himself instead).

Lord Curzon did at least manage to get a decent joke out of the murals in the end: he was fond of pointing out the nudes to each of his overseas visitors and telling them that they were 'typical, both in appearance and clothing, of the ladies whom he will encounter in London'. As he told officials, 'this will not fail to impress him, at first with delight and only later with disappointment, both poignant and profound'.

Fight for your right to party – 1924

In 1921, the Financial Secretary to the Treasury made some tentative suggestions for changes to the Government Hospitality Fund, 'in view of the great increase in expenditure on Hospitality resulting from international meetings arising out of the war, and from the greater frequency of Imperial Conferences'. They included the not unreasonable suggestion that those administering the fund should 'have sufficient notice as to the numbers of guests (principals, suite and servants separately); the accommodation required; and the length of the proposed stay in this country' before handing over cash, and that 'the maximum expenditure on occasional entertainments shall not exceed £150 an entertainment or £1,000 a year in all without specific prior Treasury approval'.

He also suggested it would be wise to do a six-monthly audit of 'the stock of wines, spirits, cigars etc. held for the Fund', and ensure that none of it had gone walkabout. And that it might be an idea for government departments to, er, pay their bills occasionally. 'The Financial Secretary further suggests that the balance outstanding, approximately £135,000, is unnecessarily large and he suggests that £35,000 should forthwith be surrendered to the Exchequer.' When the fund had been set up thirteen years previously, its entire budget had been £5,000.

His recommendations were accepted, no doubt with much grumbling as the port was passed around. But it was another matter three years later when Stanley Baldwin's private secretary Sir Patrick Gower dared to say he was 'tentatively considering' moving the administration of the hospitality fund into Number 10 itself. This was partly to avoid the confusion that arose from official invitations being issued in the name of the minister currently responsible for it – guests were considerably less thrilled by the prospect of spending an evening with the First Commissioner of Works than they would have been if it was the Prime Minister requesting the pleasure – but also because, as Gower diplomatically put it, 'it can be urged that the Hospitality Fund is a device intended to promote economy by acting as a check on the unbridled generosity of Departments and by substituting co-ordinated and regulated entertainment for the haphazard and exuberant lavishness of amateurs'.

The response from senior Treasury official Sir Otto Niemeyer was blistering. 'I think there is nothing to be said for the idea and I do not propose to suggest it to Ministers,' he wrote, and underlined his contempt by annotating the margin of Gower's note: 'By whom? . . . Not so . . . Not so.' So taken aback by his rudeness was an official named Beare in the government hospitality department that he appended his own apologetic covering note: 'My dear Gower, I do not know whether I am quite in order in sending you the enclosed copies of your memorandum . . . as it reached me yesterday from Sir Otto Niemeyer, with his marginal comments, and his memorandum to me, copy of which I also attach. However, as these documents are not marked confidential I see no reason why you should be in ignorance of them. It is not for me to take exception to Sir Otto Niemeyer's decision.'

Responsibility for the fund stayed where it was.

Publish and be damned – 1925

Long, long ago, rather than timetabling their policy announcements according to the rolling demands of the 24-hour media, politicians were expected to actually turn up at Parliament when they had something to tell the nation.

King George V certainly thought so. 'The King has read with attention the communications in the Press, with regard to the question of Cabinet Ministers writing articles for newspapers and receiving payment for the same,' a letter from Windsor Castle to Downing Street announced in June 1925. 'His Majesty, who has discussed this matter with you on more than one occasion, wishes again to deprecate this practice: and he reminds you that, when the Labour Government came into office and the King had reason to take exception to similar publications on the part of certain of the Ministers, the Prime Minister agreed to discontinue the practice.' That Labour government, led by Ramsay MacDonald, had fallen partly because of the *Daily Mail* publishing something that claimed to be written by a politician but actually wasn't – the notorious fake Zinoviev letter urging a revolution in Britain which was leaked by secret service agents – but Stanley Baldwin, who had subsequently taken over as PM, probably didn't think it was worth pointing out the irony. Besides, the monarch had other concerns: 'In the journalistic world there is a good deal of talk, possibly mere gossip and untrue, to the effect that in some instances Ministers receive sums far beyond what any professional writer is paid for similar contributions.'

Journalists in untrue gossip and moaning about pay shocker! Nevertheless, Baldwin put his top officials on the case. 'The attached note is a combined effort by TJ and self,' wrote back Cabinet Secretary Maurice Hankey apologetically. 'It is the best we can do, but perhaps not very conclusive.' He had established that the Tory Cabinet under Bonar Law had 'agreed to refrain from the practice' in January 1923. He could only identify two books published by ministers during their period in office: *Destruction of Merchant Ships* (1917) and *My American Visit* (1918) by the Attorney General, Lord Birkenhead, neither of which sound like the rippingest of yarns. The then Chancellor, Winston Churchill, restricted himself to bashing out best-sellers during periods in opposition, and Hankey noted that 'when in Office Mr Lloyd George concluded a contract for the publication of his memoirs, but the contract was subsequently cancelled'. By contrast, Gordon Brown bashed out no fewer than six books while serving as chancellor and prime minister. If you weren't aware of that, you're not alone. One of them only sold 32 copies.

Baldwin addressed the Commons to make things crystal clear: 'Ministers of the Crown, while holding office, should refrain from writing articles for publication in any way connected with matters of current public policy.'

Even this, however, was not quite straightforward enough for Lord Cecil, the Chancellor of the Duchy of Lancaster, who was asked by the *New York Times* in October 1925 to answer – in writing – the question 'Is the prospect for permanent peace any better this year than it was a year ago?' He wrote to Number 10 to point out that 'if a reporter asked such a question verbally there would presumably be no objection to answering . . . yet because it is to be answered in writing it goes very near to becoming an "article for publication"'. He wrote again the following April, when another paper sent out a questionnaire to a number of ministers, and got a terse reply: 'The Prime Minister has not received a similar request but if he does he will most certainly decline it.'

Over in the War Office, Lord Onslow was also confused: he was 'contemplating publishing a transcript of my Manor Court Rolls' in his capacity as 'President of the Surrey Archaeological Society . . . But I do not want to begin it if I shall be debarred under the regulation from making any use of it. Can you let me know what I am permitted to do?' Slightly wearily, Number 10 replied that

114

local history studies really weren't the sort of thing they had in mind. But Lord Cecil still claimed to be confused about what exactly that was. Could he not, he asked on 15 April, have 'some perfectly definite rule? . . . It adds a new and quite unnecessary work to public life to determine when an article is not an article.'

Exasperated, Baldwin pointed out that everything was perfectly straightforward. 'While the answer to these particular questions has a special reference to articles for which payment is contemplated, it is equally capable of application to all articles, whether paid for or not, when considered in relationship with the earlier reply of June 9th referred to in the letter which I addressed to [royal aide] Henty on the 15th instant, and was so intended.'

A sentence which, if nothing else, proves that newspapers weren't missing out by not having Baldwin writing for them.

Bishop to king 2 – 1929

Prime Minister Stanley Baldwin went on a lovely day trip to Bognor on 27 March 1929. He was off to visit King George V, who had spent the last few months there in the hope that the sea air would help him recover from the illness that had nearly killed him the previous November. And the PM was taking the new Archbishops of Canterbury and York with him, so that they could undertake

115

the centuries-old ceremony of 'Doing Homage' which was an obligatory part of them assuming their duties.

It wasn't really his job – the Home Secretary should have been the one reading out the oaths, but a pompous memo from the Home Office conceded that 'the present exceptional circumstances' meant that it would be OK for the PM to stand in (they weren't even planning to have a Clerk of the Closet present, for goodness' sake). Baldwin, who, with unemployment standing at 1.2 million and a general election in the offing, had a few more important things to be getting on with, was given two pieces of advice ahead of the ceremony. H. R. Boyd of the Home Office told him that 'The only really important thing to remember is that the Prime Minister must <u>take the two Oaths with him</u> as although both Archbishops have been furnished with copies they will probably leave them at home.' And George's private secretary wrote to say that 'The King told me to say that there is no necessity for him to travel in a top hat, as long as he brings a frock coat in a bag just for the actual ceremony.'

Churchill's goose is cooked – 1952

On 5 December 1952, Winston Churchill wrote to William Ross, the Labour MP for Kilmarnock, on a matter of grave national importance.

Dear Mr Ross,

I thought your remark on December 3 was a misquotation. The expression is 'to say Bo (as in Bo-Peep) to a Goose', and not 'Boo'.

I find this confirmation of my view:

'A Scholard, when just from his college broke loose,

Can hardly tell how to cry Bo to a Goose.'

Swift, Grand Question Debated, line 157 (1729).

I thought that you would like to know.

I must also point out that I should be anyhow a gander.

Yours very truly,

WSC

If the Prime Minister was willing to take spelling advice from someone who spelt 'scholar' with a D at the end, he was welcome to. But Ross – who had used the phrase when Churchill complained about the booing on the floor of the Commons, and had been threatened with suspension before the authorities confirmed that 'the word "goose" is not in the list of unparliamentary expressions in Erskine May' – begged to differ.

'*Dear Prime Minister,*' he wrote back on the 11th:

I must seek acquittal of the suggestion of misquotation – a much more serious offence than that of Parliamentary misbehaviour.

For more than a hundred years before Swift, and two hundred years since, the expression 'bo to a goose' has been in common use, and subject to the natural variations of time and dialect.

I have never heard it used in Scotland otherwise than 'Boo to a goose.' Jamieson's Scottish Dictionary noting the expression adds 'This is probably the same term with the Scots "bu" or "boo" used to excite terror.' Further, the Scottish National Dictionary lists 'Bo, Boo' together.

Churchill stood corrected. 'Your kind letter leaves me in your debt,' he wrote on 17 December. 'We shall certainly not quarrel on the differing usage of "Boo" and "Bo" north and south of the Tweed.'

Lost in Downing Street – 1964

George Wigg's job title in Harold Wilson's first government may have been Paymaster General, but this covered a multitude of sins. His real role was to be the PM's link man to the security services, keeping him abreast of any fermenting scandals that might bubble up, like the previous year's Profumo affair, as well as feeding gossip about the Conservatives in the opposite direction. The veteran political journalist Ian Aitken described him as being 'in overall charge of rumours, scandals, and general deviousness'.

And, as it turns out, helping Wilson with his homework. A plaintive note from Wilson's private secretary Derek Mitchell on 22 October 1964, exactly one week after the general election, informs Wigg that 'The Prime Minister mentioned to me last night that he would be grateful if you would give him a little personal help with the geography of defence matters. I think that this may have been prompted by discussions on Indonesia: Item 5 of yesterday's meeting of the Defence and Overseas Policy Committee.' Wilson had studied philosophy, politics and economics (PPE) at Oxford; Wigg was no geographer, but as one of the PM's closest political confidants, he was one of the few people Wilson could trust not to reveal the embarrassing gaps in his knowledge to anyone else.

'You may like to discuss this with him some time,' Mitchell tactfully continued, 'but I think what he has in mind is that you could look at the maps and then have a word with him just before a meeting in case you thought that his knowledge of the geography involved could do with a little strengthening. I myself suggested that it would be quite easy to arrange for charts to be brought into the Cabinet Room as a visual aid for the Committee as a whole and I think he was quite attracted by this idea.'

For readers in any doubt: Indonesia is most, but not all, of those bits just above Australia. If you get to the Philippines, you've gone too far.

Philip Larkin famously declared that sexual intercourse began in nineteen sixty-three, but he obviously hadn't checked with Bob Boothby. By that point Boothby had been conducting a passionate affair with the Prime Minister's wife, Lady Dorothy Macmillan, for more than 30 years, undeterred by the fact that he had been a Conservative MP and then a peer for nearly the whole of that period. He liked boys too – but the fact that homosexuality had yet to be legalised (despite his political efforts in that direction) didn't spice things up quite enough for him: that same year he embarked on an affair with Leslie Holt, a teenage rent boy and cat burglar. Whom he shared with the psychopathic gangster Ronnie Kray.

And the following July, it nearly all came out in the papers. The *Sunday Mirror* ran a front-page story under the headline 'PEER AND A GANGSTER: YARD INQUIRY'. Although it didn't name either man, it did say that police were investigating a gay relationship between them. It was the sort of thing voters tended to object to. And it was an election year.

But Boothby was not the only politician availing himself of the services offered by Kray's young friends. Tom Driberg, one of Labour's highest-profile MPs, had also attended sex parties at Ronnie Kray's flat. His sexual antics were nearly as spectacular as Boothby's (although focused in just the one direction: there's no evidence he ever had sex with his own wife, let alone anyone else's). If Boothby was exposed, Driberg was bound to be too. And so, not long after the Conservative chief whip had arrived on Boothby's doorstep demanding to know what he intended to do about the story, a close friend of the Labour leader also called and suggested he employ Harold Wilson's own lawyer, Arnold Goodman, to represent him.

The result was a letter to *The Times* in which Boothby 'outed' himself as the subject of the story, called it 'a tissue of atrocious lies' (itself an atrocious lie), and threatened that the *Sunday Mirror* would 'take the consequences'. Five days later, the tabloid apologised for the story and paid him a whopping £40,000 in damages. The editor, Reg Payne, was sacked.

At this point most people would have retired, embarrassed, and kept their head down for a bit. Not Boothby, for whom the adjective irrepressible might have been invented. On 12 November he dispatched a letter to Wilson, now safely ensconced in Downing Street following a scandal-free election campaign. Was he writing to thank him? Was he heck. Boothby complained that 'I have been pestered pretty badly by the Press during the last few days about the possibility of my going to Paris', after a story had appeared in the *Evening Standard* suggesting that he was about to be appointed as ambassador to France, a rumour he had been doing his best to spread himself. 'I have, so far, fended them off with success.' He then pushed his credentials for the job – 'I feel that – although I worked for him for nearly three years during the war – there is not much to be done with de Gaulle in his present mood' – before signing off with an utterly shameless demand:

> One final word, if I may. It is not an impertinence. After forty years of unbroken public service in Parliament, I have not got what I ought to have. This, I know, means little or nothing to the public. But if, at any time, you could see your way to put it right, it would give very great satisfaction to
> Yours ever sincerely
> Bob Boothby

It was breathtaking. Boothby had already bagged a knighthood and a peerage: the only honours still open to him were the stonkingly prestigious orders of chivalry like the Order of Merit or Companion of Honour, which are limited to a certain number of the nation's highest achievers in the arts, science, politics or the military at any given time.

Never mind another gong: Wilson didn't even grace the brass-necked baron with a reply. A note on Boothby's letter reads: 'Prime Minister: Can these be regarded as having answered themselves, do you think?' Underneath is a single word: 'Yes.'

Ducking the question – 1970

When the breathtaking scale of MPs' looting of public funds to furnish their second homes and enviable lifestyles became apparent in 2009, one image stood out as a symbol of their excesses; so much so that the paper responsible, the *Telegraph*, put a quacking mallard on the front cover of its highlights supplement. Everyone remembers the duck house, even if few people recall the unfortunate MP who claimed its £1,645 cost on expenses (Tory Peter Viggers, who stepped down as a result, saying he felt 'ashamed and humiliated'). Even fewer people remember that his claim had actually been turned down.

But the government very nearly faced a duck house scandal almost 40 years earlier; it was only thanks to some determined stonewalling that it remained a secret. Arthur Lewis, the Labour MP for West Ham North, one of London's poorest areas, laid down a series of parliamentary questions during 1970 on the perks available to both ministers and civil servants. His demand that the PM should pay a market rent for Number 10 (£2,400 a year by his calculations), or at least pay tax on its value, may have failed to gain much traction, but his attack on other ministers' grace-and-favour apartments in Admiralty House was ahead of its time. Since the 2010 election, the three flats in the building have been left empty by a coalition government running in fear of bad headlines – in 2012 they even flogged off the neighbouring Admiralty Arch to become a luxury hotel, which sends slightly mixed messages about the age of austerity.

Having extracted admissions about the cost of ministers' homes and chauffeur-driven cars (three of them complete with 'radio telephones' rented at an annual cost of £453), Lewis turned his attention to those lower down the ladder. In November, he submitted a written question asking 'the Secretary of State for the Environment whether he will bring up to date the list of occupants of State-owned accommodation occupied as private residences by publishing similar details to those given for Ministers' accommodation for those servants of the State who are not Ministers'.

This caused some awkwardness behind the scenes. 'There are a large number of civil servants who are <u>required</u> to live in official accommodation,' protested a pen-pusher at the DoE. 'They are called "key staff" . . . Exactly how many of them there are we do not know, but I would put them at not less than a thousand. A key staff officer pays either the economic rent for the accommodation or a standard rent according to his salary if that is less. The reason for this is that many of our properties are old, rambling and in out-of-the-way places, i.e. they are not the properties our people would occupy if they had any choice in the matter.'

Sounds reasonable, doesn't it? Only he then blew it with his chosen case study: 'an example on our doorstep is the Keeper of the Ducks in St James's Park'.

'!', someone has written in the margin.! indeed. The Keeper of the Ducks was a sinecure created by Charles II for his pals in 1671 and it came complete with 'an house and yards in our Parke, built for the keeping of pheasants, gunny hens, partridges and other fowle'. Three centuries on, it was hard to argue that the job could not be done by a bird-lover with a bus pass commuting from the suburbs. Instead, some lucky ornithologist got to live at one of the best addresses in London, just across from Horse Guards Parade, in the pretty little cottage that now serves as the park office (although apparently it was pebble-dashed and much more 'utilitarian' in 1970).

Clearly, there was only one sensible course of action. And so junior minister Julian Amery replied to Lewis's question on 10 November: 'No. This would involve a disproportionate amount of staff time.'

But this policy of silence didn't stop uncomfortable issues being aired within his department. 'During the briefing meeting on the Parliamentary Questions by Mr Arthur Lewis, the Parliamentary Secretary commented that he was not altogether happy at having to defend the case for rent-free housing,' admits a 'Restricted Note'. Fortunately, he had the perfect solution: pay rises all round. 'He thought it would be tidier for salaries to be adjusted to take account of rent.'

Nut worth it – 1974

On 24 October 1974, the Prime Minister wrote to the Chief Whip about an article in that day's *Daily Telegraph* in which Labour MP Willie Hamilton, a virulent republican, declared that he had 'absolutely no allegiance to the Crown'.

'We are not concerned with Willie Hamilton, who is a well-known nutter,' Harold Wilson assured him.

He also wrote to Buckingham Palace to reassure the Queen. 'Mr Willie Hamilton is past praying for.'

The incredible disappearing MP – 1974

Seven days after the Labour MP and former minister John Stonehouse disappeared from a Miami beach in November 1974, leaving his clothes behind, a Downing Street private secretary thought it wise to make an official note for the record. 'No information had reached the Prime Minister's Office about the circumstances of Mr Stonehouse's disappearance, about which we knew no more than we had ourselves seen in the news-papers.'

It didn't stay that way for long. On Christmas Eve, a flash Foreign Office telegram arrived at Number 10 from the embassy in Australia. 'Consulate-general Melbourne were told by Victorian police that A) on basis of Interpol circular message Victoria State Police had yesterday detained a man using the name Markham and questioned him on suspicion of being Mr Stonehouse. B) within previous hour Markham had admitted to being Mr Stonehouse and police were now virtually though not completely satisfied of his identity.' It came as a bit of a disappointment to the cops. They'd hoped they were arresting Lord Lucan.

Just hours later, another message came in from Canberra. 'Mr Stonehouse has asked Consul-General Melbourne to arrange for following message to be passed from him to Prime Minister:

'Begins. Please convey to the Prime Minister my regrets that I have created this problem. And to all others concerned . . . My wish was to release myself from the incredible pressures being put on me, particularly in my business activities and various attempts at blackmail. I considered, clearly wrongly, that the best action I could take was to create a new identity and attempt to live a new life away from these pressures. I suppose this can be summed up as a brainstorm, or a mental break-down. I can only apologise to you and all the others who have been troubled by this business.'

Whatever was going on – and there were lurid allegations about espionage activities, as well as an ongoing inquiry by the Department of Trade into a number of Stonehouse's companies – it was pretty clear that Stonehouse was not in a position to represent the people of Walsall North, 10,000 miles away. 'Much the best way of settling this quickly will be for Mr Stonehouse himself to apply for the Chiltern Hundreds,' wrote Harold Wilson to the Leader of the House of Commons on 10 January 1975, invoking the bizarre tradition that MPs are not allowed to resign, but merely be appointed to a non-existent job loosely connected to some hills in south-east England. 'Is there anything to be said for a communication to him from you or the Chief Whip, urging him to make such an application at a very early date in order that his constituents may not be effectively dis-enfranchised for what might be an indefinite period of time, in terms which would make it clear to him that, wherever his future prospects may lie, they do not now lie in a parliamentary or political career in this country?'

Stonehouse – who was still in Australia while the authorities tried to work out if there was anything they could charge him with – refused to oblige. Having vanished once, he was not about to do so again. He would be sticking around, however much it might embarrass the government or baffle the parliamentary committee that had been appointed to look into his behaviour.

What the hell was he playing at? A clue arrived at Downing Street via a rather naughty route, in the form of a letter marked 'IN STRICT CONFIDENCE', penned by a diplomat who declined to sign his name to it. 'You may like to know that an official in the Australian Department of Labour and Immigration in Canberra has given the High Commission, in confidence, a summary of a psychiatrist's report on Mr John Stonehouse. Mr Stonehouse sent the report to the Australian Minister of Labour and Immigration to back up claims that his recent actions had been brought on by a form of a mental breakdown. <u>It is clearly important that Mr Stonehouse should not find out that we have been given an account of the contents of this report and it is not for us to indicate to the Select Committee that we have knowledge of it.</u>'

Stonehouse had told the shrink that his bizarre behaviour had begun in 1973 as a result of the 'particularly shattering experience' of suspicions being raised about his business affairs (suspicions which would later result in 18 charges of fraud, theft, forgery and conspiracy and a seven-year jail sentence). He had dealt with this pressure by the entirely logical method of stealing the identity of the deceased husband of one of his constituents and spending his leisure time pretending to be him.

> He spent short periods posing as Mr Markham, a private and 'honest' individual, which apparently led to reduced tension. In June 1974, Mr Stonehouse suffered a degree of depression which led to deterioration in his judgement and some irresponsibility though he was at all times intellectually

aware of his actions. He began to dislike the personality of Stonehouse and came to believe that his wife, colleagues and friends would be better off without him. He therefore devised his escape to get away from the identity of Stonehouse. The psychiatrist's opinion was that . . . Mr Stonehouse suffered significant but 'atypical' depression. He thought of suicide, but, deciding that this was not the answer, devised a 'suicide equivalent' – his disappearance from a beach in Miami. His detection, which he all along probably subconsciously desired, has had the benefit of reconciling him with his family.

The report rather glosses over the fact that it had also involved his family meeting the 28-year-old mistress he had let them think he was dead in order to be with. His wife divorced him not long afterwards, and he married the mistress after she had served her own suspended sentence for her part in the fraud.

The behaviour detailed in the rest of the Downing Street dossier – which runs to three folders, several inches thick and firmly marked 'SECRET confidential filing' – does not get any more rational. By March, Stonehouse was applying for a Swedish passport and telling the authorities in Stockholm that his breakdown had been 'due to the frustration of my idealism in a hostile political and business world'; he was also informing journalists that he would soon be representing his constituents from Bangladesh. By June he was petitioning the Queen to stop 'the British Government's actions in frustrating my return to the House of Commons' (the Governor of Victoria was praised for 'quite properly' refusing to pass on his 18-page letter). And by July he was back in Britain – in Brixton prison – demanding that the Home Secretary arrange for him to be 'taken to the House under escort and returned similarly in order to vote'. The Chief Whip describes a series of whingeing letters from Stonehouse about his parliamentary rights as 'almost breathtaking'. He finally resigned from the Labour Party in April 1976, shortly before his trial – by which point the government, now led by Jim Callaghan, were quite keen for him to stay on and preserve their majority of two.

Despite this, the PM declined to attend what promised to be a very entertaining few days at the Old Bailey. 'You very kindly offered to make available two tickets for the trial of Mr John Stonehouse MP,' wrote Callaghan's private secretary Ken Stowe to court officials on 15 April 1976. 'I have consulted – very quietly – about this. We have concluded, reluctantly, that although it could well be useful to have someone aware of the Prime Minister's and the Government's interests in Court for this case, it behoves us to behave with the greatest possible prudence. So, with many thanks for your thoughtfulness in suggesting it, we would prefer to let this opportunity pass by.'

Bootle? Computer says no – 1979

One of the first actions of Mrs Thatcher's government was to send large chunks of the country's administration into exile. Under a dispersal programme inherited and extended from the previous administration, London began spitting out civil servants to all corners of the country. The Manpower Services Commission powered off to Sheffield. The Export Credits Guarantee Department were exported to Cardiff. The Council for Small Industries in Rural Areas went to the relatively rural area of Salisbury, while the Stationery Office Laboratory proved it wasn't stationary by moving to Norwich. But no one, it seems, wanted to go to Bootle.

'Given the needs of Merseyside and the existence of the Crown Offices at Bootle which would soon be ready to accommodate 2,300 staff, the Ministerial Group on Dispersal considered that there would be advantage in the Government's committing itself to dispersing 2,300 posts to Bootle,' Lord Soames told the Cabinet in July 1979. 'But there was no prospect of this number of posts being volunteered.'

This was something of a problem. 'Dispersal to Bootle was,' the Cabinet concluded, 'desirable on regional policy grounds,' given the depressed state of the area following the decline of the local docks. Not that you'd see any of *them* upping sticks to move there.

So which unlucky buggers were to be Bootle-bound? Having crunched his numbers, Soames reported back in October that 'the least inconvenient option for Government' would be to move nearly the whole of the Health and Safety Executive from London, although he warned the Prime Minister that 'The Secretary of State for Employment is sure that the move to Bootle would meet with strong objections from the HSE.'

It wasn't just them. The heads of the CBI and TUC, who didn't tend to agree on many things, both pronounced themselves 'dismayed by the decision', on the grounds that it would make 'face to face meetings' much more difficult and expensive. 'The problem is that everyone supports dispersal but no-one wants to be the one to go,' sighed Cabinet Secretary John Hunt in a confidential briefing note for Mrs Thatcher. He could see even bigger problems with Soames's plan B, which was to shift a selection of staff from a number of different departments including the Foreign Office: 'You may recall at the last Cabinet discussion, Lord Carrington invited his colleagues to imagine telling a diplomat on return from Phnom Penh that his next posting was to Bootle, and got instinctive support from them.' Yes, even the Killing Fields were preferable. Hunt still held out a remote hope for a plan C when Thatcher presented the proposals to ministers: 'It is always possible, though highly unlikely, that you will get a volunteer.'

There was at least an unarguable reason for the shifting of 300 Home Office staff to Bootle – 'they needed to be near the computer. The computer in turn needed a new home on the termination of an agreement with the Metropolitan Police, and the computer suite at St John's House [a newly built government office in the town] was the only location available.'

The computer in question filled a large room and weighed several tons. It was responsible, amongst other things, for tracking immigration and deciding on whether or not prisoners should be granted parole, by weighing up the likelihood of them racking up further convictions on release. The process took around three months per prisoner. Like all other automated processes in government, it aroused great suspicion: the previous December the *Economist* had looked into 'the widespread anxiety about the threat to civil liberty posed by number-crunchers and their technological toys', but was able to reassure its readers that 'the machines have not taken over [government] completely. A lot of information is still stacked in tin shoe boxes.'

The first 'portable computer' (it weighed 24lb, but it did have a handle on it) would go on sale two years later. Nowadays, of course, they have shrunk to the size of laptops, BlackBerries and flash drives. Which makes it considerably easier for civil servants to leave them on trains or lose them in the post.

The lady's not for leaking – 1981

On the morning of 20 October 1981, Mrs Thatcher's Cabinet talked at length about proposed cuts to public spending of a further five billion pounds. And then, that afternoon, at least one person who had been present at that meeting talked at length to a journalist on *The Times*, so that they could report on the following morning's front page that 13 out of 21 Cabinet members had voted against the measures.

It was a leak. And as far as the Prime Minister was concerned, it was unforgivable. She had, after all, specifically pointed out at the end of the meeting that 'it was essential to preserve the confidentiality of the discussions, and to avoid any misleading and premature publicity'. That was hardly surprising. The official minutes reveal that even ministers had spotted that proposing to slash the health service and social security benefits and put up the rent on council houses could open them to the 'charge of implementing socially divisive policies bearing more harshly on the poorer members of the community'.

There were three suspects for the leak. 'Speculation seems to centre round the names of Prior, Walker and Lawson,' wrote the Cabinet

Secretary, Robert Armstrong, in a long memo to the PM, whose red 'SECRET' stamp was appended with a handwritten 'AND PERSONAL'. 'But the Home Secretary told me that he did not think the Secretary of State for Northern Ireland had been one of those responsible.' James Prior, who had been exiled to Ulster just the previous month in revenge for his 'wetness', or lack of ideological commitment to the Thatcherite vision, was off the hook. (There is no evidence that either of the other two was actually the guilty party either.)

'If you knew for certain who was responsible, you could ask him or them to resign,' Armstrong continued. 'But you do not know and I doubt whether we can find out for sure. The second possibility is another reshuffle, say at Christmas time, which enables you to drop from the Government the Minister or Ministers you suspect of systematic leaking of Cabinet proceedings.' Norman St John-Stevas had already been booted out of the Cabinet that January partly because he couldn't stop gossiping. The fact that he often did so just out of Mrs Thatcher's earshot at the far end of the Cabinet table hadn't helped.

'In the short term, all of us who have been discussing this think that it is very difficult not to do something,' Armstrong concluded. 'All you can do immediately is to read the riot act to your colleagues. This course has disadvantages. Presumably it would not prevent a repetition of the offence, and you would have used one more shot from your locker. But the fact that you had done nothing would also become known. If you are to do anything, this is the least you can do.'

The question remained of whether this should be done in writing, or face to face. On this topic, Mrs Thatcher's adviser Alan Walters had changed his mind. 'Having started off by being against your articulating something in writing (largely because when the next major leak occurs your authority will have been even more visibly flouted than would be the case if your warning had been an oral one), I have come to the conclusion that there would be advantage in sending a minute on the lines of the attached draft,' he scribbled on a note which used the words 'lamentable', 'gross breaches of confidence', 'self-inflicted and unnecessary wounds'. It ended with an order to jolly well buck up: 'We can avoid these dangers if each of us practises the sort of self-discipline in these matters which has usually been taken for granted in members of a Conservative Cabinet.'

But his boss was, as ever, resolute. She was going to deliver this dressing-down face to face. 'I imagine that you will wish to raise this at the <u>start</u> of Cabinet rather than the end. Is this right?' asked a nervous private secretary. 'When you mention it, I imagine that you would prefer not to have the Secretaries present, other than Sir Robert Armstrong himself. Am I right?'

And so, as the ministers filed in to the following week's Cabinet, the secretaries filed out, and Mrs

Thatcher put on an even more frightening face than usual. What exactly she said is unknown. Not a trace of the bollocking is recorded in the minutes of the meeting. And strangely enough, this time the details did not leak.

LANDMARK DECISIONS

A blight on Battersea – 1929

Everyone loves Battersea Power Station. Rock fans love it because of Pink Floyd's pig. Architects love it because it's the biggest brick building in Europe and the fiddly bits were done by the same bloke that designed the red telephone box. Graphic designers love it because its silhouette, along with Big Ben and the London Eye, makes an instantly recognisable shorthand symbol for London. Journalists love it because 'new developer has big plans for power station site' and 'bankrupt developer sells power station site' have been two of the most reliable stories in the news cycle for decades. Everyone loves Battersea Power Station. Don't they?

They didn't in 1929, when it was being built. The alarm was first raised in Downing Street that February by the backbencher Edward Hilton-Young, who, despite being MP for far-off Norwich, had grave concerns about the 'danger of fumes from the new power station in Battersea . . . With what little intelligence I have, I am convinced that unless something is done, this will kill every green thing within two miles of Battersea, rot all the buildings, and bleach all the babies.'

'If all they say is true, you and I and our families must immediately escape to Wiltshire leaving, like Lot and his wife, the city of the plain to its inevitable destruction,' wrote back Stanley Baldwin's private secretary Geoffrey Fry, who may not have been taking this entirely seriously. But he did speak to his boss about it, and agreed to forward the material the MP had sent to him to the Department of Scientific and Industrial Research, 'asking them to treat it as a matter of urgency'.

It certainly sounded urgent. Hilton-Young, whose expert opinions had been culled from the technical press, warned that 'while it is possible in a modern station to minimise the emission of smoke, up to the present, no effective means of preventing the emission of sulphurous and carbonic acid fumes have been found'. This was seriously alarming: not only was Battersea on a different scale from any coal-burning power station yet built (thanks to a government order that electricity supplies should be consolidated and standardised across the country), it was slap-bang in the centre of the capital. Its position meant that 'as the prevailing winds are south-west, the normal flow of the fumes will take the line over the Tate Gallery, Houses of Parliament, St James's Park, Whitehall, National Gallery, British Museum, and the EC and WC districts'. That got the politicians sitting up and taking notice. The slum-dwellers of Battersea being exposed to noxious fumes was one thing, but their own clubs and offices?

The government's boffins did not take long to confirm that 'our unanimous opinion is that there is a strong <u>prima facie</u> case in support of the contentions of the objectors to the proposed Battersea Station . . . If no precautions are taken to remove sulphur dioxide from the flue gases there may be, under quite normal atmospheric conditions, a concentration of sulphur dioxide in the air in the vicinity of the Station some four times the average concentration which exists at present.' Somehow, no one had thought of this when planning consent was given: 'at the Inquiry little mention was made of the question of fumes which had not then attracted attention'.

Clearly, decisive action was now needed. And so on 26 February Sir John Snell, chair of industry watchdog the Electricity Commissioners, was summoned to Number 10, where he persuaded the Prime Minister to do . . . absolutely nothing. 'Sir John convinced him that a good case had been made out for building the station on the site and told him that the work had been in progress for about a year,' records a note from the Scientific Department to Fry. 'Mr Baldwin, in all the circumstances of the case, decided that there was no step which he could take.'

But not everyone was so easily convinced. On 12 April, after the controversy had burst into the correspondence columns of *The Times,* a letter bearing the royal coat of arms landed on Health Secretary Neville Chamberlain's desk. George V was recuperating from problems with his lungs, and he was very keen that his subjects should not have to suffer the same way. 'The King has been reading the recent correspondence in *The Times* on the subject of the proposed erection of an enormous Generating Station in Battersea, and is in entire sympathy with the views expressed,' wrote his assistant private secretary Alexander Hardinge. 'His Majesty feels the greatest concern at the prospect of the atmosphere of London being still further polluted by the large quantity of noxious fumes which this station must inevitably emit . . . His Majesty asks why it should not be possible to follow the example of foreign countries where power stations are erected at a considerable distance from the towns which they serve . . . His Majesty considers this project of the London Power Company particularly ill-advised, and trusts that the Government will take steps, before it is too late, to prevent it being carried out.'

Chamberlain forwarded the letter to the Prime Minister's office, assuring them that 'His Majesty quite realises what a terribly strenuous time Mr Baldwin must be having.' They wrote back pointing out slightly tersely that 'the Prime Minister had already directed his mind to the problem before the agitation was raised in the press' and assuring the King that 'the whole question is now being investigated by the Departments concerned'. But if Baldwin expected any comfort from that direction, he was disappointed. H. T. Tizard of the Department of Scientific and Industrial Research had established that there *were* actually ways of removing sulphur dioxide from fumes – but 'the fact is that all these methods involve expense and quite considerable expense, and the question is whether you can force the Battersea Scheme Promoters to go to any expense in removing sulphur'.

Yet more letters rolled in, from the Royal Institute of British Architects objecting to the effect fumes might have on London's buildings, and from Westminster City Council, who had passed a resolution of 'considerable alarm' and demanded that the power station be shifted to 'a site outside the Metropolis where the emission of fumes, smoke, soot and dust cannot prove to be injurious to health and property' (or at least not that of their voters). That was out of the question for financial reasons: the Cabinet were told that transmitting electricity from a site outside London would cost an extra £3 million, not to mention the 'very serious' problem of finding space for thirty-six 66,000-volt cables beneath 'the already over-crowded roads of London'.

On 6 May, the chairman of the company building Battersea weighed in with his own magnificently huffy letter to *The Times*: 'It is no doubt true that the problem of dealing with sulphur fumes is a comparatively new one in its application to Power Stations, but it is manifestly unfair to the London Power Company to pronounce it in advance to be incapable of solution, and to do so casts an unmerited slur on the present state of advancement of the arts of engineering and chemical science.'

And, amazingly, it turned out he was right. The company came up with an effective method of gas-washing later that year; the following November the government's scientific advisers confirmed that 'we are satisfied that the elimination of sulphur gases at the exit in these experiments was nearly complete'. Construction continued, and by 1933 Battersea was generating electricity, its twin chimneys standing proudly on the London skyline.

Two chimneys? Yes. The ruin we all know and love is actually that of two power stations: the mirror-image Battersea 'B' did not begin operation until 1953, the year after the 'Great Smog' caused by a combination of exceptional weather and excessive coal-burning in the capital killed more than 4,000 of its inhabitants. It closed exactly 30 years later, meaning that it has now been falling down as long as it was ever producing electricity.

Tunnel vision – 1929

In 1929, the Cabinet considered a proposal to connect Britain and France by tunnelling under the sea between them. It wasn't a new idea. 'It appears that the proposal for a Channel Tunnel is over one hundred and twenty years old,' advised a briefing paper by the Committee of Imperial Defence, which handily enumerated all the previous attempts to get digging and the objections that had been raised by them. They included schemes backed by Napoleon, Isambard Kingdom Brunel and Robert Stephenson, and Queen Victoria, who told the French in 1872 that her 'Government would be well satisfied to hear that the British and French railway systems were likely to be connected by means of a tunnel'.

In 1880, the South-Eastern Railway Company had even got as far as sinking experimental shafts between Folkestone and Dover, before 'military objections were raised'. Sir Garnet Wolseley, one of the army's most senior commanders, had declared 'his conviction that the hour when the Tunnel is sanctioned will be for England a most disastrous one', and the sticking point ever since had been the failure of various committees and military figures to agree on how best to blow it up.

Yes, before building it, they had to work out how to take it out of action swiftly and decisively. 'I do not believe that we should ever be so prepared beforehand for an emergency as to have the Tunnel destroyed in time to ward off the danger which I foresee,' Wolseley warned. 'That danger is briefly this, that the French, or whoever for the time being held the Calais end of the Tunnel, could by a *coup de main* seize our end of it, and the very moment they had done so, Dover would become a *tête du pont* for their army [they appeared to have already invaded his vocabulary], from which they could issue forth with any large army they chose to bring through. In other words, from that moment we should cease to be an independent Power.' Not to mention the *Dad's Army* title sequence looking totally different: those Nazi arrows would just disappear beneath the waves and pop up right in the middle of Captain Mainwaring's back yard.

Wolseley's dire warning was enough to ensure government opposition when the subject came up in Parliament in (deep breath), '1883, 1884, 1885, 1886, 1887, 1889, 1890, 1891, 1892, 1893 and 1894', and the idea was quashed by committees of enquiry when it resurfaced in 1907, and again in 1914. The last of those attempts saw a Heath Robinsonesque idea floated by Winston Churchill, then serving as First Lord of the Admiralty: he proposed that any tunnel should 'be brought to the surface of the ocean not less than a quarter of a mile to the shore, and that the railway should run from the tunnel-mouth to the shore on a bridge . . . fitting it with drawbridges' to ensure the defensibility of our shores.

Interestingly, he was opposed by Field Marshal Sir John French, who supported the idea of a tunnel on the grounds that it would ensure 'a strong bridge-head on the French coast with effective means of passing and repassing across the Straits' for British troops, should they happen to need one. Just months later he would have found such a thing very useful indeed when he led his British Expeditionary Force to the defence of France; however, a footnote on the 1929 report states that 'Lord French revised his view as a result of his experience in the war.'

Come 1919, the proposal was back on the table once more, with Prime Minister David Lloyd George showing unexpected enthusiasm. This time it was the turn of the Home Ports Defence Committee to come up with the frightening scenarios; they announced themselves worried about 'attempts to destroy the Tunnel by means of explosive charges placed on the bed of the Channel or by boring' and 'attempts by secret agents to place explosive charges with clockwork mechanism in trains passing through the tunnel'. Their demands for expensive additions, including a fake entrance 'protected by obstacles as well as armed troops' in order to confuse saboteurs, and such an enormous military guard that the country would have to reintroduce conscription, were enough to ensure that Chancellor Austen Chamberlain swiftly ruled the whole thing out. Apart from a bill estimated at £60 million at a time of post-war 'financial stringency', he may also have been swayed by the warning of Foreign Secretary Lord Curzon: 'Nothing can alter the fundamental fact that we are not liked in France and never will be, except for the advantages which the French people are able to extract from us.'

By 1924, when Ramsay MacDonald received a deputation from MPs claiming that 'virtually some 400' of their colleagues supported plans for a tunnel, the military objections were less acute, although the Chiefs of Staff Committee did come up with a new angle that would put paid to any future Dunkirk: 'From a naval point of view there would be the disadvantage that if the Channel Tunnel were constructed, in all probability a large proportion of the cross-Channel steamer services would disappear, and these services include a number of fast, small craft and a personnel which are of great value . . . an important element in our sea-power.' This time the PM called in the big guns: he assembled a committee of his predecessors Arthur Balfour, Herbert Asquith, David Lloyd George and Stanley Baldwin alongside senior military and political figures of the day. 'The unanimous opinion of the Committee was against the construction of the tunnel at the present time.' Five years on, it was decided that 'if such a project is proceeded with it must command a backing which is sure of itself and is not only lukewarm', and it was rejected once again.

The Chunnel, as no one seems to call it any more, would not open until 1994.

Special deliveries – 1935

It was an early example of political correctness gone mad. As P. M. Stewart, the 'Commissioner for the Special Areas', noted in July 1935, the parliamentary bill appointing him 'was introduced under the title of the Depressed Areas (Development and Improvement) Bill, but in response to criticism the word "Depressed" was deleted in the House of Lords and the word "Special" substituted'.

Stewart's job was to come up with proposals on how to tackle those parts of the country worst affected by the Great Depression (or, as we're probably supposed to call it now, the Great Specialness). 'Tyneside and the Northern Part of Durham County', 'West Cumberland and Haltwhistle' and 'Parts of South Wales' had seen their traditional industries collapse and unemployment and poverty rocket. But this was not just about economics. 'What seems to me even more important than the improvement of the physical condition,' Chancellor Neville Chamberlain told the Commons, 'we are to effect the spiritual regeneration of these areas . . . to inspire their people with a new interest in life and a new hope for the future.'

How did Stewart propose to do so? He had plenty of ideas, including the clearance of former industrial land to build open-air swimming baths, which would provide construction jobs for locals as well as 'the opportunity for healthy exercise in the fresh air [which would] do much to improve the standard of health in the areas'.

But he also strayed outside his brief with

recommendations for other areas, advocating a number of bigger construction projects for 'works of great national value . . . Much needed schemes such as the tunnel under the Thames near Purfleet, the construction of an orbital road round London or of a bridge over the Severn at Chepstow.'

The Thames tunnel – better known by the name of its southern exit at Dartford – would not arrive until 1963, and the Severn Bridge in 1966. It took half a century for London to get its orbital road, the M25.

Something in the air – 1943

In October 1943, at the height of World War II, the Secretary of State for Air, Archibald Sinclair, penned a secret memo to his colleagues in the War Cabinet. 'The Air Officer Commanding-in-Chief, Transport Command, and I are gravely concerned about the inadequacy of the present facilities near London for transport aircraft,' he informed them. 'Transport Command requires a new airfield near London capable of accommodating heavy transport aircraft of the latest type . . . Croydon is confined to limits which are long out of date. Hendon is incapable of extension, and is so risky for Dakotas (the medium twin-engine type standard to the Americans and ourselves) that the Commanding General of the United States Air Transport Command has forbidden his Dakota pilots to use it. Northolt,

Hornchurch, Biggin Hill, Kenley and Heston are all required for operations.'

Clearly, a new site had to be found. And Sinclair thought he had discovered the perfect place. 'Exhaustive search in the London area shows only one district suitable for an airfield of the dimensions required – the triangle formed by the Bath Road and South-Western Road from their junction at Cranford to a line just east of Stanwell, the whole lying just north-east of Staines. This district, which includes the present Heath Row airfield, is well graded and well served by road and rail communications.'

But a military airfield was not all Sinclair had up his sleeve. 'The project is so planned that the airport could, after the war, be used immediately for civil transport purposes and could be developed further so as to provide an international civil airport for the capital of the Empire, which would be capable of accommodating the largest post-war types of long-distance aircraft. Unless we take steps to plan for such an airport now, our civil aviation will be seriously handicapped by the lack of this essential asset in the post-war period.'

Not that he was about to announce anything of the sort just yet. Sinclair requested that his colleagues merely give the go-ahead to the compulsory purchase of the land that was needed for 'military requirements'. But at the same time, he asked that they also set aside 'the additional land which would be required for the civil scheme to make provision for later expansion to meet the requirements of a modern civil airport, with multiple runways capable of accommodating dense traffic . . . At this stage it would be necessary to demolish a further 1,373 houses and 47 other buildings, including a number of factories, shops, garages, a school and a chapel.'

The Ministry of Agriculture objected that 'the area is eminently suitable for market gardening purposes' and 'one of the great nutritional problems facing the country post-war will be the provision of adequate supplies of fresh vegetables'. The Secretary of State for Scotland worried that it might 'prejudice the development of Prestwick after the war as a major international airport' (he was right about this – although the tiny Scottish airport did get the consolation prize of being the only place where Elvis Presley ever set foot on British soil). But in February 1944, War Cabinet minutes noted that 'the Minister of Town and Country Planning has been invited to sterilise all the land required for the full scheme'. Which is why Heathrow, the biggest airport in the world, came to be built without the need for a public inquiry, or, thanks to emergency wartime measures, the paying of compensation to those whose land and homes were taken away from them. It opened for business in May 1946. It had no terminal buildings – passengers had to check in and wait in tents. But amazingly, it did already have a branch of W. H. Smith.

Clement Attlee's post-war Labour government nationalised the hospitals and doctors' surgeries to ensure that all the sick were looked after, no matter how wretched their circumstances, handed out family allowances to everyone with more than one child regardless of their means, ensured that unemployment, sickness, maternity and widows' benefits would be available to all, and gave tax breaks to aristocrats so they could carry on living in their lovely big houses in the manner to which they had become accustomed.

Hang on . . . not that last one. While Labour were quite happy to follow up each and every one of the recommendations of the Beveridge Report of 1942, they had rather more of a problem with the Gowers Report of 1948. The result of a committee on 'Houses of Outstanding Historic or Architectural Interest' appointed by Chancellor Stafford Cripps in response to the increasing number of stately homes being demolished by their cash-strapped and short-staffed owners, it provided his successor Hugh Gaitskell with a severe headache three years later. 'The report is not at all easy to deal with,' he grumbled to colleagues in April 1951. 'Many of the recommendations are open to strong objections of principle. Further, a scheme of preservation on the scale which the Committee envisage would be far too expensive in present circumstances. Therefore, there is very little of what they recommend which can be accepted unaltered.'

Ernest Gowers, a former senior civil servant and serial chairer of official committees, had been horrified by the number of ancestral piles that had been 'broken up for the sake of the lead, timber and fittings' in the years following World War II (by my reckoning, *Downton Abbey* should make it to this point by about series seven). 'Present rates of taxation make it impossible for the private owner to maintain the largest of the houses out of income,' he pointed out. 'Staffing difficulties and rising cost of repairs and maintenance, not to speak of the physical restrictions of the last decade, have all made the task more difficult.' But never fear, he had the solution: not just emergency injections of public cash but a series of tax breaks for owners too. They should, he recommended, be free not just of 'income-tax and sur-tax in respect of approved expenditure on repairs to and maintenance of the house and contents' while they lived, but also death duties when they passed them on to their heirs.

'I find the main proposals unacceptable as they stand,' stormed Gaitskell. 'I need not stress the political difficulty of giving specially favourable treatment for this purpose to the owners of large houses . . . We have always tried, so far as possible, to avoid measuring a man's liability to tax by his particular choice of commitments.'

He had a specific objection to the way that the

committee had approached the problem: 'The proposals of the Gowers Committee were founded mainly on the desire to keep historic houses in private *ownership*; and they went to great lengths in proposing means to this end. There is a strong case, elaborated in their Report, for encouraging private *occupation* in many cases. Private ownership is another matter, and I see no reason why we should encourage it. I am more inclined to encourage ownership by the State or by the National Trusts for England and Scotland, who already have long experience and great public goodwill. This is not in the least incompatible with private occupation, as the experience of the National Trusts shows.' Gowers had at least suggested that owners should agree to 'show their houses to the public' in return for their tax privileges, but this woolly obligation (how often? From what distance?) was a rather different thing to the National Trust model of decamping to a granny flat while day-trippers traipse around your best rooms looking forward to a cream tea.

Gaitskell therefore decreed that there should only be 'some small exemptions from death duties' for those families who left their property to the Trusts or the state. As for Gowers' recommendation of lavish maintenance grants, 'in present circumstances we shall have to limit expenditure on historic houses to the minimum; we cannot possibly afford, in terms either of money or of

155

man-power, as much as could usefully be spent on this purpose'.

And it was emphatically *not* up for discussion. Gaitskell issued a written parliamentary reply which rejected all Gowers' recommendations, without, as MPs (several of whom admitted they lived in rather expensive-to-maintain country homes themselves) complained, the chance to debate the matter or ask any supplementary questions. It was not until a year later – following a Conservative victory in the general election and the return to power of a prime minister who had been born in Blenheim Palace – that the subject would limp back on to the political agenda. By that point demolitions had accelerated. Historian Giles Worsley, author of *England's Lost Houses*, estimated that 'about 300 houses are known to have been lost in the Fifties'. Still, at least we've got all those lovely 1960s tower blocks to make up for them.

Demolition man – 1965

One of the best things about London is the way they've put pretty much everything tourists want to look at slap-bang in the middle. Downing Street is just across the park from Buckingham Palace; Horse Guards Parade is just around the corner within sight of Trafalgar Square, and on the short stroll down Whitehall to the Houses of Parliament and Westminster Abbey you pass a horde of government departments housed in buildings as architecturally imposing as they are administratively important. You could call them the Great Offices of State.

So obviously, in the 1960s they wanted to knock the lot down and put up concrete office blocks instead. And it was a matter of urgency, as Charles Pannell, the Minister of Public Building and Works, lectured his colleagues in a confidential memorandum on 6 July 1965: 'If we do not lay down general principles and disciplines now, all this effort will be lost in the quicksands of detailed criticism and aesthetic argument. Piecemeal development will follow, to the general detriment of the area.'

Instead, he proposed they must instantly endorse the plans of Sir Leslie Martin, the architect responsible for the Royal Festival Hall on the South Bank. He planned a programme of 'general rebuilding' which would create 'efficient accommodation for housing Government Departments'. And to do so, he intended to remove almost everything that was already there. In fact, Pannell actually found it easier to list the buildings he wasn't going to demolish:

> Sir Leslie envisages the retention of the Westminster Central Hall (but the eventual removal of the Middlesex Guildhall and the buildings on the south side of Great George Street); of Downing Street, the Old Treasury,

Horse Guards, 36 Whitehall, Admiralty House and the Admiralty Screen group of buildings; of the Banqueting House (but the removal of the Royal United Services Institution and Gwydyr House); and of the Scotland Yard building by Norman Shaw as part of the redevelopment of the site from Bridge Street to Richmond Terrace.

Pretty much everything else – including the Foreign Office, designed in the classical style by George Gilbert Scott as 'a kind of national palace or drawing room for the nation' a century earlier – was to fall to the wrecking ball. Gwydyr House, now Grade I listed and the home of the Welsh Office, dated back to 1772 and sits alongside Inigo Jones's Banqueting House, outside which Charles I was beheaded. Although the latter would be spared, it would be left stranded on a traffic island under Martin's scheme. The Middlesex Guildhall – now the Supreme Court – is noted for its ornate stonework, wood panelling and stained glass, designed in what architectural onions-knower Nikolaus Pevsner described as an 'art nouveau gothic' style. But it was to be swept away, along with the equally imposing neighbouring HQs of the Royal Institution of Chartered Surveyors and the Institution of Civil Engineers. 'Sir Leslie Martin does not consider that Government offices or the Headquarters of Professional Institutions are appropriate uses for the site,' Pannell loftily intoned.

What did he intend to put in their place? Everything between Bridge Street and Richmond Terrace was to be replaced by 'a Parliamentary building . . . linked by a covered way to the colonnade at the foot of the Clock Tower so as to form part of the present Palace of Westminster'. If bolting an extension on to Big Ben was not enough, Martin also had some big ideas for the Houses of Parliament themselves: 'A number of ways are suggested in which additional accommodation might be provided for Parliament within the Palace of Westminster, e.g. by building out over existing buildings, and by adapting space now unsuitable for use or unsuitably used.'

North of this, a series of concrete ziggurats would rise over Whitehall, their stepped design meaning they could house tens of thousands of civil servants 'without exceeding the height of the present buildings' (because obviously that was the main problem). '462,000 sq. ft net of offices could be built on the Foreign Office site, with 800 parking places . . . A further block of offices would run south of Richmond Terrace and Downing Street, and possibly cut back in front of No. 10 Downing Street to create a small "place". Other blocks of offices would run at right angles.' The whole shiny new mini-city 'could be linked by a main gallery running just south of King Charles Street and Derby Gate, crossing Whitehall and so linking the

159

riverside with St James's Park. On the Bridge Street site at ground level, the gallery would provide a public pedestrian way with a shopping concourse. On the upper levels of the gallery, there would be a separate pedestrian way for official traffic.'

And that wasn't all that Martin had his eye on. 'The present Admiralty, War Office and neighbouring ministries could make room for an additional 10,000 or so Government staffs in the area. The last group of buildings he considers should be considered further as part of a study of the Trafalgar Square area . . . The report comments on the uneconomic design of the buildings . . . The opportunity of general rebuilding should be taken to rationalise building lines and the layout of public services, and to provide adequate underground garaging, service roads, etc.'

Pannell presented the plans to the Cabinet on 13 July. They loved them. Not a single dissenting voice was raised. 'In discussion there was general agreement [on] the imaginative quality of the proposals for the development of the centre of the capital . . . the Government should declare their firm intention to develop this area in the longer term in accordance with the principles of Sir Leslie Martin's report.'

Did they even have any qualms about the demolition of the Foreign Office? Yes, that it might not be done quickly enough: 'The wording of the proposed statement should not be such as to prejudice the rebuilding of the Foreign Office Block as soon as possible . . . It would be preferable to make it clear that both sites would be redeveloped as soon as practicable.' The timetable Pannell proposed saw construction beginning in 1968 and stretching into the 1980s. As for the fact that the plans actually broke the government's own rules on construction in the capital, Pannell was pompously dismissive: 'I see no conflict between my proposals and the present policy of restricting office development in London. Whitehall and Parliament Square, as the administrative centre of the Commonwealth, must be in a class apart from other office development.'

Thankfully, none of it came to pass, though that was more down to a lack of public money than an appreciation of old buildings. Even the Victorian Society, spearheaded by John Betjeman, announced in response to Martin's vision that 'at least seven-eighths of the Whitehall area remains suitable for clearance', a stance they are slightly embarrassed about now. They were at least determined to fight like hell for the Foreign Office, and they were right to do so: not only is it still functioning exactly as it was built to do 145 years ago, but it has become one of the most popular venues at the capital's annual Open House weekends. Visitors can ooh and aah at the marble statues, gilded ceilings, friezes and ormolu chandeliers, reflecting on the building's lucky escape from the mid-sixties planning madness that temporarily gripped the nation, and how unthinkable it is that such a thing could happen again.

Then they can pop across the road to another popular Open House venue, Portcullis House. The ultra-modern parliamentary overflow building was opened in 2001 after a number of listed nineteenth-century buildings were swept away to make room for it and the Jubilee Line extension beneath it. It sits slap-bang on the site that Martin had earmarked for the first stage of his redevelopment.

Harold Wilson's big idea – 1975

Harold Wilson was very excited. The Queen's Silver Jubilee was approaching, and he had hit on the perfect way to celebrate her 25 years on the throne.

He was, he informed the Department of Trade in July 1975, very keen on one particular aspect of his friend Illtyd Harrington's plans for 'a Festival of Britain'. Not the 'repertory season of classic comedies for the dazzling Maggie Smith' that the GLC deputy leader proposed for the National Theatre. Not the Albert Hall staging 'a "popular" concert with all the old-fashioned patriotic songs'. Not even his idea that the V&A should put on an exhibition predicting 'how we will be living in the 1980s and beyond'.

No, the bit that got Wilson going was 'the provision of a large conference centre in London'.

'Please tell Peter [Shore, the Trade Secretary] I'd like to talk about it,' he scribbled on top of a memo in which Shore had expressed some doubt and pointed out that the government had already stumped up £1.5 million for the National Exhibition Centre in Birmingham, then under construction. 'Richard Attenborough's discussion clarified things for me,' the Prime Minister enthused. 'We should get him linked with the new high-level committee planning the Jubilee.'

When Harrington went public with his plans in the *Evening Standard* that August, Wilson's enthusiasm knew no bounds. 'An imaginative project on which I have been kept in close touch, though without of course any Government commitment,' he frothed in a letter to colleagues. 'The plan envisages the building of a large Conference Centre in London, big enough to host the largest international conference, business or otherwise, but built on a basis which would enable the use of the large hall in the evenings as a concert hall, for opera, ballet, and other public performances. The idea will be a hall capable of accommodating something like 6,000. The proposed site would be on the south bank, between County Hall and the Festival Hall, on land not currently used except as a car park.'

He even had some exciting ideas of his own to throw into the pot. 'There ought to be, for example, a European Hall, financed perhaps in part by Community Governments, and named in a way

163

which commemorates the European connection. We might hope that the Americans might establish their own building, which they might or might not want to relate to, and possibly name after, the Bicentennial.'

The rest of the Cabinet were sceptical. A working party chaired by Environment Secretary Tony Crosland reported that 'there appears to be comparatively little demand for a conference centre on this scale, and that there is virtually no chance of overseas Government capital being provided'.

The PM wasn't happy. 'I do find this very negative,' he scrawled sulkily across the front page of the report.

Then, as sometimes happens, Carlos the Jackal intervened. The terrorist leader stormed an OPEC (Organisation of the Petroleum Exporting Countries) meeting in Vienna in December 1975, killed three people and took 70 hostages on a magical mystery tour by plane to Libya and Algiers. Although all the hostages were eventually released unharmed, it did rather disrupt proceedings – and the Department of Energy thought it might be an opportune moment to invite the group to continue their negotiations in London instead. Trouble was, they didn't really have a suitable venue to offer. 'All these refs about inadequate conference facilities read oddly in view of the unanimous negative reaction by all the Depts to my minute of last autumn for concert hall/confer-

164

ence centre,' wrote a stroppy Wilson on the paper-work informing him so.

He sent out an even more petulant memo in February 1976: 'I had in mind a hall for evening musical performance, to be used by day by <u>any</u> organisation not govt; though we cd use it too. Cd this all be looked at again, preferably by people who don't start from the assumption – now refuted – that nothing is needed.'

It would never happen. On 16 March Wilson announced his resignation as prime minister. It came out of the blue, and has never been properly explained, but it probably wasn't because his colleagues wouldn't let him have a conference centre.

And what of the site that Wilson and Harrington had earmarked for their enormous white elephant? Although the car park was gussied up and greened over to become the Jubilee Gardens in time for 1977, it is now better known as the location of the country's most successful millennium memorial, the London Eye.

DIPLOMATIC SILENCES

Britannia doesn't want to rule beneath
the waves – 1929

Way before the Ban the Bomb campaign – way, indeed, before there was a bomb to ban – activists all over the world were campaigning for the abolition of a 'terrible weapon' that was 'perilous in Peace or War': the submarine. And in July 1929, after two British subs collided off the coast of Wales, resulting in the sinking of one of them and the deaths of 24 sailors, they gained a very eminent recruit.

'The King wishes me to call your attention to an article in today's "Daily Sketch" by Commander Kenworthy, deprecating the employment of submarines and asking whether the time has not come when some effort should be made by international agreement to abolish this terrible weapon,' runs the letter on Buckingham Palace notepaper. 'The King knows you will remember that at the Washington Naval Conference in '21 and again at Geneva in '27 we did propose their abolition, but

I imagine the French are strongly in favour of keeping them. Yours very truly.'

Stanley Baldwin's private secretary Patrick Duff wrote straight back to his Buck House counterpart Lord Stamfordham, apologising that the PM had 'just left for Chequers', and pointing out that while Britain remained willing to get rid of their own submarines, they could hardly do so unilaterally. 'France would never entertain the abandonment of what they consider their primary arm of Naval Defence, and so long as they will not give up submarines it is impossible for others to do so. Apart from this, other Powers besides France believe in the submarine as a cheap defensive weapon of a weak naval power.'

His Majesty was unimpressed. 'The King hopes that his present Government will not be content with the non possumus attitude of France and will endeavour, in cooperation with America, to over-come the opposition from our friends across the Channel.'

Since President Coolidge had recently let it be known that he was 'in favour of an inhibition on submarines', this was not beyond the realms of possibility. But Baldwin didn't hold out much hope. 'The Prime Minister asks you to assure His Majesty that he has the subject much in mind and does in effect intend to take the steps desired by the King,' Duff wrote back to the Palace. 'He does not feel confident of the result – which is very natural.'

Don't let's be beastly to the Germans – 1937

In May 1937, Foreign Secretary Anthony Eden had some rather worrying news. That nice Mr Hitler was apparently under the impression we didn't like him. His concern arose from a remark by Hermann Göring, reported back by the British Ambassador to Berlin, about 'the danger of allowing the German people to continue indefinitely to regard England as the enemy in their path'.

Eden instructed the ambassador to get straight back to Göring for clarification. 'Sir N. Henderson has, on my instructions, sought to obtain from General Göring a clear definition of Germany's aims and a precise statement as to the manner in which, and the occasions on which, the action and policy of His Majesty's Government have, in the general's opinion, prevented or are preventing the German Government from obtaining their objective,' he reported to the Cabinet on 30 July. Unfortunately Hitler's far-right-hand man had failed to 'furnish a clear or satisfactory answer to our enquiry'.

The telegraphed reports of Henderson, an Eton-educated diplomat who had the same Christian name, moustache and very indulgent attitude to the Führer as the Prime Minister, Neville Chamberlain, were attached to Eden's memo. His first detailed something rather more serious than the average falling-out: Göring had told him that 'until now he had always refused to allow the German air force to indulge in war games with England as the enemy, on the ground that he did not wish to encourage even the idea of such a possibility. He had, however, recently been unable to resist pressure brought upon him to provide against a contingency which had begun to appear to Germans as inevitable, and he had recently and reluctantly authorised this precaution.' That would be the air force – the Luftwaffe – that Germany was explicitly banned from having in the Treaty of Versailles, but which it had re-established two years earlier without much more happening than the League of Nations agreeing to be Very Cross Indeed.

At the same time, Göring was doing some serious flirting. 'Italian friendship was not at all popular with the German people,' he told Henderson, 'but Germany had no alternative but to make friends where she could find them. In spite of this, there was, he asserted, still nothing binding in Germany's relations with either Italy or Japan.'

While Eden just about managed to resist this transparent plea to declare his country BFFs with the Nazi regime, he did instruct Henderson to do some serious sucking-up. 'I feel that to let this remark pass without comment would be practically to acquiesce in the view that His Majesty's Government have recently been pursuing an anti-German policy.' The very thought! 'I will be glad if you will seek an early opportunity of telling General Göring that, in the opinion of His Majesty's Government, the German people are harbouring an imaginary grievance . . . You should make it clear that you are seeking elucidation, not for the purpose of sterile recrimination, nor in order to controvert his views by argument, but simply so that His Majesty's Government may be in a position to know what exactly is in General Göring's mind, to remove any genuine misunderstandings which may exist, and thereby to . . . ameliorate the situation between Great Britain, Germany and France and to secure a closer measure of co-operation between the three Governments in the interest of European stabilisation as a whole.' He should take pains to ensure that it should not be 'an acrimonious discussion with General Göring. I should be prepared to examine with interest and all possible sympathy what may be said on the German side.'

Henderson reassured his boss that since his arrival in Berlin he had done little else but affirm to the Nazis that his country had nothing against them – 'It was entirely on this account that I made the speech which I did on the occasion of the German–English Society dinner on the 1st June. Most of the Nazi party leaders attended that banquet and it afforded me an opportunity of publicly refuting before a large audience this dangerous grievance.' And he was delighted to be able to report on 20 July that 'General Göring received me this morning at his country place about an hour and a half from Berlin.' Unfortunately, their conversation 'was not very enlightening either as regards Germany's definite ambitions or as regards specific cases in which England had shown herself hostile to Germany's aspirations. It was, said General Göring, difficult for any country to say openly in advance what its ultimate ambitions were.' That was presumably especially true when they involved invading most of your neighbours and establishing a thousand-year Reich.

Göring did talk about one specific point: Germany's desire for Anschluss, the annexation of Austria, which he insisted 80 per cent of that country's inhabitants would vote in favour of if given the opportunity. 'Yet, if the German Government did persuade the Austrian Government, as they were constantly urging the latter to do, to agree to a plebiscite, the British Government would rise up and say no.' In this he was quite wrong. When Austrian Chancellor Schuschnigg *did* call a referendum on the issue the following March, Hitler pre-empted the result by just invading instead – and Britain did nothing about it.

'I intervened at this stage,' reported Henderson. And what form did this decisive intervention take? Er, he told Göring that 'Looking at Germany's situation quite objectively I was able to appreciate certain great qualities of the Nazi regime . . . Certain of its spiritual qualities, such as its teaching of the dignity of labour and the moral value of service, were admirable. But Time was required to lay solid foundations for Germany's new experiment. I could not believe that Hitler desired to risk all his work on the chance of war. To this Göring replied that I could set my mind at ease; there would be no more surprises for several years.'

Surprise! Austria would be part of the Reich within eight months. Six months after that, Czechoslovakia in turn was invaded, with the ink barely dry on Neville Chamberlain's piece of paper. Two months on from that, 30,000 Jews would be rounded up and carted off to Dachau and Buchenwald to experience the 'dignity of labour' that Henderson so admired at first hand.

'Hitler had clearly indicated in *Mein Kampf* how earnestly he desired England's friendship,' Göring told the ambassador at their meeting. 'He was bitterly disappointed and resentful at England's unwillingness to reciprocate. It was, Göring assured me, the bitterest experience of Hitler's life. Nor could he, Göring, understand it. German soldiers, German airmen, German sailors, all told him how friendly disposed the British military forces were towards Germany. The British public, if the reports which reached him were correct, was equally so. It was only the British Government and the British politician who were so hostile.'

As this correspondence shamefully demonstrates, the exact opposite was true.

Irish nationalist Roger Casement was executed for high treason in 1916 after travelling to Germany at the height of the First World War to try to solicit enemy support and munitions for a rebellion in his home country. This was scandalous enough, particularly given that he had enjoyed a long and very respectable career in the British consular service, with various postings in Africa and South America. But after Casement was arrested, freshly disembarked from one of the Kaiser's U-boats, the police seized a great deal of evidence from his home, including a set of diaries that revealed that . . . well, let's just say his trip to Germany was far from the first time he'd tried to get his hands on massive foreign weapons.

The diaries – generally referred to as the 'Black' diaries, because he kept a contemporaneous 'White' set that were sanitised for public consumption – are filled with surprisingly detailed notes on the various penises he encountered during his travels, from 'black and thick and stiff as a poker' ones in the Congo, via 'Huge Irish thick as wrist' ones in Dublin to 'enormous about 7 inches and 4 thick' ones in parks in London. He documented what he liked to do with them, too: 'In Bath, splendid. Millar into me . . . Into Millar and then he came too.'

None of this, of course, had any relevance to his trial. But the authorities were damned if that was going to stop them from using it. A secret Home Office briefing reveals that when the American Ambassador dared to ask if Britain really wanted to hang a man on the strength of a rather ambiguous treason law that dated all the way back to 1351, one of Scotland Yard's assistant commissioners took a copy of the diaries – which they were refusing to publicly confirm even existed – round to the embassy to shock him out of making any public noises about a reprieve. 'The diaries did show that Casement was a sexual pervert . . . The Ambassador undertook to report to the President.'

This all came up again in 1936, 20 years after Casement's execution and 14 years after the establishment of the Irish Free State under British rule, when the president of the latter's Executive Council, Eamon de Valera, wrote to Prime Minister Stanley Baldwin to request that the remains of his former revolutionary colleague, buried in the grounds of Pentonville prison where he had been executed, be returned to his homeland. Baldwin's reply was as eloquent as it was emollient: 'the publicity which would inevitably ensue would be bound to lead to a recrudescence of controversy and would make for the embitterment of relations rather than for the appeasement which we both desire'.

But de Valera refused to forget about it. He wrote again as Taoiseach of a fully independent Ireland in 1953, obliging Winston Churchill's government to cast around for another excuse. It was the Prime Minister himself who came up with one. 'Let me have the facts about Casement's diary, showing his homosexual excesses,' reads a handwritten note to a Home Office official (it rather suggests Churchill had a quota for exactly how much homosexual activity was acceptable). 'Does Mr Valera know anything about this aspect? It might be conveyed to him in confidence. He is very careful to respect confidences and this might alter his outlook.'

Six years later, there was no chance of confidentiality on either side. A copy of the diaries, as transcribed by police typists four decades previously, somehow made its way to Paris-based publisher Maurice Girodias, who pepped up his Olympia Press's range of literary *causes célèbres* (Nabokov's *Lolita*, William Burroughs' *Naked Lunch*) with as much filth as he could lay his hands on (he instructed one author to include a sex scene 'of at least five pages for every ten pages' of his manuscript). He put them into print in 1959. As Irish nationalists struggled to assimilate this new information about their hero – or, for the most part, loudly insisted that it must all be a forgery aimed at discrediting him – the British government was obliged to confirm the diaries' existence and place them in the Public Record Office, although they did insist that they remain sealed for 100 years except to 'historians and other responsible persons who have made a study of Casement's life'. Seventy applications for access were made in the following five years: only half were granted, archivists presumably deeming the other 35 to be insufficiently qualified dirty old men.

Alec Douglas-Home made a further attempt to dismiss the requests from Ireland after his Home Secretary pointed out that '48 years having passed, there may be little left in the way of remains' to return. But in 1965, Harold Wilson's government finally acceded to Ireland's request for Roger Casement's corpse to be repatriated. The final details were agreed over Winston Churchill's dead body, with a meeting between Wilson and Irish officials who had travelled over for the war leader's funeral that January. He also agreed to find out 'whether modern science would enable us to check the allegation that while the diaries were in the possession of the police, additions were made to the text designed to give the impression that Casement was a homosexual'. It did, and they weren't, although to this day many people continue to believe that the whole thing was an attempt to blacken the name of a fine red-blooded patriot.

President Eisenhower's artist friend and the trouble with Winston Churchill's trousers – 1955

December 1954, and the bromance between Winston Churchill and US President Dwight D. Eisenhower was at its height. After the Prime

Minister finally persuaded Eisenhower during his visit to Washington that summer to agree to nuclear disarmament talks with the Russians, the pair had enjoyed a 'riotous evening' at the White House. They were in regular contact by mail. Churchill signed his letters 'with every good wish – Believe me always your sincere friend.' Eisenhower reciprocated even more gushingly: 'With my continuing warm regard, and with my sincere wishes for your health, strength and happiness, as ever, IKE.'

In fact, things were going so well that Eisenhower asked if he could take their relationship a bit further. 'As you know, I occasionally flatter myself by attempting to paint likenesses of friends,' he wrote on 15 December. 'I would be tremendously intrigued by the effort to paint one of you. Would it be an intolerable burden on you to allow an artist friend of mine to visit you long enough to take a few photographs and draw a few hasty colour sketches that I could use in such an attempt? The final result would, of course, not be good, but also it might not be so bad as to be unendurable.'

Churchill, a keen painter himself, sent a 'Top Secret Private & Personal' telegram back via the Foreign Office. 'Should be delighted to see your artist friend and am much honoured at the prospect.' He followed this up with a longer letter in January: 'I need hardly say I shall be greatly honoured to be one of your subjects in an artistic sense. Although my experiences as a model have not been altogether agreeable lately I submit myself with great confidence to your well-balanced love of truth and mercy.'

This was a bit of an understatement. As his official present from the House of Commons for his eightieth birthday the previous November, Churchill had been presented with a portrait by the distinguished painter Graham Sutherland. 'This portrait is a remarkable example of modern art,' he announced at the unveiling at Westminster Hall. 'It certainly combines force and candour.' In other words, he hated it. 'I think it is malignant,' he told friends. 'It makes me look half-witted.' He shoved it straight into the attic at Chartwell, his family home, where it remained until his wife Clementine took it out and burned it a year later.

Still, perhaps the President, who had converted one of the rooms in the White House into an artist's studio, would do a better job. He would at least be assisted by a professional, in the form of the artist friend in question, Thomas E. Stephens. It was quickly arranged that he would come to Chequers for lunch at the end of January, and take some photos and do some preliminary sketches of his host between mouthfuls. 'I have earnestly instructed my artist friend to be as sparing of your time as possible,' wrote Eisenhower. 'Right now I have put in some odd moments I have in attempting to copy a photograph I have of a portrait painted of you some years ago . . .

But I would far rather work on something that was not a mere slavish copy.'

Stephens was a hit. 'I had a very agreeable meeting with Stephens today. I hope the results will inspire you,' wrote Churchill to the White House that very afternoon. (That didn't guarantee anything; 'Graham Sutherland is a Wow,' Clementine had written to her daughter the previous September.) Things were looking good, though, according to the American Ambassador: 'The President has asked me to deliver to you the following message: "Dear Winston. My grateful thanks. The inspiration is guaranteed: the big question mark is the result."'

At that point, as they tend to, events intervened. The President wrote to Churchill again on 4 March, apologising that he hadn't had time even to look at Stephens's sketches, 'because of the pressure we have been under here – and lately it has seemed heavier than usual'. This was no understatement. Eisenhower spent much of the early part of 1955 dealing with the crisis in Formosa, now known as Taiwan, which China's communist regime were threatening to invade; there was serious discussion in the White House of whether or not to launch a nuclear strike. He did, however, claim to 'look forward eagerly to seeing how his artist's eye has captured your spirit and personality. I am certain no artist can ever do it to my complete satisfaction.'

But Churchill was impatient. 'How are you

getting on with the portrait?' he wrote in a PS to a Top Secret telegram on military matters on 18 March. 'I hope you will show it to me when it is finished and I warn you I shall claim full rights of retaliation.' Eisenhower, probably by now regretting ever having brought the topic up, fobbed him off with the version he had perhaps forgotten mentioning earlier. 'Since Mr Stephens has come back, I have had no opportunity to meet with him to go over the work he did on my behalf. However, in the meantime I discovered a small black and white print of a portrait of you that was painted some years ago. I have painted a small canvas, using this photograph as a guide.' He had at least made a safe choice. The portrait was the famous one of Churchill at the height of his powers that Arthur Pan painted in 1942: it was one both he and his family thoroughly approved of.

Eisenhower was quite pleased with his version, too. 'Considering my lack of qualifications in the field, it did not turn out badly and I have had a color photograph made of it, which I am forwarding with this letter.' The photo has long since been detached from the file of correspondence – let's be optimistic and suggest that Winston liked it so much he took it home for the mantelpiece – but the painting itself was presented to the Walter Reed Army Medical Center in Washington, where it hung until the building was closed in 2011. A photo from 1959 shows a visiting Churchill and Eisenhower sitting and admiring it propped up on a chair in front of them: it looks a bit like two confused residents in an old people's home wondering why the telly isn't working.

Eisenhower had one final confession to make. 'Actually, I have not had time to complete every detail of this particular canvas because I must say it is difficult for me to give a fairly realistic impression of the stripes in a statesman's trousers. I could wish that, at least for the day you sat for that portrait, you could have worn your wartime "zipper suit".'

Next time, just get tokens – 1957

One of the problems with giving up an empire is that it all gets so damn *expensive*.

'The Federation of Malaya is due to achieve independence within the Commonwealth on 31st August,' noted a memo to the Cabinet on 10 July 1957. 'We shall, therefore, shortly have to decide what gift might most appropriately be made by the United Kingdom Government to mark the occasion.'

Socks? A nice scented candle? In the end they decided to plump for 'a Post-Graduate scholarship. This might be tenable by a suitably selected, locally born resident of the Federation for a two year period at a leading University in this country.'

It was a nice idea – 'an imaginative gesture', the Secretary of State for the Colonies reckoned – but a thrifty one too. 'The annual cost of such an award should be not higher than £600 per annum at present prices . . . The total cost over whatever period the Scholarships ran – and we think it is unnecessary to specify this in advance – would be higher than for the plaque or piece of statuary which we have offered as a Government to Government gift (at a cost of some £2,500) to Ghana. But we shall not be repeating in Malaya the air display costing some £35,000 which was authorised at the time of Ghana's Independence.'

Big nope to pope hope – 1959

Selwyn Lloyd, the Foreign Secretary, brought a ticklish diplomatic problem to the Cabinet in January 1959: the government had received a letter from the Duke of Norfolk, writing at the request of the Catholic Union of Great Britain, to request them to take an internuncio. This was not quite as painful as it sounds – it was a diplomatic representative from the Vatican, one step down from the equivalent of an ambassador – but given that the UK had had barely any official relations with the Holy See since Henry VIII's new-wife-new-church clearout more than four centuries previously, it would still be quite a big step.

It was far from the first time the subject had come up in Cabinet. Winston Churchill had dismissed the idea in 1953, and Lloyd had prepared a similar memo back in 1957, although he had advised that 'we should not disclose the fact that the Cabinet have discussed the matter'. Now, however, they had to face a very public request: the Duke of Norfolk was not some eccentric aristocrat whose letters could safely be ignored; he had inherited along with an awful lot of other titles the role of Earl Marshal in the Royal Household, with responsibility for organising the Queen's coronation seven years previously. He was, like the 15 dukes who had preceded him, a Catholic. And he was convinced that 'the beginning of a new Pontificate' – Pope Pius XII had died the previous November and been replaced by the more boringly named John XXIII – provided the perfect moment for full diplomatic relations to be resumed – not least because there was already a channel going in the other direction. The UK had been sending representatives to the Vatican ever since the outbreak of war in 1914, when they figured that if the Germans got to have an official word in one of the Pope's ears, they really ought to be whispering into the other one.

Others thought differently. The Archbishop of Canterbury, Geoffrey Fisher, had 'made it plain informally that he would object to the reception of an Internuncio', and several MPs and 'Protestant bodies' had also made their 'objection to a change' clear to the government. Rab Butler, the Home Secretary, opined that 'while recognising that the granting of diplomatic status would undoubtedly give pleasure to Roman Catholics in this country, who are believed to number 4½ millions, he is doubtful about the Duke of Norfolk's belief that it would meet with wide support from the rest of the country'. He also objected on the grounds that senior Catholic figures had turned down their invitations to the Coronation despite the fact that it was being organised by one of their own. Vainly did Lloyd protest, as the Cabinet Secretary records in his notebook, that 'they went to a place outside Abbey: and to banquets etc.'. Butler was having none of it: 'Strong anti-Catholic feeling in UK – don't provoke it.'

Was this really the case? Certainly of Lloyd and Butler's generation. 'Anti-Catholic prejudice was rife in polite English society until surprisingly recently,' noted the *Economist* during the 2010 papal visit to Britain. 'Countless families can tell tales of scandals or feuds triggered by a mixed Anglican–Catholic marriage, up to the 1960s or 1970s.' It lingers on in odd pockets to this day: wander the streets of Belfast or go to an Old Firm match in Glasgow and you will realise that in certain crowds this is an issue that is still very current indeed.

Lloyd persisted: he would, he told his colleagues, 'like to make a gesture'. Apart from anything else, the Vatican would make strong 'allies against Soviet subversion . . . full co-operation and under-standing between all anti-Communist forces is most desirable'. But Prime Minister Harold

184

Macmillan was having none of it. The government was already in trouble over its policy on church schools: as the official minutes record the Cabinet's discussion, he felt that 'the Government's proposal to increase the rate of grant to denominational schools had already aroused opposition, particularly among the Free Churches, and any action which might aggravate denominational feeling would be liable to endanger the Government's educational policy'. The Cabinet Secretary's hand-written notes are rather blunter: 'PM: We would do better to give them something on schools. Dangerous to do both at same time. Leave this for a year.'

It was an overoptimistic timetable – and rather a disingenuous one, given that Macmillan would give the subject a couple more kicks into the long grass when it came up again in 1960 ('opinion in the Cabinet was so equally balanced that it would be preferable to defer a decision') and 1963 ('arrange for further consideration to be given to the implications of the proposal'). In fact a full exchange of ambassadors would not happen until 1982, when Pope John Paul II came to Britain and got up close and personal with the tarmac at Gatwick. There has been an apostolic nuncio to Great Britain – why say ambassador when there's some perfectly good Latin you can use instead? – ever since. He lives in a nice big house next to Wimbledon Common.

Commonwealth doesn't have to mean common – 1960

The problem with throwing good parties is everyone wants to come. And once you start letting the riff-raff in – well, then the parties just aren't as good any more.

This was the problem that faced the Commonwealth, that ragbag affiliation of post-Imperial nations, in the summer of 1960. A working party of officials from six out of the ten countries that were then members (Canada, Australia, New Zealand, India, Ghana and the UK itself) had got together at the PM's country residence, Chequers, for a chinwag about the group's constitutional development. This rather self-congratulatory bunch put on the record the fact that their countries shared 'the following common characteristics – a certain weight of population; political, financial and economic viability; the ability to play a role in world affairs and to carry weight in world councils; and the capacity for self-defence, at least against local acts of aggression. It is, in short, a relatively small group of relatively large countries.' Now, however, the small fry wanted in. Not only were African countries like Sierra Leone, Tanganyika, Uganda and Kenya gearing up for independence in the next few years, but smaller dependent territories like Malta, British Guiana, British Honduras and the Aden Protectorate looked likely to follow, and all were likely to apply for membership. Cyprus had already demanded to join the gang, 'and its admission would constitute a precedent making it difficult to exclude other small countries because of their size'.

Everyone agreed that Commonwealth membership was a good thing, but the group's main concern seems to have been the havoc this might play with the established members' social lives. 'The Meetings of the Commonwealth Prime Ministers themselves have always been characterised by a frankness and intimacy of discussion unparalleled in international gatherings,' they noted. 'These occasions for free and informal discussion of the international problems of the day and the opportunities which they provide for personal contacts have been highly valued . . . This atmosphere of intimate discussion could be impaired if the membership of the independent Commonwealth were very greatly enlarged . . . There would be something like 100 people in the conference room.' There might not even be enough Ferrero Rocher to go round!

The solution? One idea was essentially the equivalent of those 'you must be this big to ride me' signs at the fairground: 'Smaller territories which attain independence might be accorded all the privileges of Commonwealth membership except that of attendance at those meetings . . . it has been suggested that a line might be drawn at a population figure of 1 million.' Maybe the newcomers could have a sort of kids' table, well away from the grown-ups, with 'the development of a system of regional Commonwealth Meetings, by which the smaller countries would participate only in the regional gatherings and not in the main Meetings'. Or they could take turns, coming along to join the PMs from the bigger countries 'on some system of rotation'. The main objection to this? Not so much the blatant unfairness of a 'two-tier' system, as the fact that 'it would introduce a rigid formula into Commonwealth procedure, which has always been characterised by its informality and the absence of rules of procedure'. You bet it had. Reading between the lines of the official account, it all sounds like one colossal jolly: 'The Meetings' value derives very largely from the personal relations between the Prime Ministers and the frankness and informality of their discussions . . . If these suggestions were adopted, they would call for a somewhat more detailed advance preparation of the agenda and the programme of Meetings than hitherto.'

In the end, officials concluded that their PMs were just going to have to grin and bear it – at least for the next ten years, during which they concluded that 'the increase in numbers may not be unmanageable . . . analysis suggests that by 1970 the membership of the Commonwealth will have increased from the present number of 10 to, at most, a total of 24'. The old-schoolers could probably put up with that many new faces, providing that 'as the number of Prime Ministers increases, they might wish to reserve more "free" time for informal contacts' when they got together.

As it turned out, there would actually be 30 countries in the Commonwealth by the end of the decade – but by that point, the prime ministers' shindigs themselves were a thing of the past. In 1969 they were replaced with biennial Commonwealth Heads of Government Meetings, hosted in different locations around the world. By then everything had been put on a more formal basis with the establishment of the Commonwealth Secretariat, a deliberate attempt to stop the older nations hogging all the power for themselves.

Attitudes to the get-togethers, however, did not necessarily change. In her 1996 biography of her father Denis, Carol Thatcher revealed that her parents had a particularly charmless explanation for the initials CHOGM: 'Coons Holidaying On Government Money'.

Nelson Mandela's bookshelf – 1962

'You will perhaps have noticed reports that Nelson Mandela, the former Secretary General of the African National Congress, was arrested by Security Branch police on Sunday,' wrote Lord Dunrossil, a diplomat in the British Embassy in Pretoria, in a confidential dispatch back to London on 10 August 1962. 'There are two stories going around about how he was captured. One says that he was in a house near Howick in Natal, the other says that he was caught driving in a car in which he was posing as a chauffeur . . . Mandela has evaded the Security Branch for more than two years and with his nickname "the Black Pimpernel" had become an almost legendary figure.'

It was a mark of how slowly the Foreign Office moved in the days before email and rolling news. Five days had passed since Mandela's arrest. He had been hauled in front of magistrates and remanded in custody by the time this official notification had been dispatched. Newspapers, as Dunrossil noted, had already written about it. And one particular newspaper editor had decided to do more than just report the situation.

'May I bother you, please, about the possibility of getting books sent to a man in gaol?' wrote David Astor, editor of the *Observer* in London, that very same day. His letter was addressed to Sir John Maud, the High Commissioner for those enclaves of the British Empire that remained within the borders of South Africa, namely Basutoland, the Bechuanaland Protectorate and Swaziland.

'Many people I know have a particularly high opinion of Nelson Mandela and feel it is of great importance to keep him provided with something to read,' continued Astor, a passionate campaigner against apartheid and supporter of the banned ANC. 'I would very much like to send him books, but I imagine that the only hope of their reaching him would be if this could be done with your support . . . Obviously one would not want to send books that were deliberately provocative of the South African authorities. The idea would be to send him historical and scholarly works to enable him to continue his general intellectual growth.'

'I'm so glad you wrote,' replied Maud on 20 August. 'Nelson Mandela is, of course, not a British subject, and I have no <u>locus standi</u> towards him.' But he was damned if he was going to let that get in the way of what he thought was a great idea. 'I am very ready to ask the South Africans to pass the books on . . . It would probably be helpful if I could explain that the general trend of the literature being supplied is not in any way in support of Communism, but rather seeks to occupy Mandela's mind with a Western alternative.'

And that was exactly what Astor supplied: a sort of social and political science 101 reading list; precisely the volumes you would expect to find dog-eared and tastefully piled up in every *Observer* reader's knocked-through sitting room. They should really have been bundled up and given away free with every Habitat coffee table. That first batch in full:

The History of Europe by H. A. L. Fisher,
 vols. I and II (Fontana Paperbacks)
The Sleepwalkers by Arthur Koestler
The White Nile by Alan Moorehead
Essays in Biography by John Maynard Keynes

Making of a President by Theodore White
Life of Gladstone by Philip Magnus
My Early Life by Winston Churchill
Short History of Africa by Roland Oliver
(Penguin Books)
New Architecture of Europe by G. E. Kidder
Smith (Penguin Books)
*Patriotic Gore: Studies in the Literature of the
American Civil War* by Edmund Wilson
Anatomy of Britain by Anthony Sampson

The six that the local bookshop in Pretoria had in stock were swiftly dispatched via Sir John, with the others to follow. Given that the *Observer* was notorious within South Africa for its vocal criticism of the apartheid regime, he and Astor agreed that it would be best not to say who they came from.

On 14 September, prisoner 13260/62 wrote a thank-you letter.

The Jail
Johannesburg
14th September 1962

Sir John Maud GCB, CBE
The British Embassy

Dear Sir,
I have received the six books which were sent to me by a friend in England through your Embassy.

I thank you for making it possible for me to receive them, and I should be grateful if you would kindly inform the friend, should you be in possession of his or her address, that I greatly appreciate this valuable present.
   Yours faithfully
   N. Mandela
   NELSON MANDELA
   AWAITING TRIAL PRISONER
   13260/62

On 7 November, Mandela was sentenced to five years' imprisonment, three of them for inciting ANC supporters to go on strike, and two for leaving the country without a passport while on the run from the authorities. He would be back in front of a judge the following July alongside nine other ANC leaders, charged with 193 acts of sabotage and attempting the violent overthrow of the government. It was at this trial that he received the life sentence that would keep him in Robben Island until 1990. But it could have been far worse – and his then wife Winnie Mandela believes that it was down to Astor that it wasn't. 'Had it not been for the coverage of the *Observer*, those men would have faced the death penalty. We knew that, and they knew that too: it was the *Observer* that saved the leadership of the ANC,' she said in 2011.

Already, however, Mandela had begun to put his time to good use. 'Amid the other letters on sabotage, riot, murder etc., that we are sending you by this bag, you might like to know of a minor piece of consideration and helpfulness on the part of the South African authorities with regard to political prisoners,' Dunrossil reported back to the Foreign Office on 7 December 1962. 'The prison authorities have now been in touch with the British Council to say that Mandela wishes to read for an LLB (London) [a law degree]. Raymond Butlin [of the British Council] is accordingly sending over the appropriate guidance to enable Mandela to make his proper application to the University authorities and to embark on his studies . . . Mr Astor, through Amnesty, would like to send law books to Mandela to enable him to continue his studies.' Mandela was already a lawyer; he and his fellow ANC activist Oliver Tambo had run their own firm in Johannesburg during the 1950s, but as Dunrossil pointed out, 'It is interesting that the South African authorities are not standing in the way of these men taking London degrees and there seems to have been no insistence that they should try for South African qualifications. Indeed, one is tempted to wonder if this readiness on the part of the prison authorities to assist indicates that there is no future for these men in South Africa and that they may ultimately be encouraged to leave for Britain!'

He concluded that 'Perhaps none of this has very great significance though in the long run we may get some good will from Mandela for having helped him.'

A Chile reception – 1966

As Home Secretary, Jack Straw infuriated lots of ghastly old right-wingers in 1998 by ordering the arrest of the former Chilean dictator General Augusto Pinochet when he visited London. Then, two years later, he infuriated lots of ghastly old left-wingers by letting him go again. But Straw was an old hand at pissing off important people over Chile.

'The British student visit was a thoroughly disorganised venture which I recommend should not be repeated unless radically different arrangements can be made,' wrote a livid Alexander Stirling from the British Embassy in Santiago on 23 September 1966, not long after a group of 21 youngsters including Straw had departed the country after helping to build a youth centre there. 'The party of students was nearly sent home in disgrace,' he frothed. 'They came with inadequate briefing, without having tied up the details of their programme in Chile, and without having planned their return journey to the United Kingdom . . . A projected trip to southern Chile fell through altogether, which was probably just as well, since their tour in the north was nearly disastrous. Two students were gravely ill (at least partly as a result of the conditions in which they had to travel) and the party broke up half-way through the tour.

'The students were, as individuals, pleasant and intelligent; but they were depressingly immature. I understand that about half of them have aspirations to office in the National Union of Students and most seemed more interested in advancing their own or their associates' candidacies than in the job on hand . . . As a group they were somewhat less than ideal representatives of British youth.'

Still, Straw, then studying law at Leeds University, must have been a calming influence on his student pals, mustn't he? After all, this was the man who would become so well known for his strictness as Home Secretary that Tony Blair used to threaten his kids with a visit from him if they didn't do their homework.

Er, no. 'I ought to add that we had the impression that Jack Straw, the appropriately named chief trouble-maker, was acting with malice aforethought,' continued Stirling. 'This impression might be entirely mistaken and I should hate to start a witch hunt, but he seemed deliberately to have brought matters to the point where the British Council had to intervene. His apparent objective was to cause a minor scandal which would demonstrate that the present NUS Executive was incapable of proper organisation – unlike its predecessor, which had, I gather, a strong Communist flavour. All this may, as I say, be quite unfounded; but

Straw's actions and attitude strongly suggested that the trouble among the party did not happen altogether spontaneously.'

Straw was elected president of his own university union the following year, staging some spectacular sit-ins, and then of the whole NUS in 1969, prompting fears of a 'leftwing takeover'. Three decades later he had become such a devout New Labourite that he managed the successive leadership campaigns of both Tony Blair and Gordon Brown.

Good grief – 1974

French President Georges Pompidou succumbed to a particularly nasty form of bone marrow cancer on 2 April 1974. Right up until the end, he had refused to admit he was ill.

The Foreign Office swung into immediate action. 'Apart from the message to monsieur Messmer [the French PM] the Prime Minister may also wish to send a private message to Madame Pompidou,' they advised Number 10 in a telegram. 'I assume that this will not be for publication. You may like to consider something along the following lines: Quote my wife and I mourn your husband's death and send you our deepest sympathy. For him it required the greatest courage and determination to carry on. For you it must have required no less to suffer in silence. Our hearts go out to you. Unquote.'

Someone – not the Prime Minister – crossed out 'Our hearts go out to you' and pencilled in 'We have the highest respect for his ~~achievements~~ memory, and admiration for your fortitude. Please accept this expression of our sorrow.' This version was typed, and then sent as a telegram to Paris.

There is no evidence in the file to suggest that either Mr or Mrs Wilson ever saw the sentiment, let alone felt it.

Tricky Dicky no-mates – 1974

Ahead of his attendance at President Pompidou's funeral in April 1974, Harold Wilson was given extensive briefing notes of topics to bring up with the various world leaders he was bound to bump into over the sherry and sausage rolls afterwards. Never mind the mourning, there was important diplomatic work to be done. Except with the Canadians. 'There are no specific points to raise with Mr Trudeau,' the Foreign Office advised.

They did, however, have some advice about what to expect from Richard Nixon: 'The President is bound to be in an edgy and worried state.'

He certainly was. By that point the Senate Watergate Committee had been sitting for nearly a year. Nixon was fighting a desperate legal battle to avoid handing over tape recordings that exposed just how heavy his personal involvement was in the criminal conspiracy – tape recordings that only existed because he had, in the grip of paranoia, secretly bugged his own office. It was looking increasingly likely that he would be impeached and booted out of the White House.

Still, Wilson found him on quite good form. 'He spoke at some length over a very wide range,' the Prime Minister reported back in a dictated account of his trip to Paris. Despite this being his second stint in Downing Street, and a long-standing habit of sucking up to celebrities in the hope that their glamour would rub off at the ballot box, Wilson doesn't seem to have got over being star-struck. He proudly points out that 'Throughout the conversation, from the moment when he first shook my hand to the time he left me outside the British Embassy, it was Christian names throughout.'

And what of the . . . unpleasantness back home? 'There was no reference by either of us to Watergate, though he made a tangential and identifiable reference to the subject when he said something about his internal difficulties which he described as a "load of crap" (sic).'

Well really! 'The Prime Minister's account is a document which clearly needs to be given a very restricted circulation,' warns a shocked official in a covering note.

But the President's language was not the most awkward aspect of the meeting. Nixon was scheduled to visit Moscow for security talks that summer; he suggested that it would provide an ideal opportunity to pop into London for an official visit on his way home. 'Mr Wilson told me that he had deliberately steered the conversation away from this possibility,' reads a Top Secret Note for the Record dated 19 April. 'Nevertheless, the Prime Minister was concerned by the possibility. He did not relish the idea of a visit by President Nixon for what were evidently domestic electoral purposes.' Not least because being pictured alongside the man pretty much everyone was coming to recognise as the commander-in-thief would be a disaster for Wilson's own domestic electoral purposes (with a hung parliament, he knew he would be heading for the polls again before the end of the year). Nixon had already tried the same trick in Paris: the British Ambassador reported back that he gave the French 'the impression of trying too obviously to step from shifting domestic sands onto the firmer ground of international reputation . . . He made rather too much of a beanfeast of it. He stayed two nights and showed too exuberantly his gratitude for public applause in the streets. And the French were of course only too ready to find this vulgar.'

Wilson was not about to let himself be used the same way. His instructions were clear: 'The Prime Minister therefore told me that he wanted the FCO to take any measures open to us to ensure that Mr Nixon did not come to London.'

This might be more difficult than it sounded, reported top diplomat Sir John Killick. 'Any country, and particularly the first, which <u>visibly</u> allowed Watergate to affect its dealings with the Administration, would inevitably be the target of the President's bitterness and perhaps retribution,' he warned. 'His ill-will could cause us serious difficulties. This all points to the general conclusion that we would probably have to pay a high price if we appeared deliberately to rebuff the President by avoiding a visit . . . He is a vengeful man.'

Killick had an idea, though. 'We should work hard to arrange a multilateral European occasion – e.g. just before a possible CSCE Summit Meeting or a meeting in Brussels at which the President might brief NATO leaders on his return from Moscow – as a substitute for bilateral visits.' That would at least disperse the poison – and it would be worth it just to see the desperate scramble as every leader tried not to be the one standing next to Nixon in the official photographs. But it was not good enough for Downing Street. Someone scribbled despairingly in the margin 'but he is still likely to want to come here'.

So then Killick offered his most cunning plan: if Nixon insisted on paying a visit, they would just have to make sure the Prime Minister wasn't in. 'Once the date for the President's visit to Moscow is firmly announced, we should examine whether the Prime Minister could not himself undertake some visit abroad, shortly before and after the Moscow visit.' Failing that, maybe he could just switch all the lights off in Number 10 and hide when the doorbell rang.

If he did so, the Queen would probably end up behind the sofa with him. When the Moscow trip passed and the American Ambassador started sounding out Jim Callaghan about the possibility of Her Majesty hosting a state banquet if Nixon did happen to drop by in November instead, the Foreign Secretary bit the bullet and told him that 'If the question of impeachment still hung over the President a visit could cause some embarrassment to the Royal Family and no doubt Mr Annenberg would want to avoid this.' His report back to Downing Street has an intriguing annotation in Wilson's favourite green pen: 'JC could not have put it better. You know this view is not limited to our house.'

Fortunately for everyone, Nixon resigned in disgrace that August. Wilson was saved the embarrassment of being linked with him, and got to spend more time with his own upstanding and respectable friends like Joseph Kagan and Eric Miller instead.

Well done, Mr Mugabe! – 1980

'I send you my warmest congratulations and good wishes, and those of my government, on the assumption of your high office,' wrote Margaret Thatcher to Zimbabwe's newly elected Prime Minister Robert Mugabe on 8 March 1980. 'Now we can look forward to a happy and prosperous future for Zimbabwe, in which the wounds of the recent past will be healed in the spirit of hope and reconciliation which you have set as a guiding principle.' The original draft talked about the 'spirit of humanity', but Thatcher struck that out, possibly on the grounds that it didn't come naturally to either of them. She also took out a line saying 'you and we have had our disagreements': maybe she had a premonition that when it came to fallings-out between Mugabe and the British government, you ain't seen nothing yet.

'The landslide election victory for Mr Robert Mugabe was not perhaps what some sections of British opinion would have wanted, but we committed ourselves to holding free and fair elections, seeing whom the people of Rhodesia wished to lead them, and handing over power to those people,' admitted an internal briefing a week later. 'Mr Mugabe has spoken in a statesmanlike and moderate way of working within the Constitution agreed.' And to be fair, he had actually won 64 per cent of the vote this time: it was only later on that he started blatantly rigging elections and having opposition leaders arrested and their supporters beaten up. Around the time he decided that growing a little Hitler moustache would do wonders for his image.

But there was plenty of bright side to look on in 1980. As Lord Soames, appointed by Britain as transitional governor to ease Zimbabwe into independence, pointed out: 'The underlying economic potential of this country is considerable and provided that the government pursues reasonable policies (and in particular does not scare off the whites) this potential should begin to be realised within a few years.'

In the meantime, he was more concerned about keeping Mugabe's biggest rival happy. Joshua Nkomo, who had come a very distant second in the elections, was very cross indeed. 'An indignant Nkomo telephoned this morning,' Soames telegraphed on 15 March. 'It was monstrous, he said, that he had been left to learn of the independence date of Zimbabwe from the radio and newspaper (published this morning). He had fought for independence for years. Was this the way to reward him? He would not accept it. I fear this is a reflection of Nkomo's current frustration. He is disappointed at obtaining only a small share in government.'

Soames suggested to Mrs Thatcher that 'it might help smooth ruffled feathers and anyhow be an agreeable gesture if you would send him a private message'. His draft was a master class in sycophancy: 'I should like to take the opportunity of the announcement of the date of independence of Zimbabwe to offer you my warmest congratulations and sincere good wishes . . . your determination and courage have earned the admiration of the world . . . your role has been long and distinguished . . . fitting that you will be taking a leading part . . .' 'If you approve, could we possibly have it by Monday?' the Governor pleaded.

It worked – at least for a while. Nkomo accepted a post in the Cabinet and lasted nearly two years before Mugabe accused him of plotting a coup, drove him into exile and sent troops in to kill thousands of his supporters in Matabeleland. Things kind of went downhill from then on.

The Falklands, brought to you in association with Argentina – 1982

'It was the worst, I think, moment of my life,' Margaret Thatcher told the official Falkland Islands Review Committee of the point she realised that Argentine troops were about to land on the British Overseas Territory they preferred to call the Malvinas in April 1982. 'I never, never expected the Argentines to invade the Falklands head-on. It was such a stupid thing to do, as events happened, such a stupid thing to even contemplate doing . . . I never believed they would invade.'

The resulting two-month war, which resulted in the deaths of 255 British servicemen, at least 650 of their Argentine counterparts and three of the islanders themselves, transformed Mrs Thatcher's political career, turning her into an election-storming amalgam of Winston Churchill and Boudicca. Rather than ask awkward questions about the victory, the British people were firmly instructed to 'just rejoice at that news and congratulate our forces and the marines'. So it was extremely lucky for Thatcher that it never leaked out that less than two years previously her government had – with her full approval – been involved in very advanced negotiations to hand over the sovereignty of the Falklands to the enemy.

So sensitive was the topic that paperwork relating to it has been marked 'please destroy this after reading' or 'TO BE DESTROYED when weeding 1980 file'. But what survives makes it clear that it was all agreed at a meeting of the Cabinet's Defence and Oversea Policy Committee on 2 July 1980. Nicholas Ridley, the Foreign Office minister responsible for, as he described it, 'the whole of the Western hemisphere, including the Caribbean and various islands in the Atlantic', was authorised to 'explore confidentially with the Argentines the possibilities for a solution to the dispute, including that of a surrender of sovereignty and simultaneous lease-back'. This would mean that the government in Buenos Aires would realise their long-held claim to ownership of the Falklands, as long as they agreed to rent them back to Britain in the same way that (at that point) Hong Kong was leased from China. The Downing Street account records that 'The Committee agreed that it would need to decide, in the light of the outcome of these exploratory talks, whether the prospects were sufficiently promising to seek the views of the islanders them-selves and then enter into more formal negotiations. The Foreign and Commonwealth Secretary's paper is very discreet about the details of the discussions so far. But his conclusion is that initial Argentine reactions to the concept of a transfer of sovereignty accompanied by lease-back have been sufficiently encouraging to justify Britain going further down this path.'

It had taken Mrs Thatcher some time to come round to this view. A memo from 1979 suggesting such a plan has been annotated with one of her fiercest underlinings: 'I cannot possibly agree to the proposed course of action . . . No.' Ridley told the review committee chaired by Lord Franks – which took evidence in secret before producing a report derided by many as a whitewash of the government – that it had taken 'much discussion and argument', but he had managed to convince her that sharing nicely was the only practical solution. 'My basic position was that one either had to declare, as it were, a "fortress Falklands" and take the necessary steps on the defence and economic and resupply side, or one had to find a solution involving an agreement with the Argentine Government . . . The resultant costs [of not negotiating] both in terms of defence and in terms of economic aid and communications aid to the islands, would have been so horrific that one would have been laughed out of court. Certainly that was the argument which perhaps persuaded the Cabinet to authorise me to try and solve the problem.'

Even after she had personally authorised her minister to open negotiations, Thatcher appears to have had her doubts. Robert Armstrong, the Cabinet Secretary, set out some 'points to establish in discussion' for her that July, including 'What would the international reactions be if the United Kingdom showed itself willing to negotiate with the Argentines over the sovereignty of the Falkland Islands? Would this be regarded as another example of enlightened statesmanship, or simply another sign that Great Britain is on the skids?' The last six words have been underlined by the prime ministerial pen.

But Ridley pressed on. He already had an 'in'. 'I became very friendly with Comodoro Cavandoli, who was my opposite number in the Argentine government,' he told the Franks committee. Indeed, I made it my business to get to know him personally and we had a relationship beyond our formal negotiating one.' His confidential telegram of 10 July was certainly a cosy one. It proposed 'an entirely private meeting during which we would explore each other's ideas freely without any pressures from publicity. You may agree that it would not be possible to do this in your country or in mine. I should therefore like to propose that we try and meet in privacy for a frank and personal talk.' Venice or Rome were suggested as agreeable venues. 'Since my camouflage will be a private tourist visit, I propose to take my wife at my own expense. The risk of publicity should be very small . . . We shall each be accompanied by one official only, in my case Mr Harding.'

Ridley's boss, Foreign Secretary Lord Carrington, was worried. 'Why Venice?' he has scribbled on his own copy of the correspondence. 'It will look very odd if it comes out. All looks very hole in the corner.'

Officials agreed. 'Security advice is that Italy is extremely risky, both for reasons of personal safety and for maintaining secrecy,' Ridley was told on 21 August. 'Alternatives suggested are i) a Dutch provincial city, ii) Brussels.' Mrs Ridley, however, doesn't seem to have fancied cooling her heels in Groningen or Tilburg. Somewhere rather grander was agreed on, as an extremely cloak-and-dagger Foreign Office memo of 27 August makes clear: 'Person concerned is ready to agree to Geneva. He asked what excuse his counterpart will be giving for such a trip, so that a suitable rendezvous can be arranged.'

They agreed on the Hotel du Lac, with Ridley booking his room personally to avoid arousing any suspicion that this might be an official trip. 'It is imperative that knowledge of this meeting be severely restricted,' Foreign Office staff in Switzerland were informed. 'There must be no publicity and you should not inform the local authorities of Mr Ridley's presence. If questions were to arise, you should say only that Mr Ridley's visit to Geneva with his wife is private for a short holiday break and that he hopes to do a little water colour painting.' A 'defensive press line' was prepared in case the two ministers were spotted together – 'Comodoro Cavandoli appears to have been making a visit to a number of European countries, including Switzerland. He knows and contacted Mr Ridley. They met briefly on a personal basis. We do not know what they talked about' – but even this was dismissed as too revealing. 'Mr Ridley agrees very strongly that News Department should avoid giving the impression that they have answers too pat . . . they should pretend to know nothing about any meeting, and should in the first instance merely offer to inquire.'

The talks kicked off in Ridley's hotel suite on 9 September. Just how much the British government was willing to give away is evident from the text of an 'exploratory proposal' which the minister handed to Cavandoli two days later.

1. Titular sovereignty over the Falkland Islands (Islas Malvinas) and their maritime zone would be transferred to Argentina, with effect from the date of signature of the Agreement.
2. Continued British administration of the Islands and their maritime zone, with a view to guaranteeing to the Islanders and their descendants the uninterrupted enjoyment of their way of life under British institutions, laws and practices, would be simultaneously assured by means of a lease-back to the United

Kingdom for a period of 99 years. The terms of such a lease would be subject to periodic review, by agreement between the two parties.

3. The British and Argentine flags would be flown side by side on public buildings on the islands.
4. The British government would be represented by a Governor who, together with a locally-elected Council, would be responsible for the administration of the Islands and their inhabitants.
5. The Argentine Government would be represented by a Commissioner-General.
6. There would be a Joint Council to arrange co-operation over the economic development of the Islands and their maritime zone.

Argentine flags flying over the Falklands! Even the terms of the lease had been a matter of vast concession: Ridley had suggested a period 'of the order of 200 years'; Cavandoli had suggested 75 before they compromised on a term much closer to the latter. It's hardly surprising that the British Ambassador in Buenos Aires described Cavandoli as 'bubbling with pleasure and very pleased' on his return from Switzerland.

Throughout all this, however, there was one stumbling block: the Falkland Islanders themselves. Ridley visited the territory in November that year specifically to try to sell the idea in principle (without admitting just how far negotiations had proceeded). He admitted aiming 'to persuade Councillors (and through them islanders) that we must work towards a negotiated settlement with the Argentines; therefore to obtain their agreement that we should enter into negotiations with Argentina to explore the scope for a settlement based on lease-back'. It was a no-go. The Islanders were determined to stay British – fully, one hundred per cent copper-bottomed British – at all costs. And those costs were likely to be severe. A Treasury note to Number 10 from 1981 complains of the 'obdurate attitude of the Falklanders, and the great difficulty of bringing them to acceptance of some compromise arrangement for the future with Argentina. This issue has <u>considerable financial implications</u> for the UK.' Again, the underlining is Thatcher's.

'I decided that we did not have the authority to impose a solution of lease-back without the consent of the islanders, nor would we have had the support of parliament had we done so,' Ridley told the Franks committee. 'The Argentines were being very understanding, they were being as helpful as they possibly could because they too had an interest in a negotiated settlement and wanted to see one . . . I would never have been happy to carry on the negotiations on the basis of stringing them along and playing for time because I felt that their patience was exhausted and that they might easily have done something violent. So it was for that reason that I thought it was right to play for a real solution, which meant that we made concessions of a sort.'

Ridley had moved to the Treasury by the time of the invasion in 1982, leaving his successor Richard Luce to carry the can with Lord Carrington and resign in response to the 'humiliating affront to this country'. Cavandoli had gone too, after yet another of the military coups the Argentines were prone to brought General Galtieri to power and ushered in his more direct approach to the Falklands problem. Called in front of the Franks committee later that year, Ridley was unapologetic about his past actions. 'The more I did in this business, the more convinced I became that whatever the merits or demerits of the lease-back solution, there was no other conceivable solution which would bring agreement and so I made it my business to pursue obtaining a lease-back solution.' But that didn't mean he wanted anyone – particularly the Islanders themselves – to know just how far the government had been willing to go. 'I did not tell them about the meeting in Switzerland, and I hope that nobody ever will.'

ENEMIES WITHIN

We're the IRA, we're new – 1919

On 14 June 1919, six months after 73 Sinn Fein MPs who had been elected to the House of Commons in London decided to stay home, set up their own parliament and declare independence from Britain instead, Lloyd George's Cabinet received a report from its Chief Secretary for Ireland at Dublin Castle. It contained the first mention in Cabinet papers of a terrorist group whose name would become all too familiar over the following 80 years.

Ian Macpherson was writing to refute – at length – the report of three Irish-American delegates who had visited the country to investigate the political situation, and to present their findings to the post-war Peace Conference which was then piling up problems for the future in Paris.

The Americans – who had nailed their colours to the mast at the outset, declaring that 'the object of their journey is to help the cause of Irish freedom' – detailed horrendous-sounding abuses of political prisoners at Mountjoy prison, all of them denied by Macpherson. But they also claimed to have discovered that 'There is a military organization of approximately 200,000 men of fighting age, poorly equipped as to arms and without artillery,' operating in Ireland. 'They appear to be well officered, and seemingly maintain a perfect organization, engaging in daily drills and frequent manoeuvres. Upon all sides may be heard declarations that they are ready to fight and die for the right of self-determination no matter how great the odds against them may be. Guerrilla warfare of the character which usually precedes major conflicts is now going on in Ireland.'

Macpherson was having none of it. 'There is, it is true, a quasi-military organization which calls itself the Irish Republican Army, and it is known that this organization secretly plots murders and outrages against persons and property in many parts of Ireland,' he told his colleagues. 'There is no such thing as guerrilla warfare in Ireland. But if the Delegates mean that members of the so-called Irish Republican Army in a cowardly and dastardly manner assassinate unsuspecting policemen or other loyal persons it is only too certain that "guerrilla warfare" in this sense exists . . . The suggestion that there is daily "warfare" between His Majesty's troops and the Volunteers of the so-called Irish Republic is grotesque.'

More detail on the new group came with the Home Office's monthly 'Report on Revolutionary Organizations in the United Kingdom' the following month, although they still rated very low on the list of potential threats, after such subversives as Russian anti-interventionists, 'Labour leaders organising opposition to peace celebrations', the Bolshevik Herald League, militants in the Iron Founders' Trade Union and of course the suffragettes. 'The re-organisation of the Cork Brigade of the Irish Republican Army shows that the Military side of Sinn Fein is not altogether idle,' wrote Basil Thomson, head of the Directorate of Intelligence, 'and this example is likely to be followed in other districts.' He was not wrong.

Hark the Herald – 1919

Every government is obsessed with what the papers say. And in 1919, the contents of one particular newspaper were causing serious concern at the highest levels. 'The policy of the *Daily Herald* has always been to encourage strikes in vital industries, to applaud revolutionary movements, to foment unrest among the troops, and persistently to misrepresent the motives of the Government,' frothed a Confidential Special Report prepared that November by the Home Office's newly formed Directorate of Intelligence, which kept a weather eye on the enemy within for Lloyd George's administration. Leaked military material had appeared in the paper, and there were concerns that it 'was offering inducements to persons employed in the War Office to steal other documents'.

Who was the sinister puppet master behind this scandal sheet? George Lansbury, former MP and future leader of the Labour Party (and, perhaps most impressively, grandfather of *Bagpuss* creator Oliver Postgate). He had helped found the *Daily Herald* as a voice for the Labour movement in 1912, and edited it throughout the First World War, during which it had confused readers by being produced weekly and enraged the War Office by implacably opposing the conflict. The Directorate, however, seems to have been convinced that others were responsible for the paper's worst excesses: 'Mr Gerald Gould was acting as Foreign Editor a few months ago and probably still occupies that position; he is helped by his wife and probably the two Goulds supply most of the acrimony which characterises the paper.' Gould had got what the report's compiler clearly considered his just deserts for being a conscientious objector during the war: 'He undertook work of national importance on the land, where he failed to get on terms with the dumb animals under his charge – he is reported to have been tossed by a bull and bitten by a pedigree pig.'

A familiar name pops up in the staff list. 'Captain Siegfried Sassoon, MC is responsible for the Reviews, but probably he is only an occasional contributor. It will be remembered that while a commissioned officer he protested, in a circular sent out in July 1917, against the continued sacrifice of fighting men in the war by politicians.' He

217

also wrote quite a lot of poetry – eight volumes of it had already been published by 1919, much of it making a similar point – but this went unrecorded by the Directorate. Literary criticism was obviously outside their remit.

They were far more impressed by one of Sassoon's colleagues: 'Mr Francis Meredith Meynell is a pushing, rather good-looking young man.' He was, however, that most suspicious of figures, a champagne socialist: 'He invited his English colleagues to champagne supper parties when champagne cost £3 a bottle. The sources of Meynell's lavish entertainments were much commented upon among his colleagues, who knew that his means were limited.' Other reasons were found to distrust reporter Vivian Brodsky: 'He is an Australian Jew . . . His father is a Jew, resident in New York.' He was also apparently 'unscrupulous in his methods of obtaining news', which sounds like a fair description of the other deeply unrespectable J-word: journalist. It is at least cheering that investigators had been unable to dig any dirt whatsoever on one member of staff: 'Miss Bridges is the "Aunt Kitsie" of the Children's Corner.'

But the rest of the report was crammed with any and all bits of gossip the Directorate had managed to pick up in the pubs near the paper's office (they'd have made quite good journalists themselves). The business manager's secretary was 'strongly pacifist', the advertising manager was 'extremely advanced in his views' and 'very intimate' with a man who was writing a book on 'the Coming Revolution in England'. Most intriguingly, 'a man named Deserne spends most of his time in the cellars where he is supposed to be looking after photographs'.

As for cash, 'great mystery is preserved about the sources of the capital' behind the paper, particularly given that 'Mr Lansbury has always expressed a sovereign contempt for advertisements, which are to his mind one of the evils of the capitalistic system.' Much to their evident frustration, the Directorate was unable to finger any actual Russian paymasters lurking in the shadows, but there were certainly some rum coves amongst the shareholders, including 'Miss Dodge, a wealthy American lady who also financed the Suffragettes, and who now, owing to her age and state of health, allows herself to be exploited by the promoters of any advanced movement', and an Indian Nationalist and director of the *Bombay Chronicle* by the name of Mr Bomanji. Herein lay a mystery. 'It was reported that as Bomanji was not in the position to give so much money, that there was someone behind him and that that person was the Gaekwar of Baroda.' This particular Indian prince had introduced such dangerously revolutionary measures as free primary education and a ban on child marriage in his own corner of the subcontinent: he was notorious in Britain for failing to bow properly to King George V at the Delhi Durbar in 1911, which had earned him a place in the pantheon of foreign villains right up alongside

Lenin and Kaiser Bill. The conspiracy theories the report offers to explain the paper's finances give an idea of just how global and comprehensive the British establishment considered the threats against it to be in 1919: during a paper-buying trip to Sweden the champagne-loving Meynell was accused of having 'got into communication with Strom, the Swedish extreme Socialist, who is in touch with the Russian Bolsheviks and who was formerly a German agent; this is the same man who gave money to the young Norweigan Zachariassen, who brought money over to Miss Sylvia Pankhurst'.

For the moment, though, the *Herald*, which claimed a circulation of 320,000, seemed to be limping along thanks to handouts from a motley crew of trade unions, despite Lansbury's own warnings that 'no Labour daily could be made to pay'. He was right. The *Herald* had an uncharacteristic burst of popularity in the 1930s when its circulation rocketed to two million, thanks largely to the genius idea, hastily copied by the *Daily Mail* and *Express*, of giving away bound sets of Dickens (most of those leather-bound editions knocking around in second-hand bookshops to this day date from this particular circulation war). Not long after that, however, it went into a terminal decline. And then in the 1960s came a fate worse than death: it was reformatted, renamed, reorientated and finally sold to a pushy young Australian called Rupert Murdoch – as *The Sun*.

Cross purposes – 1944

In November 1944, Home Secretary Herbert Morrison circulated to his Cabinet colleagues a transcription of a German propaganda leaflet that had been dropped from a flying bomb over Sussex six days previously. 'Only one copy has reached this Department,' he noted.

The highlight – amongst the gloating about the 'German inventive genius' that had come up with V-1 bombs, the bountiful harvests that were 'certain to keep Germany fighting trim' and the first-person account of Upper Silesian miner Felix Rübell of why he was 'all-out for Hitler – fighting for social justice' – was a crossword. Yes, Dr Goebbels knew that the way to an Englishman's heart was through a really good cryptic clue.

Across:
1. He is your enemy, too. (9)
7. V1 is so fast, that it is hard to this. (3)
8. Partly a beverage. (2)
10. This is the beginning of a German victory. (2)
11. We hear that this is a rare commodity in England. (3)
13. This is in Latin. (3)
14. He wants all you've got. (9)

Down:
1. In the case of the air war, he has been bit by V1. (5)

2. Money but no pence. (2)
3. Men and material intended for Normandy very often finish up at the bottom of this. (3)
4. V1 contains this. (2)
5. Britain has none at inter-Allied conferences. (5)
6. At Tehran, Churchill practically did this before Stalin. (5)
9. First person singular. (3)
10. Two reprisals with nothing in between. (3)
12. Warmongers must this, if England is to be saved. (2)
13. That man. (2)

It wasn't as if the War Office weren't already having trouble with crosswords – in May that year the *Daily Telegraph*'s compiler Leonard Dawe had been interviewed by MI5 after the codewords for a number of beaches to be used in the Normandy landings, the floating harbours, naval assault phase and the entire D-Day operation itself happened to appear as clues in his puzzles. 'They turned me inside out, and they went to Bury St Edmunds where my senior colleague Melville Jones was living and put him through the works, but they eventually decided not to shoot us after all,' he recalled in 1958.

As for the Nazis' very deliberately chosen clues, the pamphlet warned that 'If you choose to regard the cross-word merely as an entertainment, no doubt you will get some fun out of it. If you take it seriously you will get more than that – you will find that it contains some very useful advice!'

The spies shine light on Charlie Chaplin – 1956

MI5 didn't think much of Charlie Chaplin. That is to say, they were unimpressed by the information that the FBI – whose suspicions that he had donated cash to 'Communist Front Organisations' ensured that the silent movie star was banned from the US at the height of the McCarthyite witch hunts in 1952 – had passed on to them. 'When resident in America [he] was the subject of several reports associating him with Communism,' noted top spook H. P. Goodwyn in a security service file released in 2012. 'These reports, the veracity of which we are unable to check, do not impress us by their prima facie quality.'

'We have no indication from the Americans of the reliability they ascribe to their information, and in the absence of this, I am inclined to consider it as being of very doubtful quality,' was the assessment of another colleague. In fact, they appear to have known hardly anything about one of the most famous men in the world: following another tip-off from America, yet another spy, W. M. T. Magan, issued instructions in January 1953 to 'follow up Chaplin's origin', specifically to discover if he was Russian, Jewish, or preferably both. He was still on the case a few weeks later: 'I would like to establish CHAPLIN's name at birth, and it would therefore be worth asking MI6 if there is any record of his birth at Fontainebleau on 16.4.89 either under the name CHAPLIN or Israel THORNSTEIN.' His underlings failed to find any – nor did his name come up in the UK's register of births, despite his lifelong claim to have been born in Walworth in south London.

The official conclusion, delivered to an unknown enquirer (like many of the names in the file, it has been redacted) that year, was 'that we have no information of our own about CHAPLIN and that we consider that there are no reliable grounds for regarding him as a security risk'.

It did not stop them from keeping a close eye on him. Chaplin's MI5 file contains a wealth of information on the artist formerly known as the Little Tramp, who spent much of the decade in Geneva working on his memoirs. There are transcripts of tapped phone calls between Communist Party staff who mentioned 'their friend Charlie', intercepted telegrams to Chaplin requesting '500 to 600 words in connection with forthcoming congress soviet writers' for the *Literary Gazette* in Moscow, copies of postcards sent to the actor from fans behind the Iron Curtain and an enormous number of newspaper clippings dealing with such fascinating topics as his holiday plans and enjoyment of travelling on the London Underground. The most intriguing oddity in the file is a page of typewritten notes on what was obviously a bugged conversation between the Clydeside trade unionist Jimmy Reid and a fellow traveller. 'BILL referred to the musicians in JIMMY's "thing" approaching CHAPLIN, BILL became very inaudible but was heard to mention HUMPHREY LYTTELTON.' Quite what the future host of *I'm Sorry I Haven't A Clue* would have brought to the table is unclear, but it could have been very funny indeed.

But after five years of digging, MI5 had turned up nothing that convinced them Chaplin was heading up a secret Soviet slapstick division. 'It may be that CHAPLIN is a Communist sympathiser,' Goodwyn concluded in 1958, 'but on the information before us he would appear to be no more than a "progressive" or radical.' His file was closed.

The failure to turn up anything incriminating about Chaplin, however, did not stop the British establishment from closing ranks to prevent him getting a knighthood in 1956. 'It is an undeniable fact that Mr Chaplin has done much to make himself a figure of controversy,' thundered the Foreign Office when they were sounded out for their views on the proposed honour. 'Mr Chaplin first exposed himself to serious criticism on the Communist score during the war when he echoed Stalin's demand for an early second front . . . In April 1949 he invited further public censure by sending a telegram to Paris, enthusiastically supporting the Communist-sponsored World Peace Congress which was being held there . . . He has also added grist to his opponents' mill by his acceptance of public marks of favour from the communist orbit.'

This, however, was not the worst of it. He wasn't just a leftie: he was a dirty old leftie. 'On the morals issue the American public is still mindful of the scandals with which Mr Chaplin managed to shock even the more broad-minded in the nineteen-twenties – e.g. his two marriages to 16-year-olds (Mildred Harris, 1918; Lita Grey, 1924).' The fact that Harris had been dead for over a decade and Grey was at menopause age by now counted for nothing: their youthful escapades were apparently still a hot topic at the Foreign Office, along with 'lurid details which dominated the headlines in 1943 and 1944' concerning a hotly contested paternity case. 'While the Queen might be prepared to overlook the political objections to Mr Chaplin I very much doubt whether she could overlook the moral charges since they are of concern to the British public as well as to the American public,' concluded official A. N. MacCleary, who sounds like he ought to have got out a bit more.

Thankfully, his successors had slightly more progressive ideas. In July 1971, the Protocol Department in Whitehall had another go. 'Charlie Chaplin has been put forward for a knighthood from highly reputable, indeed distinguished sources . . . What would the Foreign Office say? . . . Would the Americans mind, or would we?'

We would not, as it turned out. 'My own view

is that in present circumstances an honour for Mr Chaplin would do no harm to our relations with the US and could indeed do some good, in liberal circles,' Miss R. A. Vining of the North America Department daringly opined. 'I am inclined to agree that the award of a Knighthood would no longer arouse great indignation,' chimed in Lord Cromer, the ambassador to the US. He also offered an additional suggestion: 'I should like to mention that Mr Bob Hope, who is a US citizen although he was born in England, is generally regarded as the Doyen of the American entertainment world . . . The only reason I mention this now is that some sections of American opinion might well feel that Bob Hope has as good a claim for an award as Charlie Chaplin and you might wish to take this into account in your consideration of this recommendation.'

After that, things moved swiftly. Chaplin got his knighthood a mere four years later, when he was 85 and had to greet the Queen from a wheelchair (he died two years afterwards). Bob Hope did even better. He was finally invited to the embassy in Washington to receive his honorary knighthood in 1998, when he was 94.

It's a conspiracy, ma'am – 1963

Harold Macmillan and the Queen did enjoy a good gossip.

'The House of Commons is in a rather excitable

mood,' the Prime Minister confided in Her Majesty on 17 February 1963. 'The election of a new leader of the Labour Party has been conducted with a good deal of dignity in public but with a great deal of what I believe is called "character assassination" behind the scenes; one is too drunk, one is too dishonest, and so forth. Whether any of these men will prove adequate to the post of Your Majesty's First Minister, I cannot tell. However, as Churchill said on a famous occasion, "If you feed a grub on royal jelly, you may turn it into a queen bee." They have already got the smell and almost the taste of royal jelly in their mouths, so let us hope the moral and intellectual growth will follow.'

Ooh, get him! On 15 April he wrote again, this time to disparage the duffel-coated hordes who attended that year's CND demonstrations against nuclear weapons:

> Fifteen thousand people are said to have taken part in the Aldermaston March. I feel this is all rather pathetic as well as tiresome. I am sure the poor people feel that they are doing a noble work, but I fear that they are not prepared to face the realities of the situation.
>
> This leads me to give Your Majesty some account of the stage now reached in the very secret correspondence which I have been having with President Kennedy . . .

Unfortunately at this point things got a bit too interesting. 'Remainder of letter is deleted and closed under Section 5 (1), 50 years,' runs a 2002 note on the file.

Here, though, you will find Macmillan's most awkward letter, the one he dispatched to the Palace after the revelations of the Profumo scandal that summer. John Profumo, the Secretary of State for War, had resigned a fortnight previously, after admitting that he had lied to the House of Commons when he said there had been 'no impropriety whatsoever' in his relationship with Christine Keeler. She actually turned out to have been having lots of impropriety not just with him but with all sorts of other people too, including a Russian spy.

'Although I am to have the honour of an Audience with Your Majesty on Thursday next, I feel I should not like to delay so long before expressing to Your Majesty my deep regret at the development of recent affairs,' wrote the PM on 23 June. I feel that I ought to apologise to You for the undoubted injury done by the terrible behaviour of one of Your Majesty's Secretaries of State upon not only the Government but, perhaps more serious, on the great Armed Forces.'

He liked a capital letter, didn't he? But then the Prime Minister – who started each letter to the monarch 'Madam – Mr Macmillan with his humble duty to the Queen' and ended it 'With my humble duty, I remain, Your Majesty's faithful and devoted servant' – was clinging desperately to the old formalities as everything else seemed to crumble away around him.

> I had of course no idea of the strange underworld in which other people, alas, besides Mr Profumo have allowed themselves to become entrapped. I begin to suspect in all these wild accusations against many people, Ministers and others, something in the nature of a plot to destroy the established system.

Steady on, Prime Minister! Macmillan – who had first been elected to the House of Commons in 1924, two years before the Queen was even born – could only do his best to reassure the young monarch.

> All these are very distressing affairs. But I am confident that they can be overcome and that when Your Majesty looks back upon them, in the course of what I trust may be a very long and successful Reign, they will appear no more than the irritations which have, from time to time, been of concern to Your Majesty's predecessors. What is so painful to me is to think that, whether by some action or inaction on my part, I may have contributed to Your burden.

We don't get to see what the Queen wrote back to him, but it appears to have been reassuring. 'I am most appreciative of Your Majesty's kind letter to me and I shall always treasure it,' he wrote on 26 July. He confessed to feeling 'a little battered . . . It has not been, as Your Majesty knows, an easy time for me.'

Fortunately, he was back to his bitchy best by September, when he drafted an update for the Palace on the progress of the official inquiry into the scandal. 'It is likely that certain passages of the Report will be actionable in that they are defamatory of a number of individuals concerned in this matter, including, I understand, Miss Keeler (a person who seems more prone than most to issue writs in order to seek further publicity).' At the last minute, however, he thought better of this particular aside, perhaps on the grounds of accuracy, and struck it out.

Macmillan resigned the following month after he was rushed to hospital for an emergency operation which was too much to cope with on top of the continuing political storm. 'Had this affliction come upon me at some other time I could have bowed to the surgeon's knife, been stitched and recovered and resumed my toil. But I now recognise that my days, as Prime Minister, are numbered,' he wrote to Her Majesty on 9 October. His final act was a defiant blast on behalf of that established system he was so worried about: he ensured he was succeeded in Downing Street by his fellow

Old Etonian the Earl of Home, whose aristocratic title went back to the seventeenth century. Take that, plotters!

We will fine them on the beaches – 1964

It all seems so ancient now. It kicked off at the 'Whitsun weekend', a date anyone under pension age would have difficulty placing. It involved most of the country heading to Margate or Clacton for their holidays. Gangs that fought with coshes rather than guns. And Vespa scooters being a symbol of dangerous rebellion rather than of media workers having a mid-life crisis.

Type 'Mods and Rockers' into Google now and its autofill function will assume you're looking for fancy-dress costumes. But the horror invoked by the groups of youths who fought their way around the coast of Britain in the summer of 1964 is evident from the series of agonised memos which Home Secretary Henry Brooke fired off to Prime Minister Alec Douglas-Home that June.

'The Home Affairs Committee considered at their meeting on 29th May whether there was any legislative action which the Government should take to deal with the possibility of further outbreaks of teenage hooliganism at seaside resorts during the summer,' he informed the PM, who had channelled his own adolescent frustration into playing cricket and fives at Eton.

The House was up in arms, as an attached list of parliamentary questions tabled for Brooke makes clear. David James, the MP for Brighton Kemp Town, demanded 'much heavier penalties, for those who persistently wreck the peace, cause wanton damage or molest peaceful citizens'. Sir John Eden, the member for Bournemouth West, wanted 'legislation to restore the use of judicial corporal punishment as a means of dealing with persons convicted of wanton destruction'. And the unimprovably titled MP for Ayr, Lieutenant Colonel Sir Thomas Moore, proposed that 'as Vespas or motor cycles, or whatever they are, are the methods by which these young idiots get to their place of destruction, surely it might be thought wise to confiscate their licences or disqualify them for, say, five years?'

Brooke, however, had realised that legislation along the latter lines would be unworkable, since it would give magistrates carte blanche to disqualify anyone who happened to have used a vehicle before committing a crime. Instead he proposed another, hooligan-specific measure, which he sought permission to put before Parliament as a matter of urgency. Teenagers in Brighton had smashed up deckchairs and burned them on the beach; in Margate they had smashed windows and vandalised a pub and hardware shop. The maximum amount that could be demanded in compensation from those convicted of malicious damage was £20, which even Brooke had spotted was 'a figure now out of date'. He was seeking permission to urgently bring before Parliament legislation to raise the sum to £100, with a fine to match: with the average weekly wage standing at £16.14s.11d (and young workers earning considerably less), £200 would be a serious bill to be faced with. 'Not all the seaside disorders have resulted in damage to property,' Brooke admitted, 'but the proposed increase in these amounts is fully justified on every ground and would be a valuable deterrent to have.' On the other hand, it might not: as one Mod told the *Observer* that May, 'if anyone fined me £75 I'd go back and do some real damage; put a few windows through with a hammer'.

Douglas-Home agreed to Brooke's proposal, but added a further thought in spidery fountain pen. 'Is it possible to make a youth pay this fine personally, over an extended period of time? I think that this might inconvenience and shame him much more than taking out a cheque book or getting one payment out of his father.'

Sadly, Brooke concluded that this idea was unworkable too. Although court orders to pay by instalments already existed, he informed the PM in an apologetic letter, they were meant for 'defendants of limited means', and 'there would be nothing to prevent the defendant from paying off the fine in a lump sum . . . There is, I am afraid, no way that we can think of of preventing a person ordered to pay a fine from obtaining the money from father or anyone else.'

Brooke's other big idea was an 'Advisory Committee on Juvenile Delinquency' to investigate 'the true reasons why groups of boys and girls break away into selfish behaviour that is offensive to the mass of ordinary decent people'. He even appointed the crooner Frankie Vaughan to sit on it. But in the short term, the Home Secretary had something else up his sleeve. 'The police are concerting plans for reinforcing any resorts which are subject to teenage incursions in future,' he told the Prime Minister, 'but I propose to keep quiet about this, since the knowledge that the police are taking precautions merely incites youngsters to test their effectiveness.' His secret plan swung into action that August Bank Holiday when the Mods and Rockers headed to Hastings: Scotland Yard's riot squad, who had been standing ready at RAF Northolt, were flown into nearby Lydd airport to reinforce the Sussex constabulary and make around 70 arrests in what the media swiftly dubbed the Second Battle of Hastings, despite the disappointing lack of bloodshed.

But it was the beginning of the end. Both the revelries and the rivalries faded away over the next couple of summers, leaving Brooke's generation to fret about long-haired hippies instead. These days we just have Paul Weller and Bradley Wiggins, who were too young to be Mods the first time round, and are definitely too old for it now.

The Watergate that wasn't – 1975

The *News of the World* carried a sensational head-line on 17 August 1975: 'BRITISH WATERGATE SHOCK CLAIM'. As is often the case during the summer 'Silly Season', the story beneath proved not quite as spectacular: 'A sensational claim that a British Prime Minister ordered the Watergate-style burglary of a politician's home is to be made in a new book.'

The book in question was the staid-sounding *Crime in Britain Today*, to be published the following month by the academic imprint Routledge & Kegan Paul. It was by two Fleet Street crime correspondents, Clive Borrell and Brian Cashinella, who obviously hadn't thought the allegation strong enough to run in their own papers. *The Times*, where Borrell actually worked, was rather more restrained in its own coverage the following day: 'Book connects "a Prime Minister" with burglary'.

But however much the *News of the Screws* might have gussied things up, the 'W' word set off serious alarms in Downing Street. It was almost exactly a year since Richard Nixon had been obliged to resign over the 1972 break-in at the HQ of his Democrat rivals in Washington's Watergate building. It was the President's role in an increasingly frantic cover-up, rather than any direct connection to the crime itself, that had done for him. So for Wilson, whose paranoia rivalled that of his US counterpart on a bad day, it was vital to show a clean pair of hands to the public.

But first of all, he had to make sure he actually possessed them. Could a state-sanctioned burglary possibly have slipped his mind? A quick check with the Home Office confirmed that 'we have no knowledge of any activities which could account for these allegations and we can offer no explanation for them'. Robert Armstrong, Wilson's private secretary, spoke to the Commissioner of the Met and the Security Service and reported back that they too had both drawn a blank. What's more, Armstrong put on the official record that 'the Prime Minister had no recollection of ever having made an arrangement of the kind alleged'.

But it was possible the book wasn't referring to Wilson anyway. The paragraph quoted in the papers – which, although Number 10 were in no position to know it, was the sole reference to the alleged incident in the book's 200-plus pages – merely claimed that:

> Not a decade ago a certain Prime Minister even arranged for a detective to 'burgle' a senior politician's flat because he was dubious about some of his activities. It does not require much inventiveness to imagine the uproar that would have ensued had that 'crime' become public knowledge. There are times, however, especially in the fight against crime, when the ends justify the means.

Counting back ten years covered both Wilson's stints in Downing Street, but also the four years in between when Edward Heath had had his valiant stab at running the country. 'I have not spoken to Mr Heath,' ventured Armstrong, who had served under both PMs, 'but there is nothing in my recollection, which covers almost the whole of his term of office, which could provide a foundation for these allegations.'

Still, they probably ought to check. That job fell to civil servant Mark Forrester, another hanger-on from the previous regime. 'Mr Heath asked me to call this evening to discuss the article,' runs his typewritten account of 18 August, firmly stamped SECRET. 'Mr Heath said that he had never authorised any activity of this nature and the conclusion must therefore be that the story was a fabrication, so far as he was concerned.' But there was a but. 'Mr Heath said that it was being said by the two authors of the book in Fleet Street that, while they could not publish anything for fear of compromising their sources, the activity to which they were referring was in connection with Mr Heath and the Jellicoe affair in May 1973.'

The downfall of Earl Jellicoe, the leader of the House of Lords, dates from an era when they did political scandals properly. It began when his ministerial colleague Lord Lambton was photographed naked in bed with prostitute Norma Levy. As if that wasn't enough, Levy had brought along a friend, and the politician was smoking cannabis. When Lambton resigned and cheerfully 'fessed up on the BBC to paying for an assortment of drugs and women because 'people sometimes like variety', the considerably more embarrassed Earl Jellicoe was forced to admit that he too had been using the services of prostitutes – although rather sweetly, he insisted on taking his ones out for dinner first.

But the Tory leader was very clear that the confession had come unprompted by any official rifling through the good lord's drawers. 'He had at no time ever authorised any burglary and indeed, given Lord Jellicoe's attitude at the time, it would not have been in any way necessary to do so. Lord Jellicoe's activities had come to light in the course of routine police enquiries, and when approached by him (Mr Heath), Lord Jellicoe had made a clean breast of the activities which led him to submit his resignation . . . There was absolutely no ill feeling or attempt at a cover up which would have led him to act any differently than the way he in fact did.'

Forrester agreed to be discreet. 'I told Mr Heath that I would tell the Prime Minister of my call, and we agreed that, while I would not be specific about the incident to which Mr Heath had referred, I could let it be known to the Prime Minister that rumour had it that it was Mr Heath who was referred to, though completely without foundation.'

Reassured, the PM canvassed opinion on how he could proceed with legal action. Suing for libel had been one of Wilson's favourite hobbies ever since he grabbed all royalties in perpetuity from The Move's 1967 song 'Flowers in the Rain' in revenge for an unflattering cartoon on a postcard promoting the single. Others were less enthusiastic. Police and MI5 representatives who were summoned to Number 10 for their advice pointed out that 'the publicity for the allegations could have been designed as a puff for sales of the book, and the issue of a statement . . . would be an additional puff'. And while the Treasury Solicitor advised that the allegation 'is clearly actionable by you and Mr Heath' he cautioned, 'I trust you will not infer that I am an advocate of legal proceedings. I am not.'

Wilson decided to press on anyway. The Friday after the *News of the World* report Downing Street put out a statement that 'Mr Wilson and Mr Heath wish to state categorically and without further delay that no such operation as described in the newspaper reports has been carried out on their request or with their knowledge or authority at any time during the term of office of either of them as Prime Minister.' The headline in the *Sun* the following morning put it slightly more pithily: 'HAROLD AND TED DENY ORDERING BREAK-IN'. They had almost certainly been briefed by the Downing Street press office, whose handwritten 'line for use if asked' includes the scribbled phrases 'grossly defamatory', 'action not substantially' and 'look v. odd indeed'.

Borrell and Cashinella were defiant, telling the following Sunday's *News of the World* that they were 'willing to go to prison to defend their claim'. Their publishers attempted to snub Downing Street too. 'We propose to take no further action, as these form a very minor and insignificant part of a long book,' the Routledge chairman wrote.

This meant war. 'Consideration of the publishers' reply has led to a feeling on Robert Armstrong's part, shared by the Home Secretary who has been consulted in France, that the publishers should not be allowed to get away with it,' runs a Number 10 telex to Wilson, who had by now departed for his hols in the Scilly Isles. Heath was on holiday too, at Broadstairs, but after much drafting and redrafting Downing Street managed to dispatch a joint response from both men 'asking that a retraction and apology should be issued with each copy of the book . . . it would have to be pursued by further action if the publishers refused to comply'.

In the face of united action from a brace of PMs, Routledge crumbled. A letter from chairman Norman Franklin on 29 August proposed that 'with your approval, we will delete the last six lines on page 4 of those copies of the books in our hands, with adhesive white paper labels'. But this was not enough. Number 10 also demanded a 'statement of retraction and apology', something Routledge apologised they were unable to provide for a reason that was utterly of its time: 'Mr Franklin said that he was in practical difficulty about making such a statement, since Cashinella was on holiday in a caravan on the south coast, and could not be contacted: he could not make a statement on behalf of the authors without getting in touch with Cashinella.'

So the retraction came from the publishers alone, while Clive Borrell (presumably also speaking on behalf of his be-caravanned colleague) told the *Sun* that 'I stand by every word. I know my facts are right.' If they were, he never chose to enlarge upon them. When he died in 2004, his *Times* obituary noted that 'the book did not sell as well as expected and Borrell vowed never to write another'.

Spy TV – 1981

These days, when the MI6 building is such a landmark that the orchestra accompanying the Queen's Diamond Jubilee pageant on the Thames struck up the James Bond theme in tribute as they floated past, the official policy of pretending the secret services did not exist seems frankly weird. But it was one to which Margaret Thatcher clung doggedly. When, in 1979, a young Labour back-bencher by the name of Robin Cook (the very man who, as Foreign Secretary decades later, would give the Bond producers permission to feature the real-life MI6 building in their films) tried to flush out the spies' existence by the cunning means of putting up a parliamentary motion for the creation of a security service, since the country didn't appear to have one, she was furious. 'I think the decision <u>totally wrong</u> and <u>misconceived</u>,' she scrawled on a letter from the Chancellor of the Duchy of Lancaster assuring her that if Conservative MPs were instructed to ignore Cook's motion, it would just go away.

A year later, she was faced with an even bigger problem. The BBC's *Panorama* was making a film which not only pointed out that the security services really did exist, with buildings and bosses with names and faces and everything, but that they also did things like manipulating the press and bugging phones and possibly even assassinating foreign people they didn't like. Ministers pronounced themselves 'dismayed' by the prospect. Mrs Thatcher said she was 'very anxious to protect the Intelligence Services and she feared the purpose of those who were making the programme was to discredit those Services'. She refused even to countenance a programme limited to looking at their accountability to Parliament: beside a query as to whether a documentary 'not extending to their functions and working' would be acceptable she scribbled an enraged '<u>NO</u>'.

But there appeared to be nothing the government could do to stop it from being broadcast. 'Not a happy prospect, but short of using the veto (which Ministers have been minded not to do) there is little we can do,' wrote an adviser on one of many confidential memos which flew back and forth during the affair (many of them copied in to 'C', codeword for the head of MI6). 'I am against <u>any</u> programme being shown. I would be prepared to use the veto,' Thatcher scribbled on another.

Thankfully, the PM had a fall guy who was happy to step in and prevent the programme from being broadcast (at least in full): Ian Trethowan, the director general of the BBC, who called in a video of the 100 minutes of material that the programme team had gathered together in January 1981, sat on it for 15 days, and then announced that most of it could not be shown. He insisted to outraged journalists both within and without the corporation that he had made the decision solely on editorial grounds, and, in the words of a *Guardian* report on 3 February, 'denied that he showed it to anyone from the Government'. But he was lying.

A memo marked 'Top Secret', which the Cabinet Secretary Robert Armstrong specifically instructed should not be sent to departments 'not geared to handling papers about intelligence and security matters', revealed that actually, Trethowan had shown the film to MI5, in the person of their legal adviser Bernard Sheldon. So concerned had the Man from Auntie been about keeping this fact a secret that he 'decided that he and Mr Sheldon should watch the film privately together . . . since the role of Mr Sheldon would be liable to leak'. Sheldon, in turn, had gone to Downing Street and detailed the film's entire contents for them.

Trethowan had also met with the heads of both MI5 and MI6 while the programme was being put together, although he told the BBC governors that 'both had been comparatively relaxed about the programme' – a bit of gossip that the chairman had immediately passed back to Downing Street via Home Secretary Willie Whitelaw.

BBC executives had, a delighted Armstrong reported, 'been asked to reduce it to a 50 minute programme, taking account of the various comments made and deletions suggested by Sir Ian Trethowan following Mr Sheldon's comments'. Whether or not this included the section which apparently detailed 'the manipulation of news' is not clear. But Armstrong was able to reassure the PM that 'if those comments are all faithfully followed, the result should be a reasonably balanced programme from which most of the material to which we would have strong objection had been deleted'. Even better, Trethowan was prepared to take the rap himself: 'The main attack is on him, and he is content to take it. He is expecting to have something of a showdown with his editors next week.'

He wasn't wrong. Tom Mangold, the reporter on the programme, remembers various confrontations during which executives went 'white with fury', and Trethowan referred to *Panorama* editor Roger Bolton as a 'Marxist little shit', despite the fact that, as Mangold points out, 'Roger is neither little, Marxist or a shit'. The National Union of

Journalists passed a resolution taking 'the greatest exception to any form of censorship or improper pressure placed on any BBC journalist'. Those close to the programme took more practical measures by leaking most of the juiciest information that had been left out to the *Sunday Times* and *Guardian*. A bowdlerised version of the programme, cut according to the director general's instructions, eventually went out later that month.

Trethowan had been awarded a knighthood the previous year in recognition of his 'services to television journalism'.

STRATEGIC THINKING

The thin end of the Wedgie – 1957

I n February 1957, the Marquess of Salisbury, Leader of the House of Lords, wrote to Harold Macmillan about a programme that Woodrow Wyatt was proposing to make for the BBC about that pipe dream of politicians from Henry Campbell-Bannerman to Nick Clegg, reform of the House of Lords.

Salisbury had been asked to appear – but it was another potential contributor who was causing him sleepless nights. 'So far as Mr Wedgwood Benn is concerned,' he told the Prime Minister, 'it seems to me that he is being given far too much publicity for his scheme, which is really, so far as I understand it, quite impracticable. He seeks to do away with the existing House of Lords, and replace it by a body formed from the Privy Council.

'But first, the members of the Privy Council are all very elderly, which would mean there was no young element in the Second Chamber at all, and secondly, most of them have little or no experience

247

of politics, and probably no desire to devote the evening of their lives to that profession. I should guess that his main objective in putting the plan forward was to avoid the possibility that he himself might some day have to go to the House of Lords, a prospect which apparently fills him with deep depression.'

Anthony Wedgwood Benn eventually succeeded in reforming himself rather than the House he was destined to enter thanks to his father's elevation as Viscount Stansgate. Although he couldn't avoid inheriting the title in 1960, he managed to force through the Peerage Act three years later, which allowed him to disclaim it and carry on as an MP instead. A decade after that, he decided he still had too many names and dropped the Ant and the Wedgwood too. As plain old Tony Benn, he continued to be a thorn in the side of the Labour Party for a further 30 years before retiring from the Commons in 2001 to 'devote more time to politics'. Ironically, his interrogator Woodrow Wyatt, who had been moonlighting as a *Panorama* reporter between parliamentary seats, had long since completed his own journey in precisely the opposite direction, from Labour MP to a stridently right-wing member of the House of Lords.

Mrs Thatcher, milk . . . saviour? – 1970

Nothing she did during her subsequent 11 years in Downing Street ever managed to expunge one particular blot on the career of Margaret Thatcher, one that earned her a nickname that lived on for generations of schoolchildren long after the taste of a third-of-a-pinta left too close to the radiator had faded. It's the rhyming that did it. Just as the Tories never really laid a finger on Tony Blair until they spotted that 'crony' paired rather well with his Christian name, Mrs Thatcher remained a milk snatcher until the day she died.

Which is a bit unfair, given that it wasn't her idea in the first place, and she actually intervened to roll back the scale of the cuts. The proposal came from the Treasury, in a Public Expenditure Review in July 1970 which aimed at cutting £1.7 billion from the government's bills over the next four years so businessmen could have a tax break – 'The immediate objective is to provide scope for reductions in personal and company taxation, as part of our strategy for encouraging initiative and enterprise.'

'Publicly provided or heavily subsidised services are made too widely available,' declared Chief Secretary Maurice Macmillan. The complete withdrawal of both 'welfare and school milk, and of the subsidy on school meals' were among his proposals, as well as 'new types of charges in the Health Service', the immediate closure of the Open University and a charge for borrowing books from public libraries, on the grounds that 'a library service is basically recreational'.

Macmillan – son of former prime minister

Harold – laid out his reasoning in brutal black and white:

SCHOOL MILK. Proposal: Withdraw free milk (one-third of a pint per day) from pupils in primary schools and special schools, from September 1971 . . . Main points in favour: A substantial and continuing saving would be obtained without impairing the education service. It is out of date to give benefits in kind and to give them indiscriminately to rich and poor alike. Likely main points against: There will be opposition from those concerned with nutrition who will say that milk is necessary for the children's health.

They're so tedious, aren't they, those doctors always banging on about rickets and osteoporosis?

'I have told the Chief Secretary that in general I accept these proposals as reasonable contributions to achieving our aim of reduced public expenditure,' wrote Mrs Thatcher, the Education Secretary, in a memo of 23 September 1970, 'though the Paymaster General will be asking the Cabinet to consider the question of principle involved in the proposed libraries charge. I also wish to retain free milk for pupils of nursery and infant age.'

It was, as the figures she provided made clear, quite an ask: retaining free milk for children under seven meant that the government would save only £32.9 million over four years rather than the £52.7 million the Treasury's snatcher-in-chief had demanded. But Thatcher had found a way of balancing the books: 'I am prepared to forgo the more generous remission arrangements offered by the Chief Secretary and to increase the school meals charges to 12p in 1971.'

And she put up a fierce fight. When Macmillan pooh-poohed demands for long-term spending on school buildings which she submitted at the same time, she wrote back that 'as you yourself acknowledge I offered savings in excess of what you had asked for because I recognised our obligation, as a Government, to reduce public expenditure, but there is an equally binding obligation on us to provide more resources for the primary schools and I feel that I was entitled to expect from you an equal willingness to accept'.

As with so many other things, she got her way. So it was only eight- to eleven-year-olds who lost their free milk, as opposed to all primary school children (secondary-schoolers had had their rations removed under Labour back in 1968 without anyone making nearly such a fuss). Even so, the Education Secretary appears to have spotted the storm approaching, and attempted to spread the blame as widely as possible. 'Mrs Thatcher . . . is anxious for this to go as a joint memorandum by the Secretary of State for Wales and the Secretary of State for Scotland as well as herself,' runs a covering note on a draft for the legislation penned the following April. A 'note for lobby correspondents' written later that month throws the 'Financial Secretary to the Treasury' and 'Parliamentary Under Secretary, Department of Education and Science' into the mix as well. By that point backbenchers were already preparing motions denouncing the dairy raid as a 'malicious decision' that went against 'professional, medical and scholastic opinion', and Labour had come out against what Thatcher's shadow Ted Short called the 'new direction [the government] is giving to Britain, to save money on school milk in order to give tax remissions to wealthy people'.

So great was the outcry – the government even had to bring in extra legislation to stop Labour councils carrying on supplying milk out of their own funds – that it left the Iron Lady with a long-term lactose intolerance. Eight years later in Downing Street she scribbled an anxious message on a proposal by the Ministry of Agriculture to raise the price of a pint of milk by 1½p. 'I do not believe such a large increase is possible politically. 1½p is a great addition to the housewife's budget. 1p is all she will bear. Moreover there is the other political point – I abolished school milk in schools!'

A miner miscalculation – 1974

On 5 February 1974, Ted Heath called a powwow at Downing Street to update the Cabinet on the progress of his attempt to halt the second strike that miners had called over their pay in three years. He emphasised that 'the fact that the meeting had taken place, and still more the nature of their discussion, should be treated as entirely confidential and should not be discussed with Ministers outside the Cabinet'.

Frankly, things weren't going well. The Trades Union Congress had thrown a hissy fit when he proposed talking directly to the National Union of Mineworkers about their pay deal: 'the TUC had not liked this . . . They had added that if the Secretary of State for Employment asked to see the NUM executive he would be rebuffed.' The NUM had 'declined to come' to a meeting and brought forward the date of their strike instead. The Confederation of British Industry were 'frightened men' who had threatened to issue a 'damaging public statement' about bypassing the government entirely and talking to the TUC themselves.

There were, Heath told his colleagues, three possible options open to them. 'They could attempt to sit the strike out until the will of the NUM cracked. With average weather and no serious picketing and increased savings of electricity through the introduction of rota cuts, fuel stocks would last until the end of April on a 3-day week or until the end of May on a 2-day week.' Alternatively they could consider 'conceding the miners' claim in full. This would destroy the Government's credibility.'

Thankfully, Heath had had a brilliant idea. 'The third course was to seek a Dissolution of Parliament. It was arguable that success in a General Election would of itself change nothing but in practice it would create a new situation. The electorate as a whole would have expressed a view on the need for a firm and fair incomes policy and the unions would be dealing with a Government which had both a clear mandate and five years to run instead of a Government in their last year of office.'

His colleagues thought this was a brilliant idea. 'All the Ministers present, while recognising that the final decision was one which could only be taken by the Prime Minister personally in the light of the developing situation, indicated that they favoured the course of a General Election.'

Two days later, Heath called the election, which he fought on the slogan 'Who Governs Britain?' Turns out it wasn't him. The Conservatives lost the election to Harold Wilson, who settled the miners' dispute within 48 hours by offering them a 35 per cent pay rise, twice as much as the Tories had put on the table.

Little by little – 1974

In July 1974, Harold Wilson launched what he called his 'Little Things That Mean a Lot' exercise, inviting ministers to come up with 'points which, though they may be minor parts of overall Government policy, have great importance in people's minds and in their attitudes to social justice and fairness'. He was planning to call an election that autumn, and with no money in the kitty for the Big Things (he had given most of it to the miners to end the three-day week), he had little choice but to concentrate on cosmetic issues.

'It is important that we should show in the next few weeks that we are sensitive to these feelings and prepared to take initiatives to meet them, especially when doing so does not pre-empt any significant amounts of public expenditure,' his instructions continued. 'I attach a list of some of the points which I have asked to be considered.'

That list in full:

LITTLE THINGS THAT MEAN A LOT

- Metrication: an independent watchdog group to protect customers' interests
- Standard food packages and acceleration of their introduction
- The future of the pint
- The preservation of local breweries
- Empty office blocks
- Juggernauts
- Abolition of hare coursing
- May Day as a Bank Holiday
- Telling taxpayers where their money goes
- Protection for caravan dwellers
- Concessionary fares for the elderly
- Expansion of the Open University

Inflation was standing at 16 per cent. Companies were going bust left, right and centre, throwing yet more people into unemployment. The unions were demanding pay increases of up to 50 per cent for public sector workers, and the IRA had recently bombed the Houses of Parliament. But Harold Wilson stood ready to guarantee that the British people would continue to enjoy Watneys Red Barrel and Double Diamond by the pint and not the half-litre. Clearly the country was in safe hands.

It's now or never – 1978

Things were about as good as they had ever been for Prime Minister Jim Callaghan in the summer of 1978. All right, the pact with the Liberal Party that had kept him in power for the previous year was falling apart. But the economy finally appeared to be perking up, inflation was down, the humiliation of having to seek loans from the IMF to prop up the pound was fading into the past, and Labour was way ahead in the polls thanks to a recent round of tax cuts. All in all, the autumn was looking like a pretty good time to call an election.

He sounded out the Labour whips for their thoughts.

'The Whips have had a long, informal discussion on the options for the timing of a General Election,' Chief Whip Michael Cocks told him in a memo on 1 August. 'A clear majority favour deferring the election partly on the grounds I have mentioned, namely that the October dates have been, and are being, pushed by the Tories.'

But not everyone agreed. The Scots bruiser Jimmy Hamilton was '100 percent for October and thinks we could win, and fears there would be severe problem over wage agreements if the election is delayed'. His colleague Alf Bates proved even more of a Cassandra. 'Alf Bates tends to prefer October because of uncertainty on a number of fronts. Most of the economy should be in a reasonable shape in October, and the atmosphere should be reasonable . . . To go on would mean the need for agreement with the Unions. A winter of unrest would be damaging as would possible Parliamentary defeats even on small issues.'

Bates was bang on, even if Shakespeare's phrasing turned out to be rather more memorable. His reward was to lose his seat to the Tories as Mrs Thatcher swept into Downing Street the following May after what will forever be remembered as the Winter of Discontent.

CULTURAL DIFFERENCES

War is over . . . this is no time to party – 1919

The 'war to end all wars' was over – at least for the moment. The agreement of the 'cessation of operations by land and in the air' had been signed between Germany and the Allied forces at 5 a.m. on 11 November the previous year, although everyone agreed to keep going until 11 a.m. so they could have a nice neat palindromic moment to end things on, a gesture that was not particularly appreciated by US soldier Private Henry Gunther, shot dead at 10.58.

Curiously, the coalition government appeared to be in denial about the whole thing, given that the group that met at Downing Street on 18 June 1919 was still calling itself the War Cabinet. It was chaired by Lord Privy Seal Andrew Bonar Law in the absence of Prime Minister Lloyd George, who was off at the Paris Peace Conference ensuring the treaty terms imposed on the Germans were harsh enough to guarantee they would be up for doing it all again in a few years' time.

He had, however, sent a message back from France: 'The Prime Minister had expressed the view that as soon as peace was signed there would be a strong desire on the part of the nation to celebrate the event immediately.' Which was completely unacceptable: they should be 'waiting for the functions in August which were being organised by Lord Curzon's Committee'.

Some of his colleagues were sceptical. 'The Minister of Labour said that he did not think there would be demonstrations when peace was signed, provided the public were informed that the celebrations would be held on a specified date.' Why on earth would anyone want to make a fuss about something as minor as the official end of the wholesale slaughter, biting hardship and grief that had dominated their lives for the past four years?

Winston Churchill agreed: 'The secretary of state for War said that in his view, supposing peace was signed at the beginning of next week, it would cause no excitement. He was very keen that there should be organised celebrations in August, as it was the anniversary of the outbreak of hostilities, and favoured adhering to the policy advocated by the Peace Celebrations Committee.' Don't they sound like a group who really know how to have fun? Chairman Lord Curzon even admitted that 'personally he was against any peace celebrations' and was only going through with it because 'he felt that the country expected demonstrations, and meant to have them'.

To be fair, he and his colleagues came up with some pretty elaborate plans. When Peace Day finally arrived (a month early thanks to the Paris negotiations concluding sooner than expected), 15,000 troops marched in a Victory Parade past the wood-and-plaster cenotaph that architect Edwin Lutyens had designed for Whitehall: they liked it so much that it was replaced with a permanent stone version the following year. There was a river pageant, open-air concerts and theatre shows in the Royal Parks and a huge firework display when darkness fell. Other lavish celebrations took place around the country. At that very Cabinet meeting the Minister of Labour proposed an extra bank holiday be added so that everyone could have Tuesday off for the celebrations as well as Monday; he even proposed that 'employees in permanent Government establishments should be paid for these days', although 'he had heard that private employers did not propose to pay any wages for the Tuesday'. With all that to look forward to, there was surely no need for anyone to start partying willy-nilly, and the Cabinet agreed that 'the signature of peace should not be the signal for premature peace celebrations . . . to guard against unorganised demonstrations as soon as peace was signed, a statement should again be issued to the effect that peace celebrations would not take place until August next, as time was required for the necessary arrangements'.

There was, however, one bit of good news they

could give the public, albeit as the result of a shameless bit of spin. For weeks people had been grumbling about restrictions on beer production: they had already seen pub opening hours cut and been banned from buying rounds of drinks during the war, and now they had been told that the government intended to impose controls on the brewing process, which would mean weaker beer all round, and only a certain number of barrels produced each year. The latter statistic, however, was not quite what it seemed. 'Mr Bonar Law said he did not think it had been made clear in public announcements that, although the barrelage of beer was restricted to 26,000,000 standard barrels, that was in practice as much as the brewers could brew. He was convinced that a large part of the unrest in the country was due to the feeling that the Government did not allow sufficient beer to be brewed; and he thought that all restrictions on quantity should be removed.'

And so the Cabinet pledged that 'an announcement should be made forthwith to the effect that all restrictions on the quantity of beer to be brewed should be removed'. The fact that this didn't actually involve changing anything and drinkers would get precisely as many pints as before was not something they felt the public needed to be informed of. Better for them just to raise their glasses and rejoice! As long as they waited until they got the go-ahead from the appropriate committee, of course.

Superinjunctions. Secret courts. State regulation and censorship. Newspapers don't like them now, and they didn't like them in the mid-1920s, when parliamentarians were trying to steer the Proceedings (Regulation of Reports) Bill into law. It arose from an investigation by a select committee in 1923 into lurid coverage of the divorce courts, then entirely the preserve of the rich, who kept everyone else entertained by accusing their spouses of all sorts of appalling behaviour while the press gallery scribbled away. Sir Archibald Bodkin, the splendidly named Director of Public Prosecutions, loftily informed them that 'the existing law is inadequate to deal with reports which unnecessarily encourage familiarity with what ought to be avoided and in consequence take away half the horror of it'.

Around 200 MPs – some of whom may even not have been having sex with people other than their wives – then signed a petition to the Prime Minister demanding that newspapers covering either the civil or criminal courts be forbidden by law to 'print, circulate or publish, or cause or procure to be printed, circulated or published, in relation to any indecent matter or medical, surgical or physiological details being matter or details the publication of which would be calculated to injure public morals or otherwise be to the public mischief'. Furthermore, they insisted that in divorce cases, 'the names, etc. of the parties and witnesses' and 'the grounds on which the proceedings are brought and resisted' should all be kept under wraps.

Unsurprisingly, journalists objected to this – and not just the ones that were proud to consider the very point of their existence to be public mischief. Home Secretary William Joynson-Hicks informed his colleagues in March 1925 that 'speaking generally, the Bill is supported by social workers but opposed by the press and the trades connected therewith on the grounds that it is a slur on the great majority of British newspapers, that it is an unwise interference with the liberty of the press, that to suppress reports on cases dealing with white slave traffic, cocaine and other matters in connection with which sex questions arise will play into the hands of guilty persons by keeping their misdoings out of the press, etc. etc.'.

Precisely 80 years before Twitter was invented, the Press Association raised the objection that 'distorted accounts of the proceedings would certainly be disseminated by word of mouth' if newspapers were not allowed to report accurate ones. The Newspaper Proprietors' Association and the Newspaper Society, which represented provincial titles, both told the Home Secretary they 'regard the bill in its present form as unworkable'. By contrast, the *Daily Chronicle* and *Sunday News* took the high moral ground and announced themselves in favour of the bill. It will not surprise you to notice that those two titles have long since gone out of business.

Every other newspaper, however, was dead set against it, and Joynson-Hicks (a man so personally uxorious that he had added his wife's maiden name to his own when they married) foresaw their editors making 'great play with the contention that on many controversial questions, such, for example, as the question of birth control, there is divergence of opinion as to what publications are or are not "calculated to injure public morals"'. For his own part, he was up for a total ban: 'The main question on which a Cabinet decision is required is whether it is desirable entirely to prohibit reports of matrimonial proceedings,' he sighed to colleagues in March 1926. 'If the whole matter becomes a question of balancing the advantage of unrestricted publication to secure justice, as against the disadvantage of publication in lowering the standard of national character, the high standard of national character must be chosen.'

They plumped for a compromise. The printing of 'the names, addresses and occupations of the parties and witnesses' in divorce cases could continue, but nothing more than 'a concise statement' of what was said in court would be allowed, with any 'indecent matter' lopped out. When the bill passed into law in December 1926, a lot of people thought the *News of the World,* which thrived on what it called 'a never-ending stream of matrimonial troubles', might close down as a result.

But the man who would finally pull the plug on that paper in 2011 – after whipping it on to even more indefensible excesses and then claiming to be shocked by them (and, incidentally, ensuring that details of his own divorces never made it anywhere near the front pages) – would not be born for another five years.

The dawn of film censorship – 1928

In film history, 1928 is usually remembered for the debut of Mickey Mouse in Disney's *Steamboat Willie*. But he was not the big-screen irritant that was exercising Stanley Baldwin's government that February.

'The controversy which has arisen over the film *Dawn* which deals with the execution of Nurse Cavell will probably lead to a demand from some quarters for the setting up of an official censorship of films,' reveals a secret memo written by the Home Secretary, William Joynson-Hicks, an eminent Victorian who was already in his thirties when the first cinema in Britain opened in 1896.

What was the problem with *Dawn*, a biopic of Edith Cavell, who was shot at dawn during the First World War as punishment for helping British soldiers escape from occupied Belgium? George Bernard Shaw, whose protégée Sybil Thorndike starred as the tragic nurse, described it as a 'story on the highest plane, told by a young film poet who has been entirely faithful to his great theme', which doesn't exactly make it sound like *Cannibal Holocaust*. But the news that the film was being made had been enough to prompt protests from the German Embassy, and for Foreign Secretary Austen Chamberlain to write to its director Herbert Wilcox to say he felt 'repugnance to its production'. He subsequently announced to the Commons that it was an 'outrage on a noble woman's memory to turn for purposes of commercial profit so heroic a story'. Naturally, in the great tradition of calls for censorship, all this came before anyone had actually seen the film, which the British Film Institute says 'bent over backwards to portray the Germans in as sympathetic a light as possible'. Chamberlain refused to see it even when it was finished, prompting Cavell's colleague Ada Bodart, who had a cameo role in the film, to return her OBE in protest. But his objections were enough to pressure the British Board of Film Censors into refusing to give it either of the certifications it offered at the time, a 'U' for Universal, or an 'A' meaning it was more suitable for adults (but still 'clean and wholesome').

'In these circumstances,' Joynson-Hicks declared, 'I think it desirable that my colleagues should know what my present position is and should consider whether any change of policy is required. In this country the responsibility for controlling the character of films for public exhibition rests with the local licensing authorities who, in pursuance of the Cinematograph Act, 1909, license the premises where films are exhibited . . . In the early years many complaints were received as to the undesirable character of the films exhibited, and realising the need for protecting their own interests the trade decided in 1912 to set up a censorship of their own.' This was staffed by a small team who were, the Home Secretary assured his colleagues, 'all persons of education and experience and well suited to the work'.

They were not the only ones deciding if films could be shown, though. The local authorities could still overrule them, which, as Joynson-Hicks pointed out, 'meets the difficulty arising from varying standards. In some provincial towns public opinion is notoriously more sensitive than in London, and they object to films which are considered unobjectionable by the London County Council.' A 'good example' cited by Joynson-Hicks was 1927's *King of Kings,* which had been refused a certificate but was still allowed to be shown to the enlightened burghers of London and Middlesex, who got to witness the deeply unclean and non-wholesome behaviour of Mary Magdalene, who in Cecil B. De Mille's never-knowingly-under-blown vision was a 'beautiful courtesan [who] laughed alike at God and Man' and travelled around in a chariot drawn by zebras.

As it turned out, exactly the same thing was to happen with *Dawn* – the following April, London County Council voted to license it for the capital's cinemas, with other councils following their example, and Anglo-German relations singularly failed to collapse as a result. Wilcox, the director, later came back and had another go at the story with *Nurse Edith Cavell* starring Anna Neagle in 1939, when people were considerably less concerned about the whole 'offending the Germans' aspect.

Rather refreshingly, the Cabinet concluded that the best thing they could do was to leave things be. Joynson-Hicks outlined a vision of state-imposed censorship which was nightmarish, not least for himself. 'Some Minister – presumably the Home Secretary – would have to answer in the House of Commons for the decisions of the official body of censors, and he would be liable to meet constant criticism either as to undue leniency or as to excessive interference with freedom of expression . . . I am of the opinion that, unless it can be shown – as it has not yet been shown – that the present system is unsatisfactory, it is sound policy quieta non movere.'

And there, extraordinarily, it rested until the present day. The Board of Film Censors is now better known as the BBFC, with its final initial changed to stand for the less contentious 'Classification', and local authorities still retain the power to overrule its judgements – as many of them have done, most famously in the case of *Monty Python's Life of Brian* in 1979. The ban on showing that film in Aberystwyth was not rescinded until 30 years later, at the personal instigation of the mayor, Sue Jones-Davies – which meant, pleasingly, that her constituents were finally allowed to see what she looked like when she played the starring role of Judith.

Brought to book in the desert – 1942

On 26 October 1942, the Second Battle of El Alamein was at its height. The Eighth Army, under the command of the recently appointed Lieutenant General Montgomery, had forced their way through the minefields and deep into Axis territory, only for Rommel to return from sick leave in Germany and order his depleted Panzer divisions to counter-attack. The Secretary of State for War, Percy James Grigg, dispatched a briefing note to his Cabinet colleagues. It was headed 'TO BE KEPT UNDER LOCK AND KEY – It is requested that special care may be taken to ensure the secrecy of this document.' And it concerned . . . the lack of suitable reading material for those troops who were lucky enough not to have been blown to bits yet.

'The Prime Minister raised at the War Cabinet meeting held on 25th August the need for improving the supply of books and periodicals for the troops in the Middle East,' wrote Grigg, a senior civil servant who had been unprecedentedly promoted to the Cabinet just a few months previously, his last duty as permanent secretary being to break the news to his minister that he would be replacing him. 'I accordingly submit for the information of my colleagues the various plans I have in mind.'

One of the problems was that there was less reading matter all round: as Grigg pointed out, 'the book publishers are now restricted to 37 per cent of their pre-war consumption of paper, whilst periodicals and newspapers are only allowed about 20 per cent of such consumption'. He had, however, managed to wangle an extra 100 tons of paper from the Ministry of Supply 'on condition that it is solely used for the purpose of exporting books and magazines to overseas forces . . . This will greatly ease the position for the time being.' There would also be an increased grant to the Services' Libraries and Books Fund, which sent out thousands of books and magazines eastwards each week: these included 4,000 copies of *Blighty*, a *Punch*-esque humorous magazine which promised its military readers that it 'laughs itself to victory' and, post-war, would drop its cartoons, then military links, and finally title to evolve into top-shelf grumblemag *Parade* (which, frankly, most soldiers would probably have preferred in the first place). Around 500,000 Penguin books had also been shipped, proving that Allen Lane's revolutionary sixpenny paperbacks, launched just seven years previously, really were succeeding in their aim of reaching 'a vast reading public for intelligent books at a low price'.

Further measures included a 'newly formed Forces Book Club' which entitled each unit to a parcel of ten books per month for an annual subscription of £3, and a personal appeal by Churchill himself to the public for old books and magazines to send to the Middle East, so that those in uniform could experience that familiar dentist's-waiting-room feeling no matter how far they were from home.

As with so much else, however, the answer seemed to be to look to America for help. The Ministry of War Transport had suggested that 'it would not be difficult to arrange direct shipment from the United States to the Middle East of periodicals and magazines', a proposal which Grigg recommended, although he fretted about the 'obvious disadvantage' that 'our troops abroad might find their reading matter very largely spiced with an American flavour'.

He had one further concern: the need to 'arrange the necessary sorting at the American end to ensure the exclusion of subversive, pornographic, or unreadably dull literature'.

Pressing the off button – 1952

In 2009, Gordon Brown declared that a fast internet connection was 'as indispensable as electricity, gas and water', possibly the most idiotic statement ever made by a prime minister. His predecessors certainly did not take the same view of that great technological innovation of their own time, television.

In November 1952, the Postmaster General informed the Cabinet that since new transmitters had ensured that a signal was available to over 80 per cent of Great Britain, 'there was now pressure to extend the service to Aberdeen, Isle of Wight and Plymouth. The cost of these extensions would probably reach a figure of £200,000 and it was open to question whether it was justifiable in present circumstances to devote so much of the country's economic resources to this purpose. If these extensions were approved, pressure would then develop for extensions to the Channel Islands, the Eastern Counties and other parts of the United Kingdom.' He added that this might be 'desirable as part of the coronation amenities'.

Absolutely not, declared the Chancellor. 'This was not a time at which we should make any avoidable diversion of economic resources to non-productive projects. He considered that there should be a standstill in the provision of further television services until the country was in a position to afford such luxuries.'

Apart from anything else, if you gave people access to television, they'd only be wanting to watch it. 'One of the main objections to the extension of the service was the increased demand for television sets which would inevitably result.'

By Royal Disappointment – 1954

The Royal Film Performance is held once a year to raise money for the Cinema and Television Benevolent Fund, which looks after screen-trade workers who have fallen on hard times. The Queen, or one of her close relatives, turns up at Leicester Square, waves a bit, and then tucks into the complimentary popcorn whilst enjoying the best the cinema has to offer that year. Afterwards she gets presented to the cast and director, and tells everyone how much she enjoyed the film.

That at least is the theory. But it is not what happened in 1954.

'The Prime Minister asked me to look into this when he returned from his Audience with the Queen,' David Pitblado, principal private secretary at Number 10, confided to Sir Frank Lee, the permanent secretary at the Board of Trade, on 19 November. 'The Queen had told him what a bad film it was and he, on his own initiative, wanted to see what could be done about it for the future. Could you please get somebody to look at this and advise me upon it? It is obviously a rather delicate matter.'

The annual showings had started about as well as they possibly could in 1946, with the Powell and Pressberger classic *A Matter of Life and Death*. But they swiftly declined through a series of sentimental historical melodramas like *The Mudlark* and Walt Disney's *Rob Roy, The Highland Rogue,* and a musical, *Because You're Mine*, most notable for the fact that star Mario Lanza's weight fluctuated massively during production and he occasionally inflates to the size of a barrage balloon in between scenes.

But even this was preferable to 1954's offering, *Beau Brummel*, an anachronistic romp which rejigged history so that Elizabeth Taylor could play a heterosexual love interest to Stewart Granger's Regency dandy, and allowed for a deathbed reconciliation with the Queen's own great-great-great-great-uncle the Prince Regent (Peter Ustinov) despite his actually predeceasing Brummel by a decade. 'There is no doubt at all that the quality of the films shown to HM on the last four occasions (to mention only those which I have had the misfortune to attend) has ranged from the mediocre down to the vulgar and distressing,' Lee wrote back to Number 10. 'The whole evening is a long garish ordeal. The film is chosen early in the year by a committee . . . What has been done on this occasion is to tell the Chairman, a Mr Bromhead, that a bad choice had been made and that the Queen could not be expected to continue going to these performances unless better films were chosen.'

A few days later, Lee sent in a progress report that was entertainingly personal. 'Mr Bromhead came to see me yesterday. He is a quiet, unimpressive little man, soft-spoken, apparently lacking in personality, anxious (I should say) to please everybody.' The unfortunate Mr Bromhead's first name was Reginald. Let's cast Charles Hawtrey to play him. For Lee I think we could do worse than James Robertson Justice.

'I said that I had been asked to see him because of the great uneasiness caused by the quality of the film selected this year . . . This was not, of course, a matter in respect of which the Government would wish to intervene directly or to accept any responsibility. And there could be no question of any prior inspection of films by anyone connected with the Palace . . . A real attempt should be made to see that the evening was no longer an ordeal for HM but rather an agreeable occasion.

'Mr Bromhead said sadly that he himself had voted against the selection of *Beau Brummel,* which had been chosen by one vote, and he had insisted on certain changes being made before it was shown . . . He felt that the only possible course would be to change the whole of the present procedure for selecting the films to be shown. He asked me, rather wistfully, what I would suggest.'

It was agreed – after several weeks of negotiation between Mr Bromhead and the other selectors, the hardly disinterested heads of various film distribution companies – that a new selection committee be appointed, with two film critics and 'a chairman unattached to the Industry'. The Benevolent Fund also agreed to do away with the lengthy stage show that preceded each performance, which Her

Majesty had apparently found 'exacting' – although they did insist on a clause making clear that this would be 'without prejudice to the Personal Appearances of Stars'. Lee kept Downing Street and Buckingham Palace apprised of every stage of the negotiations, peppering his reports with news of Bromhead, to whom he had evidently taken a violent dislike – he is always 'asking very nervously' or even 'wringing his hands (as well he might)'.

Finally, in February 1955, after Lord Radcliffe, a fully-paid-up member of the great and good, was appointed to head the selection committee, Buckingham Palace let Downing Street know that 'in the circumstances, Her Majesty will be advised to agree to attend a Performance this year'.

'I think that in view of this I can now retire gracefully from the scene (or, rather, from behind the scenes),' wrote Lee, 'and pray that the industry manages to find a good film.'

They did. The Queen and Prince Philip sat down that November alongside such stars as Kenneth More and Diana Dors to watch Alfred Hitchcock's *To Catch a Thief*. Back came the report from Buckingham Palace: 'Her Majesty had enjoyed the film.' It appears, however, that she judges these things by slightly different criteria from most critics. 'She had particularly welcomed the fact that, for her, the whole occasion had lasted for not more than about 2 hours 40 minutes.'

Winston Churchill got a treat on 17 February 1954: a package of comics he had requested Downing Street officials go out and buy for him. They included examples of the ongoing adventures of Captain Marvel, alter ego of 12-year-old Billy Batson, who transforms into 'the world's mightiest mortal' whenever he says the magic word 'Shazam'; the outlaw Jesse James – 'bringing six-gun justice to the West'; *Frankenstein* (or rather a Hollywood-ised version of his monster, re-animated after many decades frozen in Arctic ice to do battle with Egyptian mummies); cowboy series *Rod Cameron Western* and *Casey Ruggles Western*; the 'Incredible All True Crime Stories' series *Famous Yank* and the horror anthology *Black Magic*.

He didn't like them. In fact, he disliked them so much he gave them to his wife. A note pencilled in the margin of the covering letter reads: 'With Lady Churchill – now returned, 20.2.'

What did Churchill object to? Surely he can't have taken against Captain Marvel, who, like himself, had devoted much of his career to battling his nemesis Captain Nazi? Possibly not, but the spectre of Jack the Ripper who rose from beneath a surprisingly definitive gravestone 'intent on DEATH' on moonlit nights may have got his dander up. Alternatively, he may have objected to his *Black Magic* stablemates the 'Vampire at the Window', 'Man with a Tail' or 'Shambling

Half-World Heap', each of their adventures stamped with the promise 'Editors guarantee that this is one of the most ASTONISHING stories you've ever read.' For the Prime Minister was deeply concerned about the effect that 'American-style comics' were having on the nation's youth. And he wasn't the only one. Cabinet memos note that the Education Institute for Scotland, the Glasgow Corporation, the Church of England Council for Education and the Church Assembly had all demanded government action on the matter, and the National Union of Teachers had raised concerns as well.

'The publications usually known as "American type comic" embrace various categories whose principal common feature is the absence, usually but not always complete, of any comic element,' claimed a briefing note that Churchill had requested from the Home Office.

> They are really collections of stories in pictorial form with only a meagre letter press. They include stories of cowboys and Indians, gangsters and other criminals, 'supermen', Tarzan etc . . .
>
> Though very crudely produced and badly printed, some of these publications are harmless enough. This is true of many 'Western' stories (e.g. those which deal with the adventures of Roy Rogers) and some of the *Tarzan* publications which have come

to notice. But the vast majority have distinctly objectionable features. Many of them have a strong element of sadistic cruelty and an undue emphasis on violence. A number have an erotic streak and abound in representations of scantily dressed women. Some of the scenes portrayed are horrifying – macabre supernatural scenes with zombies and ghouls, the frenzy of drug addicts, the grimmer aspects of modern war, and scenes of torture and murder.

They sound BRILLIANT, don't they? But the Home Office didn't think so. 'It is difficult to estimate how far American type comics have any permanent social effects, but such influence as they may have is unlikely to be beneficial,' the anonymous briefer blithely announced. 'The emphasis on violence and cruelty is heavy and unwholesome. The prevailing sense of values is shoddy and distorted . . . It is difficult to prove conclusively that they are responsible for juvenile delinquency since the factors which lead a particular child into crime are usually so many and varied that it is rarely possible to say which is the decisive factor. But their potential power of evil is self-evident.'

Oh, as if that wasn't enough, there was the danger that their 'crude and alien idiom' might make children talk funny, too. Clearly, they should be banned.

And that is what the Cabinet decided to do in November that year. The problem was how to go about outlawing 'American-type comics' – most of them actually crude versions of decades-old strips reproduced on this side of the Atlantic from imported printing matrices – without curtailing the adventures of such wholesome figures as Dennis the Menace (then just three years old) and Desperate Dan (14). 'The well-known children's comics which have been published in this country for many years also contain scenes of violence' but were 'wholly different in character', the Cabinet heard. 'The difference is not, however, readily definable, and that is what makes the problem so difficult. If legislation were introduced with the object of prohibiting the sale of "horror comics" there is some danger that, however carefully it is drafted, it might be held to expose unobjectionable publications to the danger of prosecution.'

That was certainly a danger with the first draft of the bill, which was presented to the Attorney General, Reginald Manningham-Buller, in December. It proposed an outright ban on:

> Publications consisting wholly or mainly of pictorial representations of stories about real or imaginary events in which there are depicted
> a) the commission of crimes; or
> b) acts of violence or cruelty; or

c) the actions of supernatural or monstrous creatures . . . if any of the stories contained in it are depicted in such a way that it is unsuitable for reading by a child (under 14) or a young person (under 17), as being likely or calculated to have a frightening or corrupting effect on him.

As Manningham-Buller pointed out, that wording 'may be wide enough to cover a generously illustrated edition of the Ingoldsby Legends [a popular Victorian collection of ghost stories] or some of Grimm's Fairy Tales. A Bench might hold that they would have a frightening effect on a child or young person.'

Instead, he suggested that the existing obscenity laws might already be sufficient to deal with the problem. 'I am not aware of any judicial decision restricting the meaning of "obscene" to matters relating to sex . . . While the majority if not all of the prosecutions for obscene libel have been based on matter relating to sex or sexual perversion, one should not, I think, assume that matter which is not related to those subjects might not be held to be obscene. One has to prove that the matter alleged to be obscene has a tendency "to deprave and corrupt those whose minds are open to such immoral influences and into whose hands a publication of this sort might fall".'

But that was no good at all, as Home Secretary

Gwilym Lloyd George told the Cabinet on 6 December: 'There was a growing body of public opinion which favoured early Government action to restrict the circulation of this kind of literature.' In the words of the *Beyond the Fringe* sketch that lay just a few years in the future, 'we need a futile gesture at this stage'.

And that is exactly what they got, in the form of the Children and Young Persons (Harmful Publications) Bill, which was introduced to Parliament the following year. It did at least amend the fairy-tale-encompassing point c) from the draft version above, but only in favour of an even woollier wording: publishers would now be banned from depicting 'incidents of a repulsive or horrible nature'.

It proved to be almost completely useless. The only prosecutions ever to result did not take place until 1970, when L. Miller & Sons were fined £25 for distributing horror titles they had imported from New York. But it was not for want of trying. Police had been after the Hackney-based company ever since August 1955, when three comics were referred to the Director of Public Prosecutions for the first decision under the new law.

What were the subversive titles in question? *Whiz Comics*, which featured poor old Captain Marvel again, *Master Comics*, a compendium of superhero also-rans including Minute-Man (who must have sounded even less impressive to kids who read his second syllable as 'newt' rather than 'nit') and, most subversive of all, '*Batman* no.58'.

The DPP regretfully informed the Attorney General that he did not think a case would stick. 'Apart from anything else, the fact is that right always appears to triumph in the end!'

Skirting the issue – 1968

'When a girl raises her hemline, what message is she trying to put across?' That was the question that – according to a report in the *Guardian* at the peak of the silly season in August 1968 – a Dr K. Gibbins of the Department of Psychology at Newcastle University would be attempting to answer in a project called 'Some dimensions of fashion change'.

Prime Minister Harold Wilson was not happy. Not so much about the hemlines – he liked a bit of leg as much as the next man – but about the fact that Dr Gibbins' research was being funded by a £1,432 grant from the government's Social Science Research Council. 'You rang me earlier this week about a reference the Prime Minister had seen in a newspaper to the question of the SSRC sponsoring a research project on why males prefer females to be dressed in mini-skirts,' an official in the Department of Education wrote to Downing Street a few days later. 'I have made enquiries into this and I am attaching a short note which explains the actual project. You will see that the article was well wide of the mark.'

Was it? It is quite hard to tell from the attached scholarly description of Dr Gibbins' research: 'A study of the communications aspects of clothes and the effect on attitudes towards them of the similarity of the communication conveyed by them and the impression of the self which it is desired to communicate.' Someone – almost certainly the Prime Minister – has underlined this baffling blurb and written '!' next to it. This thesis of the thigh would, supposedly, 'be the first step towards the development of a predictive theory of fashion change', which would be of great help to the clothing business, but that didn't impress Wilson. 'If this is <u>so</u> valuable to these vast industries why do they not pay for it?' he scribbled on the memo, before having a gratuitous pop at the prof himself: 'Another point: how did this get to the press? His PR suggests he's a very odd + extrovert character.'

'It is normal practice for universities to publish lists of research grants awarded, and it was undoubtedly through this means that the press got hold of the story,' an Education Department official assured his bosses on 11 September. 'I might just add that Dr Gibbins is reported to be appalled by the outcome of his interview with the press, and strenuously denies that he made any mention of mini-skirts as the object of his research.' He was probably also regretting admitting to the

Guardian that he had come up with the whole idea because 'I was trying to find something to interest undergraduates who did not seem to be very interested in psychology.'

The hemline hoo-hah was not quickly forgotten. The following February – when even the most dedicated followers of fashion had probably put on thick woolly tights under their miniskirts – the PM was updated on plans to slash the budget of the SSRC, which his own government had established a mere three years previously (it was chaired by Labour peer Michael Young, father of Toby). 'Good,' he commented on the memo detailing the cuts. 'Some of the political things are scatty. Should we be subsidising economic history?'

As one of Oxford University's highest-evermarked graduates in philosophy, politics and economics and a former junior research fellow in the subject, Wilson was probably better qualified than most to make that judgement. But his civil servants still thought it best to translate it into officialese before transmitting it back to the Education Department: 'The Prime Minister has commented that some of the "political" projects being sponsored seem to be of very limited value.'

TV dinners – 1974

By March 1974, everyone was sick of the sight of politicians. Even the politicians.

'There were some signs that, from the point of view of making sure that the issues were put before the electorate, the last election campaign was longer than it need have been,' wrote Harold Wilson, who had been re-installed in Downing Street after not only a marathon run-up to polling day but a lengthy sit-in by Ted Heath as he attempted to force the Liberals to prop him up in a coalition before conceding defeat. Was there any chance of speeding things up in future?

He was advised that the minimum time required between the dissolution of Parliament and the poll itself was 17 days (only four fewer days than the last campaign had lasted). Number 10's principal private secretary, Robert Armstrong, was sceptical about any reduction: 'the expert advice is that the arrangements for postal voting make it impossible to shorten the period', he advised the Prime Minister. 'Yes that had not escaped me,' scribbled Wilson tetchily in the margin.

Instead Armstrong proposed that 'if there were a general desire for some curtailment during the period in which electioneering takes place on television, this could be discussed by the Committee which consists of representatives of the three main parties, the BBC and the IBA'. But Wilson, who was in a particularly Eeyore-ish mood, poured cold water all over the idea: 'And the TV mandarins will, as always, reject any proposal, even if agreed by the 3 parties.'

This seems a little unfair. Ten years earlier,

Wilson had discovered that *Steptoe and Son* was due to be broadcast just before polls closed on election night: he was worried that Labour voters would stop in to watch it instead of heading to the polling station. In an emergency conference around the BBC director general Hugh Carleton Greene's kitchen table, he managed to persuade him to postpone the programme until after the ballot boxes had been sealed.

But that cosy relationship had changed. Wilson was now very cross with the BBC. He was particularly exercised about an item in *The Times* diary which noted that Alastair Burnet, the editor of the *Economist*, had had breakfast with a group of senior Conservatives during the election campaign. This wasn't quite as exciting as it might have been – there was no suggestion that he had spent the night before with them – but *The Times* had gussied up the fact that he was also employed as the frontman for the Beeb's election night coverage into a minor scandal.

Never a man to do his own dirty work when others were willing to do it for him, Wilson arranged for Ben Whitaker, a Labour activist and former MP, to fire off a letter of complaint to the BBC chairman Michael Swann (Carleton Greene was long gone). Whitaker used his home address, but the correspondence was copied in full to Downing Street. Was it true, he demanded, that Burnet 'was regularly meeting to plan the Conservatives' election campaign, at the same time as taking the leading part in the BBC's coverage of the election?'

The reply from Swann is a master class in eloquent rudeness. 'I must confess that I do not make it my business to know where, or in what circumstances, contributors to our programmes eat breakfast when not working here,' he informed Whitaker. 'If I did propose to inquire into such matters, I should certainly not rely for my information on the gossip columns of newspapers – usually, as I believe on this occasion, inaccurate.' He pointed out that Burnet's breakfast meeting had been in his capacity as a print editor, in which role he was allowed to express any opinion he wanted to, and that 'his separation of these two roles has been so complete and so successful that his integrity and impartiality have to my knowledge never been questioned – unless, indeed, you were doing so by implication in your letter'.

Whitaker immediately reported back to Joe Haines, Wilson's wily spin doctor: 'I don't know whether you think this is worth pursuing: if so, perhaps one of our allies on the BBC's Council might raise it?' Haines quickly carried the news to his own master, describing Swann's letter to Wilson as 'very off hand, almost offensive'. Wilson scribbled his own outrage on the letter in green ink: 'very offensive'.

The gruesome twosome had another weapon to hand: Wilson was due to meet with Swann on 2 April, and they agreed that Burnet's breakfasts should be top of the agenda (ahead of such small matters as the setting up of an inquiry into broadcasting under Lord Annan that could affect the entire future of the BBC).

The Beeb boss gave as good as he got: the notes of the meeting record him refusing to back down and maintaining that 'the breakfast was one given by representatives of the Conservative Party for a number of editors', and Burnet was subsequently re-hired to front 1974's second election night when Wilson was forced back to the polls that October (his campaign, by the way, lasted 20 days).

Swann was considerably more forthcoming at a dinner party at which both he and Wilson were guests the following January. It was hosted by Lord Aldington, a recent recruit to the BBC's advisory council, and appears to have been a kind of bridge-building exercise, but if Swann thought his comments were off the record, he was very much mistaken: Armstrong attended as well and managed between mouthfuls to scribble down notes which were put on file as a 'Personal and Confidential Note for the Record'. The Prime Minister kicked off by doing his Clive James act: he told Swann 'it was his impression that news presentation was better on ITV than on BBC television. Sir Michael Swann said that he agreed with this view; the BBC was going to have to do something about it.' Wilson also complained that 'he had the impression that in some respects the BBC's expenditure was needlessly lavish: he instanced the very large number of tickets required by the BBC for the Labour Party Conference'. Swann offered an excitingly hi-tech counterargument: 'the BBC was now using computers to assist in the control of expenditure, and he produced print-outs which showed a consistently high degree of capacity utilisation in various departments of the BBC'. Sounds like a cracking party, doesn't it?

It got more entertaining, though. Swann told the PM that he 'thought that too many young producers approached every programme they did from the starting point of an attitude about the subject which could be summed up as "You are a shit." It was an attitude which he and others in the management of the BBC (he particularly mentioned Huw Weldon) deplored, and they would be using their influence as opportunity offered to try to counter it.' They may not have been that successful. Fourteen years later, a dashing young recruit to the BBC's *Newsnight* programme, Jeremy Paxman, announced that he took journalist Louis Heren's words as his maxim when interviewing politicians: 'Why is this lying bastard lying to me?'

There was at least some good news: 'Talking about "hippie" influences in the BBC, Sir Michael Swann said that, while he would not pretend that the BBC was completely clear of problems of this kind, it was a picnic compared with Edinburgh University.' Swann had stepped down as Edinburgh's vice chancellor the previous year: he almost certainly had a particular long-haired leftie in mind: the Fife firebrand who had managed to have himself elected as student rector on a platform of causing as much trouble for the university authorities as possible. Swann privately described him as a 'wretched' individual. His name was Gordon Brown, and neither Swann nor Wilson would have bet that night that he would eventually take over the latter's job as prime minister.

Not in front of the children – 1976

It was a letterhead guaranteed to make the recipient's heart sink. 'National Viewers' and Listeners' Association' ran the scrupulously punctuated logo. 'President: Mrs Mary Whitehouse'.

The self-appointed guardian of the nation's morals had news for education secretary Fred Mulley on 11 May 1976.

Dear Mr Mulley

On ATV (10.50 p.m.) last night, Dr Martin Cole was the subject of a television programme, 'Ladies Night'. It started with a sequence from the film 'Growing Up' which showed intercourse and masturbation which, you will remember, caused such controversy when it was first shown in 1971.

During the course of the programme, Miss Wendy Jones, the presenter, said that the film is 'no longer banned – it is shown to 13 year olds all over the country' . . . There are certain questions which call for an immediate answer. First, why is a man who exploits children in this illegal and sick fashion allowed to have any influence in schools at all? Second, which schools have used this film? Third, who made the decision to allow this film to be shown to 13 year olds? Fourth, do you, as Minister of Education, support the stand taken by Mrs Margaret Thatcher when she was Minister for Education? She said that, as Secretary of State, she had no direct powers but that she was 'very perturbed indeed at the possibility of this film being shown to school children'.

I am sure that parents everywhere would expect that an immediate Inquiry be set up into this deplorable situation and we trust that you will take the necessary action and report fully back to the public.

Yours sincerely
Mary Whitehouse

A few points here need elucidation. The sex education film *Growing Up* certainly did cause controversy when it was first shown, but that was not to schoolchildren: it was to a specially selected audience which included Mary Whitehouse herself. Dr Cole had invited her along because he was almost as much of a publicity-seeker as she was; she obligingly provided the journalists waiting outside the screening room with the opinion that his film 'makes children no more than animals'. The second audience to see it was the local education authority in Birmingham, which banned its use in schools. Their fellow LEAs declined to show it either, making Mrs Thatcher's perturbation session completely unnecessary: historian Dominic Sandbrook could find 'no record of it having been shown to schoolchildren anywhere by the end of the year'.

At that point there was no evidence of it having been shown to schoolchildren anywhere in 1976 either, whatever Dr Cole might tell TV researchers. Mulley's staff checked with their spies on the ground, the schools inspectorate, who assured him that they 'had never picked up any indication that schools were using the film'. For good measure, the minister pulled in the notes that the Health Education Council had made on the film when Mrs Thatcher asked them to watch it in April 1971: although they had recommended it should not be used in sex education classes, that was on the grounds that 'insufficient attention is paid to personal relationships and physiological and emotional aspects' and 'no mention is made of the venereal diseases' rather than the shagging and wanking, which they thought 'appeared stilted and contrived, and lacking in spontaneity'.

And so Mulley wrote back to Whitehouse – personally, after his officials assured him she would take it as an affront to her self-importance otherwise: 'Mrs Whitehouse has usually had a

Ministerial or occasionally a private secretary reply, and I think it would probably save trouble in the long run.' He assured her that 'I have no evidence that "Growing Up" is being shown in schools' and that while 'I have not seen the film myself, from the information I have about it I can see no reason why I should wish to differ from views previously expressed about its suitability for use in schools'.

Subject closed? Was it hell. Why on earth would Whitehouse believe the word of the Secretary of State for Education and Her Majesty's Inspectorate of Schools over a sexologist given to dishing out statements to journalists like 'I think teenagers should be promiscuous'? She wrote back to Mulley on 22 June: 'I would like to point out, with respect, that you have not replied to the point of my original letter which was to ask whether you will set up an Inquiry into whether Martin Cole's film is being shown in schools, and how widely . . . Do you not agree that if, as was stated so clearly in the ATV programme to which I referred, this film is now being "widely" shown to 13 year olds, this should be, at least, a matter of grave concern to your Ministry?'

And then came the money shot. An NVALA member, Mrs Pamela Halls, discovered that her daughter had indeed been shown a copy of *Growing Up* at school in Oxford that very month. All right, she was 16, not 13, but still. Perhaps feeling that Mulley and his Labour colleagues were far too close to the communists her organisation claimed were taking over the BBC, Halls addressed her complaint instead to his Conservative shadow, Norman St John-Stevas. She was, Stevas informed the education department on 30 June, planning to employ a favourite Whitehouse weapon: the half-baked legal challenge. Not for nothing did lawyer and regular courtroom rival Geoffrey Robertson christen her the 'Director of Private Prosecutions'.

Halls and other concerned parents (unspecified ones: NVALA were a bit cagey about showing their hand at this point) planned to take legal action which would force Mulley to ban *Growing Up* from being shown in schools on the grounds that local education authorities had a duty under the 1944 Education Act to 'contribute towards the spiritual, moral, mental and physical development of the community'. And to prove it, they attached what they called a 'counsel's opinion' from one E. R. Shackleton which demanded that the head of the school in question should be prosecuted for 'corrupting public morals' and concluded by describing the film as depicting things that 'have, from time to time, been done in dark corners, but thus to degrade a youth, publicly, before the whole country and in the name of Education is scandalous. On this ground alone the Secretary of State for Education should, out of respect for Education, ban the showing of the film.' Given the strength of his legal argument, it may not surprise you that the department discovered that his 'name does not appear on the list of practising barristers'. Needless to say, his name *did* appear on the NVALA membership list.

Mulley was quick to get the facts of the case. The film had been shown at Milham Ford School, a girls' secondary, to a group of sixth formers, not as sex education but as part of their general studies course, which included the topic of what children should be taught about sex. The idea, which came from 'a probationary science teacher of fairly firm views', was to 'let them decide whether it would be a good thing to show it to younger children, and encourage them to criticise it'. Each of the girls' parents had been contacted and asked for permission: three of them had refused, so their daughters had been excluded from the class. After that a fourth-form group (14–15-year-olds) had asked if they could see it too, and those whose parents supplied the written go-ahead, and who could be bothered to give up their lunchtime to do so, had been allowed to watch. Not a single parent had complained to the LEA.

'No information has reached my Department about any other showing, and I would be extremely reluctant to meet your request that I write round to all local education authorities to ask whether the film has been shown in any of their schools,' Mulley wrote to Whitehouse on 4 August. 'I think the knowledge that I was doing this would only serve to excite interest in a film which, from all I have heard about it, appears to have no educational value and not to be suitable for use in schools.'

It was too late. *The Times* reported the following morning that 'The National Viewers' and Listeners' Association is to take legal action against Mr Mulley, Secretary of State for Education and Science, because, the association contends, he will not use his powers to prevent the showing in schools of *Growing Up*, the controversial sex education film.' Mulley's letter can't even have reached its destination, but then Mary did have a habit of issuing her press releases at the same time as her demands: why waste time waiting for a reply?

Letters were rolling in to Milham Ford School too: there are stacks of them in the file, every one supportive of the headmistress's decision to show the film to her pupils. This did not impress Whitehouse, herself a teacher until she gave up in 1964 to concentrate full-time on fighting for 'a nation which is strong and clean'. She gave an interview to the National Union of Teachers' journal later that month in which she repeated Dr Cole's claim about those '13 year olds all over the country'. *The Teacher* noted that 'rather surprisingly, Mrs Whitehouse admits she has made no attempt to contact the makers of the television programme on Dr Cole to verify the information. And apart from Milham Ford, she cannot name a school where his film has been shown.'

NVALA seem to have eventually thought better of spending their members' cash on lawyers' fees in an attempt to stop something that wasn't happening anyway: certainly the case never made it to court. Maybe Whitehouse was deterred by the short shrift she got from Shirley Williams, who replaced Mulley at the education department in a reshuffle that autumn. 'We trust that you will be prepared to make it clear that any LEA would be in default of its duty to allow a showing of this film,' Whitehouse wrote to the new girl on 16 November. After getting a briefing note from a despairing official – 'Mrs Whitehouse apparently will not accept that the Secretary of State cannot prevent the showing of Dr Martin Cole's film in schools' – Williams wrote back firmly and finally: 'I share my predecessor's view that to give this affair additional publicity serves only to excite interest in a film which appears at present to be rejected or ignored by school authorities generally.'

Changing channels – 1978

ITV2. Home of *The Only Way is Essex*, *Jordan & Peter Laid Bare* and *Top Dog Model*. But it could all have looked very different. Twenty years before the digital channel that now bears that name was launched, Jim Callaghan's Labour government were carefully considering who the contract for a new fourth TV channel should be awarded to.

We'll pause here for a brief commercial break as younger readers try to get their heads round the idea that there were only three TV channels. Best not tell them there was nothing but pages from Ceefax on for most of the daytime: their heads might explode.

Welcome back! In May 1978, the PM received a package from a distressed Sir Denis Forman, chairman of Granada and of the united front that the 15 different ITV companies that then covered the different parts of the UK were presenting against the previous year's report of the Annan Committee on the Future of Broadcasting. Sir Denis was alarmed to hear that the idea of a public access channel, funded by a mixture of sponsorship, grants and advertising and specialising in programmes that were deliberately targeted outside the mainstream, appeared to be back on the table.

'We were dismayed to read recent reports in the press indicating that the proposal of the Annan Committee concerning an Open Broadcasting Authority was now being favourably considered by the Government,' Forman frothed. 'Last year we had a number of meetings with officials of the Home Office, during which it appeared to be firmly established that the proposal was misconceived and probably impracticable . . . We believe strongly that to set up a new Open Broadcasting Authority would be a disastrously retrograde step and one that could soon be seen to be seriously damaging to the best interests of British broadcasting.'

To demonstrate just how good an alternative

they could offer, they sent Callaghan a draft schedule of their proposed fourth channel, ITV2, which the PM wrote back promising he had 'read with care'.

Its highlights included a nightly programme called *Indoors Outdoors*, the pitch for which seems to have been put together by throwing bricks through the window of a reference library and seeing where they landed: 'A daily programme about the technology and practicabilities of daily life covering such subjects as growing vegetables, interior decorating, books, records, television programmes, Provençal cooking, further education in the home, keeping pigeons, how to choose and plant a rose.' It does at least sound more interesting than Friday night's consumer programme *Money-Go-Round*, which promised to get viewers hyped up for the weekend by 'covering in particular food prices and other variable commodities but also taking each week one special topic such as carpets'. The party really kicked off at 10 p.m., with a 'short straight lecture' from the likes of 'an A. J. P. Taylor or a Wynford Vaughan Thomas'.

There would be a soap, but a very upmarket one – '*Coronation Street* and *Crossroads* have proved the lasting power of the continuing narrative. ITV2 will offer the opportunity for serials and serialisations dealing in greater depth with different social milieus (by authors such as C. P. Snow, Anthony Powell).' Half past seven on Thursdays would see

300

Cabaret, 'a solo spot for those many highly talented artists who are supreme in their own field but not necessarily top box-office attractions. Such artists as Marcel Marceau, Julie Covington, Billy Connolly.' Just imagine the hilarity when Granny tried to turn up the volume when Marceau was doing his 'walking against the wind'! And forget *Top of the Pops*: Thursday nights would soon become better known for ITV2's *Mid-Week Music*. 'The selection will be catholic, for instance James Galway, the flautist; Stéphane Grappelli, the jazz violinist; The Amadeus String Quartet; The Beach Boys.'

Downing Street was having none of it. A team of Callaghan's advisers declared that this was 'a once-in-a-generation opportunity to bring about a major increase in the <u>accountability and diversity</u> of broadcasting in Britain', and that they were more interested in appealing to 'a wide cross-section of radical opinion' than 'the existing bloated institutions'. Bernard Donoughue, the head of the PM's policy unit, declared that 'we believe that to give the fourth TV channel to the IBA [the regulatory body which oversaw commercial TV and radio] would be wrong. This is Tory policy, strongly opposed by the Labour Party, and in practice it would lead to excessive influence by commercial forces on the output of a fourth channel.'

Unfortunately for them, the following year's election got in the way. The Tories routed Labour, and handed responsibility for the new channel to the IBA just as they had said they would. Which is why on 2 November 1982, Richard Whiteley was telling viewers that 'as the countdown to a new channel ends, a new *Countdown* begins' on Channel 4.

It was at least given a remit to 'appeal to tastes and interests not generally catered for'. But 31 years on, Britain's hordes of Provençal-vegetable-growing pigeon-fanciers are still waiting for the programme that will definitively solve their rose-choosing and interior decoration dilemmas.

Hurrah for women! (just not that one) – 1978

No one at Number 10 spotted the obvious problem when Jill Craigie, wife of Cabinet minister Michael Foot, first proposed an official commemoration of the fiftieth anniversary of full female suffrage in 1928. No one saw it coming when junior minister and all-round do-gooder Baroness Birk was put in charge of the project and proposed an exhibition in Parliament's Westminster Hall and a variety show at the London Palladium with an all-women cast to kick off the celebrations. No one made the connection at any of the meetings held to update Downing Street on the plans as the winter of 1978 turned to spring. Somehow, it never occurred to anyone on the PM's staff that it might be relevant to a celebration of women getting equal political rights that the leader of the opposition was a woman, and James Callaghan wasn't. Which meant that trying to exclude her from the commemorations – as the Labour leader dearly wished to do – was a bit of a no-no.

'With hindsight, the only thing one can say charitably is that we were all asleep when this proposition was first mooted: a celebration of women's suffrage can hardly exclude a political dimension or women and it is inescapable therefore that the leading woman politician of the day is going to get a fair amount of the limelight in any official celebrations,' wrote his apologetic principal private secretary Kenneth Stowe after the point became embarrassingly clear in a meeting with Lady Birk in May 1978. She had announced, to the Prime Minister's 'obvious unhappiness', that Mrs Thatcher had accepted an invitation to give a speech at the opening of the exhibition. 'The Prime Minister explained that he did not wish Mrs Thatcher to be too prominent,' the minutes of the meeting note.

Instead, he proposed a compromise that provided the best of both worlds (at least in a *Two Ronnies* sketch kind of way): get a bloke in tights and a wig to do the honours instead. 'The Prime Minister said that he thought it would be better for the Speaker [of the House of Commons] to open the exhibition and be the only speaker.'

Stowe was sceptical. 'It seems to me that in the light of the commitments given, any attempt to write Mrs Thatcher out of the proceedings will be taken much amiss and we shall have a juicy little story in the gossip columns. I think on balance the Government lose on points.'

A few days later, after extensive enquiries as to 'how Lady Birk came to believe that No. 10 had cleared the invitation to Mrs Thatcher to speak', as opposed to just stand there quietly looking decorative, Stowe suggested another alternative: they could counter the presence of the Tory leader by having Labour's speech delivered by their most senior woman, Shirley Williams. The PM spotted an obvious flaw in this plan from his point of view. 'I think we had better leave it as it is + I will open it,' he scribbled on the memo.

But if the exhibition was a lost cause, he was damned if he was going to let Thatcher muscle in on the 'Golden Gala', which would take place in the presence of royalty and feature such heroines of electoral reform as the Beverley Sisters, Su Pollard and Noele Gordon from *Crossroads*. 'Inquiries I have made suggest that the Royal Box at the Palladium may be of such a size that, by the time Princess Margaret and you and necessary suite were in, there might not be room for Mrs Thatcher,' notes a Downing Street memo. 'This would be ideal, but otherwise we might have to let her into the box, though not in the front with you. Shall we proceed on this basis?' Stowe has written some very firm instructions in the margin: 'PM says Mrs T on no account to get into Royal Box.'

And so the cream of the civil service set about

ensuring that the country's foremost female politician had to sit in the cheap seats. There were six chairs in the box: all they had to do was make sure there were bums on all of them. 'I think, with a mixture of sweet reasonableness and low cunning, we should be able to fix it,' Stowe assured Callaghan.

The Prime Minister and his wife – a woman! – took up two of them. Princess Margaret couldn't go anywhere without a lady-in-waiting, so that made four. Lady Birk was requested to invite Lord Grade, the cigar-chomping impresario and godfather of the *Muppets*, who had helped to organise the show, to join them along with his wife. Disastrously, they declined. At this point Birk, realising the seriousness of the situation, offered to provide emergency ballast herself: 'The Grades did not wish to be in the Royal Box, but Lady Birk (whose husband would be away) would be prepared to do so if need be,' notes a memo of 7 June.

But that was no good: it would still leave a spare seat that Mrs Thatcher was bound to bagsie. Clearly it was time to call in the big guns. 'I raised this morning the question of seating in the Royal Box with Princess Margaret's Comptroller and Equerry, Lord Napier and Ettrick,' runs a note dated 12 June, just three weeks before the show. 'Lord Napier said that he would expect four of the six seats to be taken by Princess Margaret and a Lady in Waiting and Lord and Lady Grade. He asked if I had anyone in mind for the other two seats and I suggested the Prime Minister and Mrs Callaghan. He said that seemed to him entirely appropriate.'

Faced with a royal order, Lord Grade had little choice but to 'express himself entirely content with this suggestion'. Which meant that Mrs Thatcher could be sent a regretful note saying she would have to muck in in the stalls with everyone else. She was at least invited to meet Princess Margaret in the interval (just after Patti Boulaye had done her bit). But even then she wasn't allowed into the inner sanctum. 'Mr and Mrs Thatcher and the Speaker should be presented to Princess Margaret in the ante room to the Royal Box,' run the strict instructions.

Doing it for the kids – 1982

Dangermouse. Tiswas. Rentaghost. He-Man. Record Breakers. Kenneth Williams doing *Willo the Wisp. Jigsaw*, complete with the unutterably terrifying Noseybonk. *Blue Peter*'s second-best-ever presenting trio of Simon Groom, Peter Duncan and Sarah Greene. And Tucker Jenkins's final year at *Grange Hill*. 1982 was surely, by anyone's measure (and particularly for those of us who were seven at the time) a golden age for children's television. Wasn't it?

Not according to the Downing Street Policy Unit, who identified the 'trivialising, mind-numbing

effect of so much television, particularly children's television' as one of the many aspects of
British life that needed immediate action if Mrs
Thatcher's quest to 'renew the values of society'
was to succeed. 'Programmes for children are
often lifeless, moral-less, mindless and themeless,'
complained its head, Ferdinand Mount, in May
that year. 'They reduce life to a meaningless buzz
of chatter. No stories, no drama, no food for
thought, no suspense – and not much laughter
either.' Mrs Thatcher – whose own children were
in their late twenties and at the getting-lost-in-
the-desert phase by this point – appears to have
wholeheartedly agreed, judging by the number
of words she has underlined in his report. 'I am
very pleased with these ideas,' she has scribbled
on the front page.

What solution did Mount offer? 'We should
not be frightened to suggest that unless the
broadcasting authorities offer our children more
nourishing stuff in the future we should consider
setting up a separate, adequately funded Children's
Broadcasting Corporation which would do the job
for them on all channels, much as ITN does now for
the news for all the independent companies. Such
a CBC would not be a Government stooge, nor
would it be grimly and unremittingly "educational" . . . we should emphasise throughout that
we wish to make children's broadcasting more
enjoyable, not less.' Given that it would be set up
specifically to help restore 'respect for law and

order; respect for property and respect for teachers and parents', it doesn't exactly sound like a bundle of fun.

Still, Mrs Thatcher thought it sounded great. 'We discussed in detail how to occupy young people during the summer holidays [and] children's broadcasting,' reads the account of a meeting she held with Mount on 11 June. 'It was agreed that an ad hoc meeting of Ministers should be set up, to include Sir Keith Joseph, Messrs Whitelaw, Tebbit, Heseltine, Fowler and Macfarlane.' Just in case this stellar line-up didn't have quite enough youth appeal, Mount suggested further names: 'Should we include Geoffrey Howe who takes a keen interest in this area of policy? . . . Cecil Parkinson would like to attend the Renewal of Values meeting on 20th July . . . Can we send him the paper?'

Cabinet Secretary Robert Armstrong was slightly less keen. 'My fear is that, if the note goes straight to Ministers, they will all come to a meeting equipped with Departmental briefs full of cold water and faint praise,' he warned. And the CBC, along with Mount's idea for a 'British General' exam testing children on their knowledge of 'our country, its traditions of civility and its historical evolution', does seem to have fallen off the 'Agenda for the Mid-80s' which was subsequently developed by what Mrs Thatcher decided should be called the Family Policy Group. We will never know what might have become of this unholy coupling of Keith Joseph and Gordon the Gopher. Although it might well have involved rebranding the adventures of Timothy Claypole and his supernatural pals as *Righttobuyaghost.*

HONOURED GUESTS

Permission to lunch – 1956

It's always the way. You meet someone on your summer holidays, invite them to come and stay if they ever find themselves in your neck of the woods, and then, when they take you up on your offer, start dreading their arrival.

That was certainly how Anthony Eden was feeling in the winter of 1956. At a Heads of Government Conference in Geneva the previous summer, perhaps overexcited to be attending after finally wrestling the prime ministership away from Winston Churchill, he had told the Soviet premier Nikolai Bulganin and the First Secretary of the Communist Party Nikita Khrushchev that they really ought to come to London some time. Instead of saying 'yes, that would be lovely' and changing the subject, they had, he informed the Cabinet on his return, 'at once expressed gratification and, immediately after their return to Moscow, had confirmed their willingness to visit this country in April'.

Now that time was approaching, and Eden was getting cold feet. The Cabinet Secretary's notes of a meeting on 16 February observe that he had consulted the White House about wriggling out of it, but the 'President agrees we can't w'draw invitation'.

So what the hell were they going to do with their guests while they were here? Selwyn Lloyd, the Foreign Secretary, pointed out that Khrushchev 'said the main object is to hold talks with leaders of UK Govt with a view to ending cold war', which should keep them busy for a while. The Cabinet had already agreed that 'an association football match would be a suitable sporting event for the Soviet leaders to attend', but there remained one very thorny issue: how much time they would get to spend with the Queen.

'Normal practice is for visiting PMs to be given lunch if they go to Windsor,' Eden pointed out to the Cabinet. Churchill had already expressed his disapproval of Her Majesty having to put up with communist table manners for a full three courses: 'WSC is against this.' Lloyd declared that 'My instinct is against it, too.'

The Cabinet Secretary drily noted the discussion's conclusion: 'General view of Cabinet: Queen shd ask them to stay to tea, visit being put forward to afternoon: if Queen is not snarled up with Boy Scouts.'

Cutting a rug – 1961

In December 1960, the King of Morocco sent a gift to say thank you to the British government for looking after his son the Crown Prince during his visit to the UK that autumn: a lovely carpet.

Staff at Downing Street rolled it up and dispatched it to Chequers, the PM's official country home in Buckinghamshire. 'Prime Minister . . . I write to express my appreciation of your gift to the Trustees of the magnificent carpet,' wrote back the official charged with looking after the house. 'I need hardly say that your very generous gift will prove a valuable addition to Chequers and will be a source of great pleasure not only to the Official Occupant but also to his guests.' Which, frankly, seemed a bit over the top. It was only a carpet.

The following May, the President of Tunisia sent a gift to say thank you to the British government for having him on an official visit that month: a lovely carpet.

'My dear President,' wrote Harold Macmillan politely. 'I have now seen the magnificent carpet which you have so kindly sent. This is indeed a generous present, and I propose to use it at Chequers, which is the official country residence of British Prime Ministers. In this way, it will be kept as a permanent memento of your visit.'

Would it heck. A Downing Street memo from his Private Secretary for Overseas Affairs, Philip de Zulueta, informed the Prime Minister that 'Lady Dorothy agrees that Chequers might have the carpet.' Beneath it, in his spidery handwriting, Macmillan has overruled both wife and officials. 'I thought, to start with, it might go to my bedroom in Admiralty House' (Downing Street was being refurbished at the time).

His wish was their command. Beneath it is noted: 'Now in PM's bedroom.'

First Lady – 1970

To be fair to the Foreign Office, Imelda Marcos and her husband Ferdinand had yet to declare martial law, abolish parliament, jail their political opponents and loot their country's coffers to pay for her shoe collection – that would all come later. But they were fully aware when they made arrangements for the First Lady of the Philippines to visit the UK in 1970 of quite how bonkers her behaviour could be.

It didn't deter them from crawling all over her. 'It would be well worth taking trouble to try and make this visit a real success,' wrote Donald Gordon of the South East Asian Department on 27 January. 'Mrs Marcos is an influential political figure in her own right in the Philippines quite apart from being the wife of the President, and she and her husband may in effect be running the country for a number of years. In material terms therefore this would be a most useful long-term investment.' The outgoing ambassador to Manila, Sir John Addis, even recommended roping the Queen in to the export drive: he 'hoped very much that The Queen would feel able to receive Mrs Marcos . . . I explained that we naturally tried to limit such recommendations to really worthwhile causes but that we would certainly regard this as falling in that category . . . We would certainly wish to receive and entertain her in appropriate style.'

It wasn't even an official visit. Imelda was coming to Britain to drop off her son at boarding school in Sussex, an English public school education for her son being as essential an accoutrement for the up-and-coming dictator's wife as the 888 handbags, 65 parasols and 15 mink coats she would gather before fleeing into exile in 1986. His name was Bong Bong, but boringly he decided to call himself Ferdinand Junior when he grew up and embarked on a political career of his own.

So, what sort of things might the Foreign Office lay on to keep Bong Bong's mum entertained while he was finding his way round the dormitories? Gordon proposed a packed itinerary to John Curle, who had replaced Addis as Our Man in Manila: 'a social welfare programme covering visits to homes for the handicapped, aged and deprived, and to orphanages: I understand that she is likely to be interested in this. Mrs Marcos might also like a conducted tour of the South Bank complex . . . Arts Council: briefing on national patronage of the arts. National Art Collections Fund and the National Trust . . . Visit to a Great House . . . Visit to the Victoria and Albert main galleries and the Percival David Foundation of Chinese Art. When you see Mrs Marcos, you might like to sound her out about some or all of these possibilities and see if she has any particular views.'

Curle might not have been in the Philippines very long, but he knew precisely how that sort of itinerary would go down. 'The sort of programme that a COI [Central Office of Information] sponsored visitor gets is not what is required,' he pointed out as tactfully as possible. 'The First Lady is highly egocentric and will in my opinion be interested less in what she sees than in what particular attentions are paid to her in the unique English setting . . . Functions which serve to show off her beauty in public will have added appeal . . . I think she would be much more interested in going to the ballet or opera as suggested . . . A Great House would be admirable, provided of course that Mrs Marcos was there as the guest of the suitably Great Owner and not just as a conducted visitor.'

At that point, just in case his bosses in London hadn't quite got the message, Curle became considerably less diplomatic. 'I should warn you that we have learned from a trustworthy source that on her official visit to Expo '70 [a World's Fair held in Japan] Mrs Marcos was as exigent, difficult, tactless and inconsiderate as it was possible to be. A private visit to England of the kind contemplated for September will of course offer less temptation to behave like a prima donna, but you may find that she may try to change at short notice whatever plans are made.'

Oh crikey. If that wasn't worrying enough, there was bad news from the Palace, on 10 June: 'The Queen will be at Balmoral at the end of August and does not like entertaining foreign VIPs there unless there are very special reasons. These do not seem to exist in the present case.'

This would not do, as Mrs Marcos's brother and right-hand man Benjamin Romualdez made clear when he came on a preparatory visit to London in early August. 'Romualdez has made very clear the importance attached in Philippine eyes to Mrs Marcos' visit, and the risk of misunderstandings and of consequent damage to Anglo-Philippine relations if she is not received by the Queen,' Gordon noted. 'Romualdez has said that Mrs Marcos will be received by the Pope, President Nixon and [UN Secretary General] U Thant during her tour. Mrs Marcos's stay in Rome is to be very brief, but the Pope is said to be coming from his summer residence at Castel Gandolfo in order to receive her. President Nixon is said to be breaking his holiday in California to fly back to Washington to give a dinner in her honour . . . There is an element of blackmail in this.'

A quick check with Washington established that Romualdez was trying the same trick with them, too: 'There are certain difficulties as Mrs Marcos wishes to be received officially by President Nixon followed by a communiqué but White House cannot agree.' But rather than call Marcos's bluff, Gordon advised giving in. 'I recommend that if the Queen, the Queen Mother or the Duke of Edinburgh are coming to London for any other period during the likely period of Mrs Marcos's visit (i.e. between 3–20 September) they should be asked to receive her.' When it turned out that Her Majesty would indeed be heading southwards – 'Her purpose is to see one of the Princes into school . . . This information is confidential to Palace staff at present and they must not know that we are aware of it' – in early September, Foreign Secretary Alec Douglas-Home bashed out a pleading letter which got the desired result. 'It is possible that The Queen might be able to receive Mrs Marcos on Friday, 11th September when she may be in London on a private visit,' reads a grudging letter on Balmoral notepaper.

Signs of panic were beginning to creep in in London. 'Mrs Marcos, her son, ADC and maid will be official guests and their bills for accommodation and meals at Claridges paid,' a telegram nervously pointed out on 1 September (a suite had somehow been secured at the hotel despite their being fully booked). 'We cannot however pay for any other members of her entourage or "hangers-on", nor for any entertainment she may give . . . You should explain that audience with the Queen is a formal occasion with minister in attendance and not appropriate for Bong Bong. Photographers of course will not be allowed in the palace.'

317

They were right to be worried. 'Romualdez, for all his faults, has the virtue of being completely unashamed and explained the background to Mrs Marcos's visit without any inhibitions about my presence,' wrote embassy official John Goulden from Manila. 'The most important point which he wished to get over to all of us is that his sister is completely uncontrollable. After the restraints of Manila she tends to behave impulsively and thoughtlessly when abroad, showing neither consideration, nor social discipline, nor even an elementary awareness of public relations. Romualdez advised not to attempt to restrain or caution Mrs Marcos since this would aggravate her mood. She must be indulged in all her whims and the host government made to co-operate with her . . . He even suggested that we might insert into the press statement a sentence implying that the initiative for the Audience at Buckingham Palace had come from the Queen.' Happily aware that he would be the best part of 7,000 miles from the ensuing explosions, Goulden advised that his London colleagues should 'refuse to put up with any more nonsense from the Marcos's' [sic].

But there was plenty of nonsense still to come. The eve of the visit brought news that 'the entourage, still stoutly limited to a maid in all official announcements, has expanded rapidly in the last few days. At the last count there were eleven "extras".' The press in the Philippines had also been informed that Imelda and Bong Bong would be flying to the UK in economy class. That wasn't true either.

The third of September also brought another worrying update, this time about her meeting with the Queen. 'Mrs Marcos has renewed request that son should be received and souvenir photograph allowed. We have regretted that this is not possible . . . It would be prudent to make plans against possible contingency that she might nevertheless arrive at Palace with son and photographers.'

The solution to this last problem arrived from a completely unexpected direction, as a rather shocked note by a Miss Makgill in the Foreign Office's Protocol Department dated 7 September makes clear. 'I am most terribly sorry about the change of arrangements, allowing Bong Bong to come to the Palace . . . I felt I must ring Balmoral and ask the Private Secretary to ask the Queen herself whether she would like Bong Bong to come to the audience and to our intense astonishment Her Majesty agreed to this request. This has never been done before, and I cannot understand why it has been allowed in this case.' Maybe the Queen was feeling guilty about packing 10-year-old Prince Andrew off to his own boarding school? She still refused to budge on the photographers, though. They turned up, as predicted, but had to wait outside the Palace.

Which meant that the only witnesses to what

happened inside were the Philippine Ambassador to the UK (who had candidly admitted to being 'full of apprehension') and Gordon himself, who provided the following diplomatic description. 'A difficult moment almost arose when Mrs Marcos was informed that she would be expected to curtsey to the Queen. Fortunately, a tactful explanation served to calm the situation . . . the Philippine Ambassador backed me and we explained that our own Royal Family curtsey to the Queen and Foreign Royalties, and this seemed to make it all right for her.'

Much to his relief, Mrs Marcos 'appeared to go out of her way to be agreeable' during her time in London. 'I think it is quite safe to say that the visit was a considerable success,' he wrote to Curle after she had finally headed home on 17 September. 'Our fears that Mrs Marcos might be a rather difficult visitor proved unjustified.'

But she never quite forgot her position relative to Her Majesty. In May 2010, long after Imelda and her husband had been deposed and fled the country, she had faced several trials for corruption and made her return to the Philippines as a widow to resume her political career alongside the artist formerly known as Bong Bong, she gave an interview to the BBC. 'You know, not even your British Queen is called just Elizabeth – she's Elizabeth the Second,' she told correspondent Kate McGeown. 'There's only one Imelda.'

'I wish they'd leave me alone,' sighed aged folk-devil Rupert Murdoch when questioned by a parliamentary committee in 2011 about his personal contacts with prime ministers over the decades. Like a lot of what has appeared in his tabloids or on his TV channels in that time, it wasn't exactly the truth.

'Dear Prime Minister – Thanks so much for making the time to see me this evening. I am very grateful,' wrote the media mogul to Harold Wilson on 14 January 1976. It was five years before Murdoch's secret lunch with Margaret Thatcher about taking over *The Times*, the earliest prime ministerial contact about which he was interrogated at the Leveson Inquiry. He had sought an audience with Wilson to discuss the wage restrictions his government had introduced to try to curb inflation. Combined with the overtime rules of the print unions Murdoch had yet to jettison from his businesses, they threatened his ability to produce even more copies of the super soaraway *Sun*, whose readership was 'on a strongly-rising trend'. And he wanted to make it absolutely clear to the Prime Minister that this Would Not Do.

> I am sure you agree that it seems enormously more sensible, and much more in keeping with the spirit of the Government's policy, to get our modern plant working,

enabling us to get the extra copies without overtime.

Your good offices in this matter will be greatly appreciated.

'Will', you note, not 'would'. They weren't, though. 'I was anxious to dictate a short note on my meeting with him to avoid any possible misunderstanding,' Wilson put on the record two days later. 'He asked to see me at rather short notice to ask my advice and help . . . I pointed out that I did not deal with these matters and it was a question for the Department of Employment (to whom he had referred – I think implying that they had turned it down or were likely to do so). One point he tried gently to suggest was that the Secretary of State was not well known as a close friend of the newspaper industry.' If that was so, the newspaper industry more than got its own back on Michael Foot (for it was he) when he became Labour leader a few years later. The *Sun* constantly ridiculed him, and instructed its photographers 'No pictures of Foot unless falling over, shot or talking to Militants.'

For now, however, it was all in Foot's hands. 'I said I could not possibly under our arrangements, and certainly would not, get involved in decisions about the consonance of particular wage arrangements with the requirements of the White Paper approved by Parliament,' continued Wilson, who was definitely more of a broadsheet than a tabloid writer. He did, though, forward Murdoch's letter on to those who would be making the decision: 'This should go to D of Emp, Tsy + all others concerned with adjudicating.'

They weren't very impressed by it either. 'By the time your letter reached me, the News Group's general manager had already called at this department,' wrote one of Foot's senior officials on 23 January. 'He was told that, on the facts so far presented, implementation of the new agreement providing additional productivity payments to *Sun* employees would be incompatible with the current incomes policy. I understand that similar advice has been given in many other cases of this general nature. The company are seeking further discussions and these are being arranged.'

In the light of this, Wilson kept up his admirable arm's-length relationship with Murdoch by, er, letting him buy him his dinner less than three weeks later. 'I had lunch with the *Sun* – all their people (including Murdoch who had flown back overnight from the US to be there),' noted the star-struck PM on 9 February. 'The point was not raised, tho in several discussions there were ample opportunities.'

The details of their encounter appear, like so much else about the management of his newspapers, to have evaporated from Murdoch's memory in the intervening years. 'Only ever met PMs when asked, believe it or not,' he announced on Twitter in 2012. 'And I NEVER asked for anything.'

That nice Mr Mubarak – 1979

The Egyptian paper *Al Ahram* brought alarming news on the morning of 29 May 1979: the country's vice president Hosni Mubarak was planning 'to visit London during the next few days to meet Mrs Margaret Thatcher'. It was the first that Number 10 had heard about it.

Thankfully, before Mrs T had even started making up the spare beds and running the hoover round, the Foreign Office telegraphed with clarification: 'The Presidency say this story is an unauthorised leak . . . he would not, repeat not, be proposing a visit this week; President Sadat is currently on holiday and the Vice President is carrying out his engagements.' He did, however, plan to come to Britain at some point during the following month: might the PM find 45 minutes in her diary to have a chat to him?

'The Prime Minister's diary is, in fact, extremely full at the time of the Vice-President's visit,' came the rather sniffy reply from her private secretary when dates had been settled. 'The Prime Minister has, nevertheless, agreed to see Vice-President Mubarak on Thursday . . . at 1715 in her room at the House of Commons. I should be grateful if it could be clearly explained to the Egyptian Ambassador that the Prime Minister will be receiving Vice-President Mubarak at a very busy time, and in the midst of the debate on the budget, and that she consequently regrets that their conversation, to which she is looking forward, will not be able to last for more than 40 minutes at most.'

So, what did Mrs Thatcher's aides expect from the man who would, 32 years later, be ousted from the presidency in the Arab Spring? He was, she was briefed, 'President Sadat's most likely successor', but according to a 'personality report' prepared by the Foreign Office, he 'generally fails to impress Western visitors and seems to lack political flair. He is no intellectual, but is always friendly and cheerful. Speaks Russian and English. His two children speak excellent English, as does his wife who is half Welsh (her mother lives in Cardiff). An attractive and amusing family who obviously enjoy good living and who make good company.' In 2011 those two children, Gamal and Alaa, would go on trial alongside their father, charged with corruption and ordering the slaughter of protesters. Mubarak would be wheeled into a caged dock in the Cairo courtroom in a hospital bed. The Foreign Office may have begun to have some inkling of his true nature by the time of his next visit, in September 1980: the report had been updated to note that 'while he is in no way profound and still apt to express simplistic views, he has become an experienced and accomplished political operator. His affable exterior evidently conceals a degree of ruthlessness since it seems likely that he has conducted some successful political infighting to maintain his position.' But they still assured Mrs Thatcher that 'his reputation is free of any taint of corruption or malpractice and he is not thought to have made many enemies'.

They had one final warning for Mrs Thatcher: 'the Vice-President will be accompanied by Mr al-Baz, who has been the chief negotiator in their peace talks with the Israelis. I should warn you that Mr al-Baz has an unusually loud voice!'

Chair envy – 1979

One major issue stood in the way of good Anglo-French relations ahead of the visit of President Valéry Giscard d'Estaing to Downing Street in November 1979. Not the newly elected Margaret Thatcher's inexperience in foreign policy matters. Nor her determination to win a billion-pound rebate on the British contribution to the European Community budget. Not even the issue of the British nuclear deterrent, which they were scheduled to discuss at the summit. No. Giscard d'Estaing was worried about the seating arrangements.

'In all seriousness' – the underlining showed just how strongly Andy Wood, of the Number 10 press office, felt about the issue – 'the Elysée party pointed out that they would consider it essential for the President to have a chair equal in status – i.e. with arms – to the Prime Minister. Alternatively would the Prime Minister swap her chair for a "regular" (i.e. armless) model? Sorry about this – the French made the point quite seriously.'

Given that the summit was to be held in the Cabinet Room – where famously only one of the 23 chairs has arms, and that is the one halfway up the table where the PM sits – this was problematic. It was clearly a job for the third most important official in the country. 'The furniture of the room being all of a piece, it would frankly be rather difficult to introduce some quite different chair for the President,' wrote Lord Carrington, the Foreign Secretary, to his ambassador in Paris, requesting his help with this 'odd complaint'. 'We have never come across this problem before despite the many Heads of State and Heads of Government who have been to No. 10, and we find it difficult to believe that the French complaint does in fact reflect the wishes of the President himself . . . We and No. 10 would be grateful if you would have an informal word to try to get this little matter sorted out.'

No such luck. 'I took this up with Jacques Wahl [the President's secretary general] and to my surprise encountered considerable resistance,' telegraphed the ambassador the following day. 'His first reaction was to think that the obvious solution was to stand the Prime Minister's chair in a corner and have her seated on the same sort of chair as the President. He thought that the President would have a feeling of surprise if it were otherwise. I said that I thought there would be an even greater feeling of surprise on our side, and spread over a far wider number of people, if the President were to find it difficult to accept an arrangement which had been accepted over very many years by heads of state and government from all parts of the world who had visited Number 10.' Indeed, as the Foreign Office were able to point out, Giscard d'Estaing had sat in just such an inferior chair when he last visited Downing Street in 1976. Could his people's new-found objections by any chance have stemmed from the fact that then PM James Callaghan had not only arms on his chair but trousers on his legs? If the diplomats suspected sexism, they were too, well, diplomatic to say.

Fortunately the French state employs someone who is entirely devoted to such vital matters. Mr Wahl, the ambassador reported, 'felt bound to consult further with the head of protocol and would let us have further comment on Monday'. Exactly what he advised is, sadly, lost to history, and the only photos of the summit show Giscard d'Estaing and Mrs Thatcher standing very formally side by side (maybe they didn't sit down at all, to save embarrassment?). But if the President had seen any of the other paperwork covering his visit to Britain, he would have found plenty else to complain about. According to one memo contained within the same file, the catering for the visit of the head of the world's most notoriously gastronomic nation was undertaken by . . . United Biscuits.

The full horrifying scale of the sex abuse committed by Jimmy Savile emerged in a joint report by the Metropolitan Police and the NSPCC in January 2013. The child protection charity named him 'one of the most prolific sex offenders in its 129-year history'. Just days previously, the National Archives released files which revealed that the paedophile received his entrée to Downing Street courtesy of . . . the NSPCC. 'Mr Jimmy Savile OBE came into No. 10 today for a presentation ceremony in connection with the NSPCC,' reveals a confidential note dated 6 February 1980. 'He has asked the Prime Minister how he should pursue the question of tax deduction for charitable donations.'

Mrs Thatcher and her new pal would follow up this topic over a series of increasingly cosy meetings in the following years. But the full details of them remain untold. An entire 'letter from Jimmy Savile to Prime Minister (undated)' has been removed from the files, and replaced with a note reading 'closed for 40 years under FOI exemption', dated 11 October 2012, days after the first allegations against the presenter became public in an ITV documentary. So too has Number 10's account of a 'Telephone Message from Jimmy Savile dated 5th February 1980'. Intriguing excisions have been made from other records. 'PRIME MINISTER: With your encouragement,

_____ Jimmy Savile has made an excellent start with his campaign to raise money to re-build Stoke Mandeville,' runs the censored version of a memo dated 6 March, 1980. The singular 'has' means it can't be another name – it can only be a description of Savile himself, or of some contact he has had with the government. One of the Prime Minister's own phrases has been cut from a letter of 25 February: 'Dear Jimmy, When you came to see me on 6 February, _____ asked me how you could take up the question of the covenant system for donations to charity.'

The details which have been left in demonstrate that Savile was not lying when he boasted of his personal closeness to the Prime Minister. 'Jimmy Savile had a private word with the Prime Minister this morning to show her the architect's plans for Stoke Mandeville Hospital,' notes the Number 10 private secretary on 28 January 1981. 'I understand that the Prime Minister is to see Jimmy Savile again on Sunday,' runs a memo of 6 March. 'Can you kindly let me know if you made any promises to Jimmy Savile when he lunched with you yesterday,' one of Thatcher's staff asks following that particular social occasion. 'For instance: i) Did you offer him any money for Stoke Mandeville? ii) Did you tell him that you would appear on *Jim'll Fix It*?' 'Will tell you in detail' she scribbled next to the first question (the government would subsequently make a £500,000 contribution to the new spinal injuries unit at the hospital, where Savile was given his own office and flat on site). 'No' is her firm answer to the second, although she did eventually give in to his entreaties and appear on his BBC children's show in both 1983 and 1985.

Savile's thank-you note for the lunch at Chequers remains on file, too. It is on notepaper bearing a colour photograph of his own face.

> *Dear Prime Minister,*
> *I waited a week before writing to thank you for my lunch invitation because I had such a superb time I didn't want to be too effusive. My girl patients pretended to be madly jealous + wanted to know what you wore + what you ate. All the paralysed lads called me 'Sir James' all week.*
> *They all love you.*
> *Me too!!*
> *Jimmy Savile OBE xxx*

He signed his name with a smiley face in the looped curl of the 'J'.

Police estimate that Savile committed a minimum of 49 indecent assaults and rapes on 'his' patients in the various NHS institutions he insinuated his way into between 1962 and 1995.

ETERNAL OUTSIDERS

Breaking up is so very hard to do – 1924

On 24 March 1924, Prime Minister Ramsay MacDonald received a deputation in Downing Street. It was led by Lord Buckmaster, the former Lord Chancellor, who had succeeded the previous year in steering a private member's bill through the Lords which extended the grounds on which women could petition for divorce from their husbands. Thanks to 'very bitter and very strong' opposition from the bishops' benches, it did not go nearly as far as Buckmaster would have liked. 'You may know that as the law stands now a man who marries a woman and finds her pregnant on the night of marriage by another man is married to her for life, and can get no relief,' he informed the Prime Minister. 'A woman who marries a man and is wilfully injected with him by syphilis on the night of the marriage also can get no relief.'

Buckmaster desperately wanted the recommendations of a Royal Commission on the matrimonial laws more than a decade previously to be enacted:

women should be able to detach themselves from a man guilty of 'desertion, cruelty, drunkenness, insanity and perpetual imprisonment' (hopefully not all five at once). But the process of these eminently sensible recommendations into law had been derailed by an event that sundered more marriages than any law could, the First World War. Now, with the country's first Labour government in power (or at least in office: MacDonald had only made it into Number 10 two months previously when the Tories had fluffed their go at handling a hung parliament), Buckmaster hoped the time might finally have come to give Britain's abused wives a break.

He had no time for naysayers who claimed this was a minority interest issue. 'I think when people ask what the popular demand behind this Bill is, they are asking an unwise question,' he told MacDonald. 'You cannot expect to get big popular demonstrations by men who have been unhappily married. It is the one thing that men would desire to conceal.' Women's opinions don't seem to have come into it, despite the fact that some of them even had the vote by now. Instead, Buckmaster proffered another expert group: his fellow hereditary aristocrats in the House of Lords, who were, apparently, far from the crusty reactionaries you might expect, but 'a body of representative Englishmen who have unusual opportunities for knowing the conditions of life in very large areas of Society. I believe it would be impossible to find a more dispassionate and a more sensible-minded body of men.' Needless to say, they *were* all men: women would not be allowed to sit in the Upper House until 1958.

At this point, according to the 'confidential and not for publication' record of the meeting, Buckmaster conceded the floor to 'Mr Silas Hocking, who is well-known in the Non-Conformist world' (not as exciting as it sounds: he was a Methodist). He pointed out that the only option currently available to those of limited means was a 'judicial separation', which parted couples but left them married in the eyes of both church and state. Any subsequent relationship could only consist of living in sin; any children would be illegitimate. 'Judicial separation directly leads to immorality,' thundered Hocking.

Next up was May Seaton Tiedeman, the secretary of the Divorce Law Reform Union, a campaigning group formerly headed by Sherlock Holmes author Sir Arthur Conan Doyle. She offered a case study which she said was 'typical of thousands of the cases that come to us . . . A woman asked if she could get a divorce from her husband, and obtain the custody of her two children. She is 33, her husband has not co-habited with her since the birth of the second child, telling her that he has no further use for women, and boasting of his friendships with young men, but defying her to prove anything . . . Her health is breaking under this abominable cruelty . . . Her grief and horror were great when I informed her that not only could she not get a divorce, but that if she established the vice of her husband he might be committed to penal servitude for a period of years.'

Dr Ethel Behnam, who claimed to have 'worked intimately with the poor', then offered MacDonald an eminently sensible argument which his successor David Cameron could have done worse than quote in his own recent efforts to get gay marriage on the statute books. 'The opposition is really from ecclesiastical persons, and I do not think that ought to be taken into consideration. It is open to any religious denomination to make its own rules over and above those of the State to which its own adherents can conform, but it is not fair that any one denomination should bind heavy burdens upon other persons' consciences who do not agree with their religious faith.'

The Prime Minister was convinced, and he said so with a frankness unusual in a politician. 'My own personal view is that the situation at the present time is perfectly iniquitous and that people who for any reason oppose a change in the Divorce Law so as to make it common sense are really doing a most sinful thing' – here the transcription notes that his guests shouted 'hear hear' – 'but if I say that, and it appears in the papers tomorrow, you know what would be the result.'

At this point, despite having brought up the topic of press leaks himself, he went off into a little rant

335

that would give any modern-day spin doctor a heart attack. 'I am only expressing my personal view, if I can afford to have such a thing now . . . I am, as it were, a person at the moment who has had his leg broken at a football match; I am perfectly appalled at the dishonest use that is made of statements sincerely made – perfectly appalled by it. I have found it is impossible to say a word about anything but it is turned into some extra-ordinary pledge, if you can call it so, and both – all the Parties are just lying like cats watching for the twist of a mouse's whisker in order to pounce upon it; and until there is some more decency in Party life, I think you will find that some of us will say nothing at all, and we will take the consequences of it. But I am sick of the whole thing. I give you my personal feelings in the matter, and if I could do anything, I would do it.'

The problem was that he *couldn't* do anything. His was a real minority administration: Labour had just 191 seats to the Conservatives' 258. They were limping along with the help of Herbert Asquith's Liberals, but without any formal coalition agreement. And they had plenty of other business to try to force through Parliament, including a budget, a housing bill and education reforms. 'My difficulty is the <u>time</u>,' he told his guests. 'I really see no hope at all of bringing any legislation of this character this Session; at least there is an accumulation of things that must be settled, and we have not a majority; we cannot closure [sic]. Our control of the House of Commons is more moral than numerical . . . I quite honestly do not see the ghost of a chance of our being able to give time for a controversial Bill like this.'

Buckmaster sadly thanked MacDonald 'most heartily for the sincere but somewhat depressing statement you have made to us'. He might have been even more depressed had he known how long the wait was going to be. MacDonald was swept from power just seven months later. The reforms Buckmaster longed for did not arrive until three years after his own death, with the Matrimonial Causes Act of 1937. By that point MacDonald had long since undergone his own divorce – from the Labour Party.

And I did not speak out because . . . – 1938

On 10 November 1938, as Nazi supporters embarked on their second night of looting and destruction of Jewish businesses, homes and synagogues across Germany and Austria, R. M. Makins of the Foreign Office submitted a report on the situation to Downing Street.

'In view of press reports about anti-Semitic measures in Germany, rioting and burning, threat of wholesale expulsions, etc. the question arises whether HM Government can say or do anything which is likely to remedy the situation,' he wrote. The British chargé d'affaires in Berlin, Sir George Ogilvie-Forbes – who would go on to help a number of Jewish refugees escape from the country – was pessimistic. 'Treatment of German Jews is fiercely and jealously regarded as a purely internal matter by German authorities. Further, Herr Hitler is in an aggressive and anti-British mood and it will be difficult enough to protect British Jews' interests, which Sir G. Ogilvie-Forbes has in mind. Foreign intervention or public protest may in these circumstances only be expected to add fuel to the flames. Possible action seems, therefore, limited to a vigorous declaration that Jews who are British subjects and their property will be protected.'

And what of the thousands of Jews who had already been expelled from the Reich? 'No hope can be held out that other countries may be prepared to give refuge to the Jews who are being ill-treated in Germany,' advised Makins, who had that summer been one of the delegates at an international conference at Evian in France, at which nation after nation had lined up to offer sympathy to German refugees, but only one, the Dominican Republic, had actually offered to accommodate them. 'The measures taken by the German government against Jews and Jewish property have at the same time made Jewish immigrants from the economic point of view less acceptable . . . It is very doubtful whether an increase in the number of Jewish immigrants into the United Kingdom would be welcomed by the Home Office.'

'PM has seen' is the only recorded response to

Makins' memo. But that same evening Neville Chamberlain received another dispatch, which can have left him in no doubt of the extent of the horror that was unfolding. 'I telephoned to the Embassy at Berlin this evening at 7 p.m. to get the latest news of the anti-Jewish disorders,' wrote W. Strang of the Foreign Office.

> In Berlin there is little or no personal violence against Jews. What has happened is that every Jewish shop and establishment in Berlin has been looted and plundered in a systematic and orderly way by gangs of young men under the eyes of the police. The public are looking on and apparently rather enjoying the spectacle. It is rather like watching a side show at an exhibition, where you pay so much to break as much crockery as you like.
>
> What has happened is not the result of a spontaneous ebullition of public feeling, but is a deliberately organised operation . . . What the Embassy now expect is that new anti-Jewish measures will be introduced. There are rumours that extensive expulsions will take place, but the Embassy have no confirmation of this.

The most extraordinary account of what would become known as Kristallnacht, however, did not arrive at Downing Street until 21 November. It was a 'Most Secret' dispatch from someone identified only as 'Major Boyle of our intelligence staff'. He had spoken to General Ralph Wenninger, the air attaché at the German Embassy in London, about the reaction in the Nazi high command to the destruction. Hermann Göring, right-hand man to Hitler and supervisor of his 'Four Year Plan' to prioritise government spending on rearmament, was not at all happy about the violence, which had been instigated by his great rival, Joseph Goebbels. And it was specifically because of that broken glass – the *Kristall* – that gave the event its name.

'He said that Goering as soon as the Pogroms had taken place tendered his resignation to the Fuehrer who refused to accept it,' wrote Boyle. 'The reason which Wenninger gave me for this resignation was that the destruction of Jewish property brought an additional strain upon his Four Year Plan, as three million marks worth of glass had to be replaced by the purchase of Belgian glass, since Germany was only capable of making a quarter of the amount destroyed. In addition, the majority of the goods destroyed in Jewish shops was the property of non-Jews and were on sale or return. Compensation therefore had to be paid to German citizens by the State . . . Since Wenninger gave me this privately I must request that the above information, if it is of any interest, must be treated with the utmost care and that we should limit the circulation of this paper.'

Göring's solution was to pile insult on injury by

imposing a fine of a billion marks, not on those responsible for the violence, but on its victims. Meanwhile, Chamberlain had received a deputation from the Council for German Jewry in his office at the House of Commons, who pleaded with him to do something to help. Chaim Weizmann pointed out that 'there were at present in concentration camps in Germany 6,000 young men . . . the position was acute, confined as they were and diminishing in numbers daily at the hands of the execution squads'.

The woolliness of the Prime Minister's response showed little regard to the urgency of the situation.

As regards the question of mass settlement in some part of the Empire, the Prime Minister thought that the only possible territory might be British Guiana . . . The possibility of making a tract of land available in Guiana would be examined by the Government sympathetically, but the Council must recognise that, while the hinterland there was probably a good one for the purpose, its development would involve a large expenditure of capital and the time factor would operate, since it would be quite out of the question to evacuate people there without adequate preparations. The grant of a tract there might, however, be a possible contribution

341

on the part of His Majesty's Government and if made it might encourage other Governments to be more forthcoming than hitherto. . . In conclusion, Mr Chamberlain reminded the Council that, while the world had the strongest sympathy with the Jews in their unhappy plight, this was not purely a Jewish problem, but part of a larger question – the refugee problem.

Weizmann could hardly have guessed that just over a decade later, he would be elected as first president of Israel. But his group's predictions about what would come before that were horribly accurate. On 7 December, they warned Cabinet minister Lord Winterton that 'from information they had received and from comments in German papers the Council was convinced that the Jews remaining in Germany were in real peril, even of destruction, and that this peril was immediate'.

Blackening their names – 1951

'For many years permanent communities of coloured persons of Colonial origin have lived in various parts of the United Kingdom,' noted a ministerial committee headed by Home Secretary James Chuter Ede in February 1951. 'Most of them are either of West African or West Indian extraction, or Moslem people, mainly from Aden or Somaliland. In general, they look to this country as their home and have no intention of returning to their countries of origin. They are thought to number some 30,000, the larger groups being found in Merseyside, London, Cardiff and Tyneside.' They calculated that only 5,000 of these had arrived since the end of World War II: somehow that seems surprising now, but only because we have a tendency to think that immigration kicked off with the docking of the *Empire Windrush* in 1948 and forget such inconvenient facts as Britain getting its first black professional football player in the 1880s.

Although the report was explicitly aimed at addressing 'the problems presented by the immigration into this country of coloured people', nowhere does the report make clear exactly what those problems might be. The committee was forced to admit that 'unemployment and destitution among these coloured people of all types are not so widespread as to have any noticeable effect on our economy'. Nor had the newly established Welfare State, which ministers feared 'must inevitably act as a considerable attraction', made much difference as yet. 'As regards reliance on national assistance, a sample check during one week in August 1950 showed that 572 coloured Colonials had applied for such assistance.' That is just under 2 per cent, and a minuscule 0.2 per cent of the jobless total of 253,000.

The committee *did* have a problem, however, and it was that most of these people, having been born in British colonies or former colonies which were now part of the Commonwealth, were British citizens. Thanks to us having considered ourselves to have a divine right to go over there and take their countries, they now had a legal right to come over here and live in ours if they wanted to. Chuter Ede optimistically proposed that 'powers might be taken similar to those now applied to aliens' – which didn't mean shooting them down with lasers, but rather refusing each new arrival entry at the border 'unless the Immigration Officer were satisfied that he was a returning resident or genuine visitor, or was coming to take up employment authorised by the Ministry of Labour or for some other approved purpose such as study'. The drawback the ministers identified was that this would involve subjecting the 30–40,000 Irish people who came to Britain looking for work each year to the same rules, 'and it would be particularly unrewarding as there would be few, if any, Irish workers whom we should wish to exclude'. Exactly why the Irish were OK, but those from colonies further afield were a 'problem', Chuter Ede and his colleagues did not specify, but you just might be able to guess.

Four pages in, they just came out and admitted it. 'Any solution depending on an apparent or concealed colour test would be so invidious as to make it impossible of adoption. Nevertheless, the use of any powers taken to restrict the free entry of British subjects to this country would, as a general rule, be more or less confined to coloured persons . . . This might possibly give rise to resentment in India, Pakistan and Ceylon and' – wait for it – 'the more advanced Colonial territories.'

And so they decided that 'in view of the comparatively small scale of immigration into this country of coloured people from British Colonial territories . . . we consider that no such legislation should at present be introduced'. But the subject was far from settled. Chuter Ede and his Labour colleagues were swept out of office that October, and the Conservatives returned to the topic the following year, when Winston Churchill asked, apparently out of the blue, 'whether the Post Office were employing larger numbers of coloured workers? If so,' he declared, 'there was some risk that difficult social problems would be created.' In vain did the Postmaster General, Earl de la Warr, protest that 'between 500 and 600 coloured people from the Commonwealth and Empire are at present employed by the Department . . . Their employment has raised no serious difficulties.' Chancellor Rab Butler insisted to the Cabinet that this 'raised rather special problems which also appeared to merit examination'. The Home Secretary, Sir David Maxwell Fyfe, was instructed 'to examine the possibilities of preventing any further increase in the number of coloured people seeking employment in this country', while Butler made a 'concurrent examination of the possibility of restricting the number of coloured people obtaining admission to the Civil Service'.

Their reports back to the Cabinet in February 1954 give some further clues as to the sort of thing they were worried about. Maxwell Fyfe pointed out that 'of 62 persons convicted in the Metropolitan Police district in the twelve months ending 31st August, 1953, of living on women's immoral earnings 24 had been coloured men', which the mathematically gifted amongst you will spot means that the majority of them weren't. He was unable to find any evidence of further nefariousness, but still insisted that 'the fact must be faced that at any time the occurrence of some shocking crime involving a coloured person might give rise to strong public feeling on the matter'.

While 'he recognised that a case could be made for measures to exclude or remove from this country the riffraff amongst British subjects from overseas . . . It had to be recognised that any action which the Government might take could easily be misrepresented as introducing a "colour bar".' Which is hardly surprising, given that that is obviously just what they were aching to do. He was forced to conclude that 'The figures do not seem to me to justify any departure from the view which has hitherto been taken that so far no such evil consequences of this immigration have appeared as would amount to a case for legislation.' Churchill conceded the point, although not without a dire prediction: 'the rapid improvement of communications was likely to lead to a continuing increase in the number of coloured people coming to this country, and their presence here would sooner or later come to be resented by large proportions of the British people'.

Let's not talk about the queers – 1954

Home Secretary David Maxwell Fyfe brought an awkward problem to the Cabinet in February 1954: the proposal for a Royal Commission to look into both 'the prevalence of prostitution' and 'the unexplained increase in homosexual offences [which] constituted a serious social problem which the Government could not ignore'.

To press his case, Maxwell Fyfe distributed a secret report amongst his colleagues. It revealed that the number of 'unnatural offences of the gravest kind (sodomy and bestiality)', along with other offences like gross indecency, had risen 'between four-fold and five-fold over pre-war figures'. Actually, the surge in prosecutions for gay sex was all too explicable: the Met had got into the habit of sending their prettiest policemen into public toilets to flirt with strangers and then slap handcuffs on those who responded. The freshly knighted actor Sir John Gielgud had been caught that way the previous year and charged with 'importuning for immoral purposes', a case which, along with the high-profile jailing of Lord Montagu of Beaulieu and two friends after a pair of RAF men testified against them in return for their own immunity from prosecution, had helped force the government into reviewing the situation. Maxwell Fyfe was quick to make clear to his colleagues that 'although he himself doubted the expediency of amending the existing law on this subject, it must be recognised that many responsible people believed that homosexual practices between adult males should not constitute a criminal offence'.

The Home Secretary's preferred course of action was to leave the law as it was – he had told the Commons the previous December that 'homosexuals are a danger to others and so long as I hold the office of Home Secretary I shall give no countenance to the view that they should not be prevented from being such a danger'. Instead, he wanted to concentrate on trying to force gay lawbreakers to, well, stop being so gay. Although he admitted that 'experience shows that only a minority of homosexual offenders are likely to benefit by psychiatric treatment', he nevertheless concluded that 'there may be some scope for development here, particularly when it is possible to open the new institution for mentally abnormal offenders . . . I think that the most profitable line of development is to improve, so far as finances permit, the facilities for the treatment of homosexuals sentenced by the courts.' Four months after this was written, the war hero, codebreaker and computer pioneer Alan Turing killed himself after the experimental hormonal treatment he was forced to undergo following his own conviction for having a relationship with another man left him impotent and growing breasts.

Prime Minister Winston Churchill favoured another tactic: to not talk about it and pretend it wasn't happening. After due thought, he announced the following month that 'in his view, the prudent course would be to take no action save to encourage a Private Member to introduce in the House of Commons, under the ten-minute rule, a Bill designed to prohibit the publication of detailed information of criminal prosecutions for homosexual offences'. Maxwell Fyfe, however, 'pointed out that such legislation, even if it had the effect of allaying public anxiety about homosexuality, would make no contribution whatever towards a solution of the problem of prostitution. This, in his view, was the more urgent and obvious problem.'

One of the reasons put before the Cabinet that March as to why action was becoming urgent was that 'Lord Winterton had been anxious to raise these questions in a debate in the House of Lords . . . he could not be prevented indefinitely from doing so.' On 19 May it proved impossible to hold him back any longer: the former Cabinet minister stood up in the Lords to denounce 'the filthy, disgusting, unnatural vice of homosexuality' and demand that rather than focus on 'whether or not the law should be changed in favour of homosexuals', the government concentrate instead on 'the moral issue of how a further rise in criminal vice can be prevented'. He went on to claim to have been reliably informed that 'there was no ground whatsoever for saying that it was true that adult homosexualists did not attack children' and that 'homosexuals, being admittedly peculiar and in many cases vain creatures, glory in a prison sentence as a form of deterrent'. Winterton, whose political career had kicked off when he was elected as an MP way back in 1904, died five years before homosexuality was legalised, railing against 'pansies' and the 'pro-pansy press' all the way.

But he was fighting a losing battle. Maxwell Fyfe announced the creation of a Royal Commission under the leadership of university vice chancellor Sir John Wolfenden that August. Wolfenden may have insisted on referring to the subjects of his three-year study not as homosexual offences and prostitution but as Huntley and Palmers, to spare the blushes of the female secretaries to his committee, but he did come up with the proposal that same-sex activity should be legalised in private for men over 21 (it took a further decade for this to be made law). That age was picked on partly 'so as to exclude National Servicemen', which suggests that legislators found a man in uniform so irresistible that they couldn't imagine them possibly being able to keep their hands off each other.

In 1979, Margaret Thatcher accepted 10,000 of the Vietnamese 'boat people' fleeing from the communist regime into Great Britain, rescuing them from months in cramped and hellish conditions on board ships and in refugee camps in Hong Kong, and giving them a chance of a new life.

But she really, really, *really* didn't want to.

She was happy to condemn the regime that was driving them out, and in the process extorting huge amounts of cash to ease their exit. On a Foreign Office briefing note which claims that the official fees demanded from departing citizens meant that 'the refugees probably constitute the country's single most profitable export' a Downing Street adviser has scrawled 'an appalling assessment'. 'Yes,' Thatcher has written beneath. 'That is Communism.' But that didn't mean she was about to welcome them into the glorious capitalist utopia that was the UK.

On 8 June Lord Carrington, the Foreign Secretary, urged her to accept 293 refugees who had been rescued by the British ship the *Roachbank* after it came across their own small boat 'in a pitiful condition' in the South China Sea. The *Roachbank* had subsequently been refused permission to dock in Taiwan, and the boat people had spent a fortnight under the grudging care of its captain and crew, who were supposed to be on their way to Venezuela. 'Agree,' wrote Thatcher, who already felt she had done quite enough by accepting 1,000 refugees who had been rescued in similar circumstances by another British ship, the *Sibonga*. 'On condition that you have a <u>defence against</u> taking the refugees on the <u>third</u> boat now known to be expected in Japan. We can't go on like this and in spite of our discussions about the need to find a defence against taking more – none has been forthcoming. Indeed I wonder if the matter has been pursued at all?'

Carrington had in fact been doing quite the opposite. At an informal meeting at Downing Street the following day, he informed the PM that after discussing the matter with the United Nations High Commissioner for Refugees he felt the UK had no choice but to offer asylum to 10,000 people fleeing from Vietnam over the next two years. Which his boss did not like at all.

'The Prime Minister said that, in that case, the UK would have to cut down on the level of immigration into the UK, and in particular the admission of dependants,' reads the official 'note for the record'. Willie Whitelaw, the Home Secretary, who was also present, pointed out that this would actually be illegal under the terms of the 1971 Immigration Act. In that case, demanded Thatcher, the 1,500 Vietnamese the UK had already accepted (a fraction of the number taken in by other countries) would have to be subtracted from the total. The record politely notes that 'Lord Carrington expressed reservations.' But there was no stopping Mrs Thatcher. In her opinion, 'with some exceptions there had been no humanitarian case for accepting 1½ million immigrants from South Asia and elsewhere. It was essential to draw a line somewhere.'

Exactly where she considered that line to be swiftly became clear. 'She thought it quite wrong that immigrants should be given council housing whereas white citizens were not . . . She had less objection to refugees such as Rhodesians, Poles and Hungarians since they could more easily be assimilated into British society.' Most of those expected to exit Rhodesia when it turned into Zimbabwe the following year would be white.

In vain did Whitelaw protest that 'his own correspondence indicated a shift of opinion in favour of accepting more refugees. The Prime Minister said that in her view all those who wrote letters in this sense should be invited to accept one into their homes.'

Just in case you're giving her the benefit of the doubt here and assuming these were words spoken in the heat of the moment, another 'note for the record' of a further meeting two days later would cheer any member of the National Front, then at the height of its electoral popularity. Not only did Mrs Thatcher tell her colleagues 'that there would be riots in the streets if the Government had to put refugees into council houses', she informed them that 'she could not accept the distinction between refugees and immigrants'.

HOME FRONT

A fair cop? – 1922

Norman Macdermott, the director of the Everyman Theatre in Hampstead, was very cross indeed. So cross that he demanded the Prime Minister's personal attention.

'On Sunday afternoon, with my wife and a lady who was our guest, I went for a walk taking my way along the public footpath leading through the grounds of Chequers Court,' he wrote to David Lloyd George on 22 September 1922, the year after Lord Lee handed over his Buckinghamshire estate to the nation to be used as a country retreat for the Prime Minister.

> We were accosted by two men with golf clubs, one of whom in a most ill-mannered fashion ordered us back to the footpath and proceeded to 'lecture' us for not being on it. I inquired his authority for ordering me about. He informed me he was a Police Officer and he continued hectoring and bullying in a manner particularly disgusting before ladies.

I told him I thought it would be advisable for him to find more courteous methods of carrying out his duties, and in a most insolent manner he remarked that 'perhaps I could teach him'. I replied that I did not consider it a necessary part of the occupation of my time . . . I should be the very last at any time to encroach on the private portions of any gentleman's grounds, but I most strongly resent the gross lack of courtesy and the hectoring and bullying of a subordinate official, and especially the discourtesy to ladies. I feel strongly that the officer in question should be reprimanded and an apology from him should be forthcoming, and I must request that this matter be taken up.

He was so cross he wrote two further letters, claiming (not entirely convincingly) that 'I am not a person who just frivolously looks for offence.' Civil servant Thomas Jones hand-wrote a note on one of them: 'Dear JT – perhaps you will smooth this out and harmonise the "artistic temperament" with Scotland Yard.'

JT clearly did so, because the next item in the Downing Street file is a note from the policeman in question, PC Groombridge. 'On Sunday 17th Sept. this person accompanied by two ladies was walking on Beacon Hill,' he reports, before revealing the security issue behind his intervention:

356

'At the same time Mr Winston Churchill was painting some little distance away.'

Churchill was at this time Secretary of State for the Colonies and a regular guest at Chequers, which he described in a letter to his wife Clementine that year as 'a panelled museum full of history, full of treasures – but insufficiently warmed'. He was taking a break from emergency discussions with Lloyd George about the Chanak Crisis, which threatened to pitch the country back into war with Turkey, and PC Groombridge was not about to let him be disturbed by a rambling luvvie. His description of the incident is rather more restrained than Macdermott's dramatic version: 'As he was trespassing I drew his attention to the fact. He appeared to resent my action in asking him to confine himself to the public footpath.' Groombridge didn't even claim to have been called a pleb, as his successors would 90 years later in a controversial incident in Downing Street which resulted in the resignation of government Chief Whip Andrew Mitchell and the subsequent arrest of a number of officers in Scotland Yard's diplomatic protection group.

The reply Downing Street sent the thespian was scrupulously fair-minded: 'My experience of all the Officers who attend the Prime Minister is that they are without exception the most tactful and courteous men I have had to deal with and the particular Officer of whose conduct you complain is no exception to the rule. I cannot help feeling when I put together his version of the matter and yours that there must have been a little feeling shown on both sides.'

You just can't get the staff – 1942

Clementine Churchill received a rather alarming note from a Downing Street official on 22 September 1942. Lord Lee, the former MP and philanthropist, who continued to take an active interest in the running of Chequers despite bequeathing it for the use of prime ministers such as her husband, was concerned about the state of the housekeeper.

> He is worried about Miss Lamont's difficulties in connection with the domestic staff at Chequers. He fears that if her difficulties persist, she will have a break-down, and it would be hard in these days to find a satisfactory substitute.
> Miss Lamont has, of course, had considerable difficulty in replacing servants who have left for one reason or another during the last year or so. There are vacancies for a kitchen maid and a pantry maid which Miss Lamont has been unable to fill.

Aware that this was a matter of *vital* national interest, the civil service had already swung into action. 'I have spoken to Mr Bevin's Private Secretary, who has promised to see if the Ministry of Labour can assist further in any way,' the official assured Mrs Churchill. Inconveniently, most of Ernest Bevin's workforce turned out to be tied up in fiddling little areas like the munitions factories and coal industry. So clearly the only answer was to send in the army. 'Lord Lee suggested that you might get women of one of the Services to run the house?'

Negotiations began with the War Office about commandeering members of the Auxiliary Territorial Service, the women's branch of the army, from their duties driving trucks, operating searchlights, keeping stores and running canteens and telephone exchanges so they could put on a pinny and polish the prime ministerial cutlery instead. But the crisis at Chequers was escalating nearly as fast as the one in Stalingrad that autumn. 'I am afraid the servants at Chequers are melting away,' runs a note dispatched to Churchill's aide-de-camp Commander Thompson a few weeks later. 'Betty, the under-parlourmaid is leaving, and I fear Doreen, a very capable second house-maid is on the wobble. I do hope that you will soon hear more about the ATS question.'

The War Office gave the go-ahead to the employment of servicewomen early in January 1943, and Chequers has been staffed by alternating members of the army, navy and air force

359

ever since. The question of whether this is really the best use of their time has tended to pop up in the Commons occasionally: the line the government used to trot out was that it had been introduced because 'it was felt better in a house in which secret and defence matters were discussed to have a staff under discipline', rather than admitting it was the only way they could make sure the toilets got scrubbed and dinner made it to the table.

A lack of servants was not the only problem affecting Chequers at the height of World War II. 'Another point which Lord Lee raised was the fuel supply and he said how important it was to keep the Prime Minister warm,' reads the same note to Mrs Churchill. 'I mentioned this to Miss Lamont, who assures me the position is satisfactory, though she has suffered from considerable thefts of coal, for which she blames the soldiers in the camp. I have asked Commander Thompson to take this up.'

Fly Attlee Air – 1946

Nineteen forty-six was a year of true austerity. Even bread was rationed, a measure the government had managed to stave off throughout the long war years. Butter, margarine and cooking fat were more tightly restricted, even dried eggs vanished for a while, and as meat of any kind became a luxury item, the Ministry of Food issued a new official recipe. 'The Ministry recommends squirrel pie for a double reason,' newspapers reported, 'it is a delicacy, and grey squirrels are a pest because they eat vast quantities of food and so far little progress has been made to reduce their numbers.'

Still, they were all in it together. Weren't they? In May, Clement Attlee's Cabinet received an exciting memorandum from the Secretary of State for Air, Viscount Stansgate, the Minister of Supply, John Wilmot, and the Minister of Civil Aviation, Lord Winster: 'The Prime Minister has asked that we should inform our colleagues of the resources now available for long-range air transport of Cabinet Ministers and other front-rank VIP's (very important persons).'

And what resources they were! 'The Royal Air Force has had for some time at Northolt a small flight of long-range aircraft prepared to a higher degree of comfort than the normal Royal Air Force standard . . . One, LV 633, was specially prepared to a standard laid down by Mr Churchill and was normally reserved for his use. It has a cabin at the back and a conference room. In addition, it has seats for 12 and beds for 5.' This was, apparently, not quite good enough for Churchill's successor, for an appendix reveals that another plane – MW 100 – was 'undergoing certain electrical and radar modifications at

Hamble and these should be completed and the aircraft ready for the Prime Minister at the end of May'. It would have 'a private cabin for two, sitting or sleeping, with a tip-up seat for use, as required, by a stenographer who would normally be seated outside the private cabin . . . The aircraft has been prepared to the highest degree of comfort possible within the limited time allowed for the conversion.'

Not every plane in the fleet was quite up to these high standards. 'The Lancastrians are not suitable for the transport of VIPs themselves, owing to the narrowness of the fuselage, which prevents really comfortable seating being arranged; but they could, for example, take clerks, typists, office equipment and luggage, accompanying a Minister to a Conference in North America or elsewhere.'

'These are the best arrangements which we can make now,' the ministerial trio apologetically concluded. 'Two Tudor I's will, however, be converted for VIP travel, possibly about the end of this year. The Tudor I was designed to carry 12 passengers and 1,840 lbs of freight across the Atlantic, and it should be able to carry a VIP plus at least 8 staff in the very highest degree of comfort by day or night.' That would appear to estimate the average Cabinet minister as taking up as much space as four ordinary mortals. They must have been eating an awful lot of squirrel pie.

How do the moves in and out of Downing Street actually work? Do prime ministers have to pack up all their belongings in carefully labelled cardboard boxes at the same time as running the final stages of the election campaign, just in case? Is the removal van waiting to slide into their parking space the moment they vacate it to drive to the Palace, handing over the keys to the big black door to the policeman waiting outside?

It's actually much more civilised than that – at least in some cases. On 26 October 1951, Clement Attlee penned his very last letter on Downing Street notepaper:

My dear Churchill,

I am proposing to go to the Palace at 5.0 o'clock this afternoon in order to submit my resignation to the King . . . On the assumption that you will be accepting His Majesty's commission I would like to ask you to permit me to spend the weekend at Chequers in order to clear up there. I will endeavour to remove from here as soon as I can, but with the weekend intervening, it will not be possible to get clear from the residential part of the house till the middle of the week.

That evening, Churchill used what was probably the very next sheet on the pad to fire back his reply from the same address.

My dear Attlee,

Thank you so much for your letter. I have accepted the King's commission, and hope to be able to present him with a list of eight or ten Ministers of Cabinet rank in time for a Council tomorrow afternoon . . .

About houses: my wife and I will not be coming to Chequers for at least a month, so pray use it in any way convenient. As to Downing Street, I do not propose to reside there for at least a fortnight, and perhaps longer. About Tuesday or Wednesday, I might want to use the Cabinet Room. I could of course use the Map Room at the Annexe, which they tell me is available, if that would be more convenient. On no account put yourself to any inconvenience.

Believe me,

Yours very sincerely

Winston S. Churchill

It was very sweet of him. Churchill hated the Annexe, the bombproofed area directly above the Cabinet War Rooms, where he had been forced to live during World War II. But as it turned out, he had no need to relive those days: Attlee wrote back straight away to say he'd already been in to tidy up the Cabinet Room and collect his favourite pens.

> *Thank you for your letter. May I congratulate you on your becoming Prime Minister for the second time. Thank you so much for your kindness about Chequers and No. 10.*
>
> *The Cabinet Room is free and I expect to be out of the rest of the house by Thursday next.*

Thirteen years later, when Labour finally returned to Downing Street, Harold Wilson extended the same favour to his own predecessor, Alec Douglas-Home.

> *16th October, 1964*
> *My dear Alec,*
> *I understand that it is your intention to go to the Palace this afternoon to submit your resignation to The Queen.*
> *On the assumption that The Queen will wish to send for me to form a new Government I am taking this opportunity to say that I do hope that you will feel entirely free to use Chequers until you have been able to make your own arrangements.*
> *For my part I shall find it necessary to use the offices at Downing Street as soon as possible for reasons which I know you will understand, but I have no immediate need to*

occupy the private quarters there. The same applies to Chequers.

I hope this suggestion will fit in with your own plans.

Yours sincerely
Harold Wilson

As the former 14th Earl of Home (he had given up his title the previous year in order to take over as prime minister), Douglas-Home had the choice of a rather nice stately home or a ruined thirteenth-century castle to retire to; nevertheless he accepted Wilson's invitation.

My dear Harold,

It was good of you to suggest that we might use Chequers until we can make other arrangements. I would like to take advantage of your offer and we propose to go down to Chequers for the weekend. We would like to return briefly to No. 10 early next week, to clear up on Monday but only in the top flat.

The Homes eventually ended up moving into a penthouse suite at Claridges until they bought a London residence of their own, so there's no need to feel too sorry for them.

Perhaps the most poignant note of all from an outgoing prime minister is the one Ramsay MacDonald dispatched to the chair of trustees of Chequers when he stood down in June 1935.

Dear Mr Messer,

This last week-end ended my official residency at Chequers. Needless to say, I am very sorry to leave, as I should like to have seen still more results from the changes I have made. I had several friends down on Saturday and Sunday, and they were all in ecstasies about the little wood; it is now carpeted with forget-me-nots; another year's work upon it would have produced still greater improvements in its appearance.

Hear, hear – 1952

When Winston Churchill returned to Downing Street in October 1951 at the age of 76, he was, in the words of his biographer Roy Jenkins, 'gloriously unfit for office . . . Cabinets were rambling affairs, and Churchill was much inclined to treat them more as dinner-table audiences than as decision takers'.

That may have been because he couldn't actually hear what his colleagues were saying. Number 10 kept a file described as 'somewhat bulky' devoted entirely to the topic of the Prime Minister's hearing aids.

The first of these – a large built-in affair involving wires, knobs and earpieces – was installed in the Cabinet Room soon after Churchill moved back in to Number 10. Similar ones were fitted in his office at the House of Commons and the Map

Room at the Ministry of Defence that November. But the PM was still determined not to display any sign of weakness to the public. 'Do you wish any special arrangements to be made in the Chamber of the House of Commons itself?' asks a memo of 19 November. 'No not yet,' Churchill has scribbled beneath.

He didn't want the special 'telephone instrument fitted with an amplifier' which arrived in early December on public show either; when staff suggested fitting it in the Cabinet Room, he wrote firmly: '<u>Bedroom.</u>' But the Prime Minister taking to his bed should not be seen as any indicator of worsening health: he had always spent much of the day in a horizontal position, dictating to secretaries from a pile of pillows for several hours in the morning and putting on his pyjamas for a two-hour nap every afternoon. His new gadget did not aid restfulness, however: Post Office engineers had to spend four days trying to eliminate the 'whistling noises' produced by the amplifier when combined with the scrambler used on the PM's confidential calls: 'It would be most unfortunate if the scrambled calls were made in any way unintelligible or awkward.'

By January 1952, Churchill's Harley Street consultant Victor Negus was gently trying to persuade him that it might be a good idea if he could hear what was going on in the Commons as well. 'In the Chamber of the House it is possible to increase the amplification of the loud speakers behind your seat if you wish, but nothing has been done so far,' he pointed out. 'It will also be possible to put in an installation with an ear piece to hear speakers close at hand, but I believe you may prefer to do without this, as it necessitates the use of a cord and insert.' Churchill requested the first, but resisted the second. But as a page from the Multitone Electric Company's catalogue and accompanying invoice make clear, he did give in and invest in a personal hearing aid that July. It cost 42 guineas, but the company's managing director was not about to charge full price to the man who stood firm in Britain's darkest hour: 'I consider it a great privilege to have been asked to aid Mr Churchill's hearing, and I have asked for the invoice for the instruments to be made out at half the normal price,' he wrote on a covering letter. 'That's very nice,' Churchill has scribbled on the bottom. 'Make out a cheque.'

He finally gave in and accepted the necessity for a Commons hearing aid the following February. It's not surprising he was so sensitive about it. A series of memos from the Ministry of Works detail just how obvious and intrusive the equipment was:

The lead will have to be long enough for you to use it both when sitting down and when standing at the Dispatch box. The plug connection could be in one of three positions.

1) at the back of your seat by your left shoulder. The lead would have to be very long to enable you to stand up in comfort and would trail on the seat when you were sitting down.
2) below the seat by your left knee. The lead would not need to be so long but when you were sitting down it would trail on the floor.
3) On the corner of the table in front of you. This would be the least inconvenient to you but would have to be unplugged if anyone wished to move in front of you. So far as I can see this happens only on occasions when the Chief Whip wishes to have a word with the Speaker.

'I don't want any connection over my left shoulder while I am sitting on the Bench,' wrote back Churchill miserably.

Thankfully, April brought good news. 'The engineers have now devised a system which requires no wire connections from the ear-piece,' his Private Secretary for Parliamentary Affairs, Peter Oates, informed him. 'Under this system a circle of wire some twenty feet across, connected with the amplification system, is placed underneath the carpet and is quite invisible.' 'Good,' Churchill has written beneath this. The earpiece, his staff were instructed, 'will be kept in the top right hand drawer in the Private Secretaries' room at the House and can be produced for him at any time he goes into the Chamber'. The following February the system was upgraded and a second earpiece acquired. 'We may have to have recourse to the spare because the Prime Minister is more prone with the new type to bring it back from the House with him in his pocket,' warned Oates.

His hearing was the least of his health problems. In June 1953, Churchill suffered such a severe stroke that he was unable to walk and kept missing his mouth with his trademark cigars. Amazingly, his staff – with the aid of some helpful newspaper proprietors – were able to keep this a complete secret for the months it took him to convalesce. To the frustration of his colleagues, he would not step down until April 1955. By that point his hearing aids had had to be upgraded several more times.

Not that it wasn't useful on occasion to be able to choose who to listen to, given the more detached approach that Churchill was now taking to government. The naval commander Lord Mountbatten remembered being summoned into Number 10 in 1953: 'In the middle of the Cabinet table he had a large hearing-aid with an amplifier. As I entered the room he held up his hand as a signal to me not to speak. He picked up the headphones, put them on, switched on the amplifier, tapped it and then said: "I'll tell you what you ought to do about the Dardanelles." After he had held forth for about ten minutes he took off the headphones, switched off the hearing-aid and then turned to me and said: "Now, what have you to say to that?"'

Ford: by appointment to the Prime Minister – 1955

In May 1955, David Pitblado, principal private secretary in Downing Street, spotted a potential scandal looming for new prime minister Sir Anthony Eden. The trustees of Chequers had, without asking anyone's permission, accepted a freebie from the Ford Motor Company: a spanking new Ford Anglia. 'I shall be glad if you will report this gift to the Prime Minister and let him know that I have, on behalf of the trustees, written a letter to the Chairman of the Company expressing their appreciation of such a generous gift,' Chequers trustee Clement Penruddock informed Number 10.

This could look very bad indeed – and not just because Sir Anthony was much more of a Rolls-Royce kind of chap. 'Like you, I do not like this very much, but it is difficult to see what could be done without giving offence to the Ford Motor Company,' fretted Pitblado's counterpart at the Treasury, whom he consulted about the problem. 'I should have thought the risk was that something may have been said or done which might be repeated and one might find a rain of washing machines, refrigerators and what-not, descending! From this angle, Penruddock might be warned that gifts of this kind present difficulties? Obviously he seems never to have heard of the troubles of Mr Ramsay MacDonald and Sir Alexander Grant.'

Grant, the boss of biscuit company McVitie's, had received a baronetcy in 1924, shortly after supplying the Prime Minister with a Daimler and £30,000 of shares in his company, the revelation of which rather took the edge off MacDonald's criticisms of Lloyd George for auctioning off peerages. But if Pitblado was looking to nip a similar scandal in the bud, he was a good couple of decades too late. It turned out that this was the third car Ford had provided 'for the use of the Prime Minister and the Chequers household': the first, during Stanley Baldwin's premiership, was a 30 h.p. model which had been replaced in 1944 by a 'Ford Saloon h.p. Car'. It is no doubt a complete coincidence that Percival Perry, the chairman and managing director of the Ford Motor Company, had been raised to the peerage in 1938.

Pitblado may not have liked the situation, but his instructions could not have been clearer: 'LEAVE.'

Clarissa Eden was a terribly modern prime minister's wife. She had studied art and philosophy, written for *Vogue*, worked in PR for the film industry and in publishing, and counted Orson Welles and Ian Fleming among her personal friends. She was also a moody bigot and a pompous stuck-up cat, had a horrid face and looked more like a washerwoman than the wife of a prime minister.

At least that was what the copious hate mail she received in January 1956 said. 'Disgusted' wrote declaring that 'all I can ask and say to you is who the hell do you think you are?' and 'One who used to be one of Eden's admirers' helpfully pointed out that 'in the eyes of a certain religious sect your marriage is not even valid' (Anthony Eden was a divorcee). 'A Farm Worker's Wife, Somerset' observed that 'I suppose your husband has to have his pants washed, and what about your own?'

The smalls-centric nature of this anger arose from the newspaper clipping that several of these missives were scrawled on: a story from the *Sunday Pictorial* of 8 January, itself a follow-up to a *Daily Mirror* story the week before. 'Lady Eden, the Prime Minister's wife, has informed Mrs Maud Butt, the cowherd's wife, that she objects to Mrs Butt's washing hanging on the line while Sir Anthony and her ladyship are in residence at Chequers,' it jauntily reports. 'Mrs

Butt, 34, informed me last night that her husband's long pants, her children's vests, and her own "bras" and bloomers would float gaily in the breeze as usual on Tuesday. "And they can take the matter to the House of Lords, if they like," said the cowherd's wife. "Who does Lady Eden think she is?"'

Maud Butt lived in Chequers Cottage, one of the buildings on the prime ministerial country estate, and her husband was employed by the tenant farmer who worked the adjoining fields. The tabloids exploited her with just as much enthusiasm as they did Jacqui Janes, the bereaved mother who took offence at Gordon Brown's handwriting on a condolence letter in 2009. 'Mrs Butt, a staunch supporter of the Labour Party, added "Workmen arrived at the cottage and put up a new clothes line in the front garden",' the *Pictorial* gleefully continued. '"This overlooks the main road. Lorries pass and would send their dirt onto my clean clothes. Lady Churchill never complained."'

The furore in the press continued all week, as did the arrival of what Downing Street official Philip de Zulueta described as 'more tiresome letters about the washing'. In vain did Clarissa protest that 'Mrs Butt was hanging her washing not in her front or back garden, but across a path where we liked to walk . . . It was so distorted by the press.' She was firmly advised to excise the line from her draft letter of reply.

In fact, Mrs Butt had been stringing up her washing between the trunks of Lime Avenue, an impressive double column of mature trees between which the Edens liked to escort visiting foreign statesmen: it was hardly unreasonable for them to prefer not to have to look at knickers when they did so. Nor had the PM's wife made the request that so offended the Butts: it came from the estate administrators, chaired by Clement Penruddock, who confirmed to the *Daily Mail* that 'there is no question of Lady Eden being involved in this'.

Things were finally settled by what the *Mail* called 'a 40-minute conference' between Penruddock and Mrs Butt in her cottage. 'Outspoken Mrs Butt agreed that her chicken-run should be moved into an adjoining vegetable patch and the offending wash hung in her back garden – with a discreet row of bushes between it and Sir Anthony and Lady Eden's aspect.' But by that point it was about more than pants. The PM had called in no less a person than Sir Hartley Shawcross, the chief prosecutor at the Nuremberg Trials, to seek legal redress both from the *Mirror* for 'this annoying petty attack', and for a subsequent broadcast of *Any Questions* in which Anthony Wedgwood Benn had delivered several crowd-pleasing gags about 'washing of dirty linen in the Conservative party' and it being 'very difficult to turn over a new sheet'.

Thankfully, Shawcross talked some sense into

him. 'Although the article was undoubtedly defamatory of Lady Eden, it would be better to ignore it. It was, of course, a most malicious and offensive publication, but I think that it is almost always better in this sort of case, if it can be avoided, not to take legal action.' There was, in other words, no need for anyone's briefs to be aired in public.

That Harold Macmillan, he knows how to throw a party – 1963

The Chequers estate was intended to help the nation's prime ministers rule 'more sanely' due to breathing in 'the high and pure air of the Chiltern hills and woods'. It was not meant for any Tom, Dick or Harry Cabinet minister to use whenever they fancied a weekend jolly.

That, however, was the prospect foreseen by its formidable housekeeper Kathleen Hill in January 1963, a note in the Number 10 files reveals. 'Last weekend's Commonwealth meeting was the first time Chequers had been used for three months. However, Mr Sandys commented on this long gap, and told Mrs Hill that the Prime Minister had given him permission to use Chequers privately whenever it was not needed otherwise. Mrs Hill is a little uneasy about this, remembering Selwyn Lloyd, who practically lived there – to the extent that Mr Macmillan finally commented that he never seemed to be able to go to Chequers himself when he wanted to.'

Lloyd had served as Foreign Secretary and Chancellor, and made himself so at home at Chequers that he had a set of overnight things kept permanently in one of the bedrooms, and was regularly photographed walking his black Labrador Sambo (we'll forgive him the name because it was a long time ago) in the grounds. When Macmillan sacked him in the infamous 'Night of the Long Knives' in 1962, Lloyd moved out and left the dog behind (which is utterly unforgivable however much time might pass). The staff looked after Sambo until his death, and reported that he never stopped looking for his master.

Mrs Hill was right to feel uneasy about history repeating itself with Duncan Sandys, the Secretary of State for the Colonies. Apart from anything else, he is strongly suspected of being the 'headless man' who was photographed naked being fellated by the Duchess of Argyll in a Polaroid photograph that would be presented as evidence of her adultery in the divorce courts that March (although to be fair, her husband estimated that there were at least 87 other suspects). Such activities were hardly suitable for Chequers. Save it for Cliveden, a few miles up the road.

'[Mrs Hill] feels that Mr Sandys should not be encouraged to do this too much, and certainly that he should not be allowed to book Chequers months ahead,' the note continued. 'Mrs Hill also feels very strongly that the Prime Minister should go soon himself.'

She got her wish a few months later, as is noted in a memo from Downing Street which reads rather intriguingly in the light of the Profumo scandal that erupted later that year: 'I do not yet know what time the Prime Minister is arriving on Saturday, April 27 . . . I expect he will, as usual, be accompanied by a young lady and a detective, and possibly a Private Secretary.' Whatever the nature of the services provided by the young lady, this turned out to be quite a weekend. Billed as 'a series of discussions with ministers', it involved some epic consumption, all neatly documented by Mrs Hill:

3 bottles	Gin
5	Whisky
5	White Burgundy (Macon la Chapelle 1957)
2	Perrier Jouet NV Champagne
4	Sherry
3	Claret (Ch. Latour 1953)
8	Claret (Ch. Haut Bages Liberal 1952)
1 bottle	Dry Martini
1	Brandy (Choice Old Cognac No.6).

100 Cigarettes were also used

Questions were asked in the House about this particular 'jaunt' after the *Telegraph* reported that 'during the Sunday tea-break [the Prime Minister] could be seen in the garden gesticulating with one hand and clutching a plate in the other'. Macmillan confirmed that it had been 'a rather special occasion'. As the PM confirms elsewhere in a bulging file of correspondence about exactly whose responsibility it was to pick up the booze bill for Chequers, 'my colleagues drank so much they were always my expensive guests. The wine list is always very high with politicians.'

The Heathmobile – 1970

Ted Heath liked to travel in style. Even when he was off duty.

'We discussed with the Prime Minister the use of the official car for private purposes now that the car is being fitted with a multi-channel radio linked into the police/Home Office network,' wrote his principal private secretary Robert Armstrong on 17 July 1970. 'The Prime Minister agreed that, given the advice that the car so equipped provided in the view of the police the best means of maintaining police protection for the Prime Minister on his journeys by car, the general rule should be that the car should be used for all journeys, whether official or private.' For private journeys, the PM would have to stump up for the 'cost of the car, the driver and the petrol'. The question was, how much?

The mileage rate was set at 1s.9d per mile, which Armstrong proposed 'ought now to be reviewed'. So it was – and the Ministry of Works came back, on 31 July, with a new price of 2s.3d per mile. Which was not welcome at all. Because Heath was about to depart for Cowes Week, which involved taking the car by ferry to the Isle of Wight, and putting up his official driver while he was off having fun on his yacht. Factor in the price of ice creams, natty little sailor hats and other necessities, and his holiday could end up costing him a fortune.

Downing Street seized on the fivepence which was included in the figure for 'driver's extra earnings' and demanded to see 'what this latter figure represents and also the calculations which show how both figures have been arrived at'. Informed that it was a premium added to represent the fact that most private use of official cars took place outside of office hours, and the drivers were therefore on overtime, Heath got in a huff. He might be on holiday, but many of his trips would still take place between the hours of nine and five. No less a personage than his Private Secretary for Home Affairs was instructed to come up with an alternative formula that took this into account. 'I would prefer to calculate the average cost of using the Prime Minister's driver (taking his total annual wage and dividing it by the number of miles we have done in a year recently), add this to the first element in the proposed charge and then to abate it by arbitrary proportion to take account of the security factor,' Alan Simcock suggested. 'This abatement might be two-fifths of the total.' Just in case he had got his sums wrong, he gave himself a get-out clause: 'If the sum comes out unpleasantly high we could always fall back on their calculation.'

Armstrong thought they could do even better than that. 'My own inclination would be to suggest to the Ministry of Works . . . a flat rate of 2s. a mile. It is also arbitrary, but I do not think this figure could easily be faulted.' The Treasury grudgingly agreed to this on 6 October – by which point the Prime Minister had already demanded his regular vehicle and cheap-as-chips chauffeur for the Conservative Party Conference in Blackpool, despite the fact that 'the rules of procedure specifically enjoin Ministers not to use their official cars for Party occasions'.

While Heath was quick to cite security reasons for travelling in such comfort, a list of the private journeys he was billed for that autumn (at a total cost of £28.2s.) gives the lie to that particular excuse. One 50-mile trip on 30 July was to transport his housekeeper Miss Crawford back to London from another regatta, all by herself.

But even this style of travel was not quite as grand as the PM would have liked, as a 1971 memo by Detective Inspector P. Radford of his personal security team makes clear. 'The Prime

Minister is still at times being driven around the country in private cars, hired cars, local authority cars and Government Car Service cars provided from regional depots,' the copper complained. 'Such cars have no radio communication facilities, and the drivers rarely have the experience required to drive the Prime Minister in the midst of demonstrations and other hazards . . . It can in fact quite clearly be shown that the public interest would be served by the regular transportation of the Prime Minister by the most direct, convenient and secure route possible. This would naturally involve more frequent travel by air, and consequently greater use of RAF helicopters and small aircraft.'

That this would also provide a much more pleasurable experience for his personal security team was quite coincidental. But just in case the bean-counters were not convinced, Radford detailed some 'examples of the stresses and strains, as well as the actual physical dangers, to which the Prime Minister has recently been subjected'. These included having to have 'a most hasty lunch' before being driven to Luton to catch a 'hastily chartered bright green plane' and then be driven 'by a slightly nervous lady, through rain-washed rush-hour traffic' to Plymouth. It was, apparently, a 'hideous journey'. And why was he going there? Er, to 'accept the Admiral's Cup on behalf of the British team' he had captained in the Fastnet Race, an impressive achievement, but not really one that could be said to fall within his official duties.

As if that wasn't enough, a 'privately chartered launch which was to have picked him up broke down mid-Solent' when he was on his way to yet another sailing jaunt. If that sounds like the sort of bad luck any of us might suffer when we are off on our holidays, the next bit definitely doesn't: 'a police launch had to be summoned, and it was almost 4 a.m. when the Prime Minister got to bed'. Perhaps most appallingly, 'the journey to Alnwick, Northumberland, to open a fete . . . resulted in the Prime Minister's being away from Downing Street for more than twelve hours'. If only someone, somewhere, had owned a map and been able to see that Northumberland is quite a long way from London!

Clearly, the only answer was upgrades all round. 'A start could be made by eliminating the many hours a year wasted in traffic jams while commuting between Downing Street and Chequers, by the provision of a helicopter . . . If for reasons of convenience and personal preference a Prime Minister wishes to travel regularly by train, then consideration should be given to the equipment of a special coach, which would include communi-cation and office facilities, as well as lockable compartments and a combination safe.' If it was good enough for Stalin . . . Somehow, Radford's postscript is unsurprising: 'train journeys have in fact been rare under this administration; if the

Prime Minister is travelling too far to go by car, he prefers to go by air'. If you want an example of how much the political climate has changed in 40 years, bear in mind that Chancellor George Osborne got in terrible trouble in 2012 just for upgrading one of his own train tickets to first class.

Fortunately, Willie Whitelaw was on hand in 1971 to nip any prime ministerial profligacy in the bud. 'I would agree that in common sense it is nonsense that he should pay at all, but on political grounds I am equally clear that he should do so,' wrote the Lord President of the Council firmly. 'My reasons are that a change in practice from his predecessors would soon be discovered and HW [Harold Wilson, once and future PM, at that point leading the opposition] would make much of it. The answer that it is necessary on security grounds, while correct, is unattractive politically because it can be represented that the Prime Minister's policies are so unpopular that he cannot mix with the people as freely as in the past. Therefore I conclude that the Prime Minister should pay a charge based on Civil Service rates when the journey is non-official.'

At least Heath managed to negotiate those rates down. A memo from early 1972 gives him the go-ahead to pay for private use of the prime ministerial car 'at the rate of 5.3p a mile, plus a supplement of 0.5p for any non-official passenger who accompanies him'. Which almost halved the pre-decimalisation two shillings a mile he had agreed to stump up two years previously. Ker-ching!

The Ironing Lady – 1979

Seven weeks after the removal vans pulled out of Downing Street in 1979, the Department of the Environment revealed how much public cash was spent getting Number 10 ready for its new occupants: £1,736. The same parliamentary answer revealed that the new Chancellor, Geoffrey Howe, had spent half as much again doing up the flat next door (to be fair, it is bigger, which is why Tony and Cherie Blair demanded Number 11 for their own brood in 1997 and forced the bachelor Gordon Brown to swap). But Mrs Thatcher was still furious.

'To the best of our knowledge no-one here was consulted about the fact that you intended to publish this information,' stormed one of her personal secretaries Nick Sanders in a scathing memo to the officials responsible. 'This must not happen again. It is all too likely that such information will be picked up and used against the Prime Minister at Question Time.' Thatcher had arrived urging thrift on the nation and spending cuts all round: so keen were her spin doctors to push her personal parsimony that Denis Thatcher had been forced to swap his beloved Rolls-Royce for a Ford Cortina.

Number 10 also demanded a full breakdown of exactly how the amount had been arrived at. It arrived from the civil service's Property Services Agency, whose chief executive, Sir Robert Cox, was really not having a good day: he had to admit that they had got their sums wrong and the total was actually £1,836. 'I find these figures impossible to believe,' remarked one Downing Street official, highlighting what are indeed hair-raising sums of £464 for replacing linen and pillows, and £209 for replacing crockery (what exactly did they think the new residents might catch from the Callaghans that a good hot wash wouldn't get rid of?). Mrs Thatcher was in full agreement: 'So do I!' reads her handwritten note on the list. She added a few frugal suggestions of her own: 'I could use my own crockery. Bearing in mind we use only <u>one</u> bedroom' – she had the habit of underlining things twice when she was cross, which was quite a lot of the time – 'we have sufficient linen . . . can the rest go back into store?'

One item in particular appears to have infuriated the woman who revelled in the 'Iron Lady' nickname bestowed upon her by a Russian journalist in 1976: £19 was far too great a drain on the public purse. She scribbled a promise on the bottom of the correspondence: 'I will pay for the ironing board.'

'Would you like me also to pass on to the officials concerned your wish that all expenditure on the flat should be as economical as possible and notified to us in advance?' asked Sanders. 'Yes – I should at least like to be given the estimated cost of the proposed charge,' wrote the Prime Minister.

But she was still brooding over that most pressing of issues. 'I have an excellent ironing board which is not in use at home. I will pay for the new one.'